# Saunders

# Saunders Lewis

## *A presentation of his work*

by
**Harri Pritchard Jones**

Templegate Publishers
Springfield, Illinois

The special contents of this
arrangement © 1990 Harri Pritchard Jones

First published in the United States of America in 1990 by
Templegate Publishers
302 East Adams Street
P.O. Box 5152
Springfield, Illinois 62705-5152


ISBN 0-87243-187-8

# Contents

# Introduction

It may be difficult for those whose reading is confined to one of the world languages to realise that important things are being said in lesser used ones. And yet Ibsen and Kierkegaard wrote in such languages, ones which are literally closed books to most people. Saunders Lewis chose to use such a language as his medium of literary expression. It was indeed his mother tongue, but his command of English, and of other languages, made it a matter of choice for him. In opting for Welsh, he chose the language of a declining population in a bilingual situation, where all his readers were also fluent in English.

In choosing thus, he also chose to join the fight for the very survival of his medium of expression; fighting, in a way, for his own continued existence. But our main concern here with him is as a man of ideas, as a fine writer and, supremely, as a great Christian poet.

Physically, he was small in stature, but concentrated like Cocteau. He was debonair and playful, and everything he did had style. He was never, never boring; it was impossible to ignore him. At times he was an intensely private person, at others a very public figure. He could be excellent company, a splendid raconteur but with a searing satirical quality. As a public speaker he was as fascinating as D'Annunzio. One could compare him with Jan Mazaryck, another integrated patriot politician, and one who shared his passion for Europe. Indeed, this European obsession, as many saw it, in one so intensely Welsh was only one of the apparent paradoxes in the person and his work. A man of considerable scholarship in classical and modern European literature, he chose to concentrate upon his own neglected, though rich, literary tradition. A traditionalist and political conservative, he was also a Christian existentialist who was committed to the imperative of choice. The son and grandson of Calvinistic ministers, he became a dedicated Roman Catholic. Devoted to Reason, he insisted with Pascal that Reason should 'humble' itself. He was one who saw everything *sub specie aeternitatis*. A character in one of his plays, the commissar husband of a clandestine Catholic in the Eastern Europe of the 1950s, complains of his wife, 'She loves me as if eternity existed'. That might well have been said of Lewis himself in the way he cherished his patrimony, as Welshman, European and artist. But then he was always one to see all sides of things, like a cubist painter. This was probably the quality, above all others, that makes his work 'modern'.

In one of his finest poems, addressed to 'The Good Thief', he counterpoints what is seen with the eye of Faith—'that a gibbet was the throne of God'—with the view of the faith-less, who saw only 'a scarecrow' 'nailed on a pole like a sack of bones' with 'flea-ridden robbers as a retinue to his shame'. He reveals the total deprivation of the God-man side by side with the glory revealed somehow, for some reason, to this thief. There we see the ex-Calvinist still supremely aware of the gulf between God and man; but there too is the Catholic, owing something to Barth, who is so conscious of the humanity of God. Lewis, like Kierkegaard, realised how blind love can be, especially God's, and also how absurd some of our beliefs can look from the proximal side of the chasm between Faith and unaided reason.

In himself and in his work he always contained these complexities and paradoxes. There is a fundamental unity in all his life and work, though it was marked by dramatic events and actions. This very private person made three fundamental choices, choices which had public reverberations, and which are relevant to us all to this day.

In the first place, the brilliant young academic and writer, living in England and with mastery of English, had chosen the smaller, more introspective world of Wales. The second decision was to involve himself in politics, to which he once confessed he felt he had a vocation. The final, and most significant, choice was to join the Roman Catholic Church. Having made a choice he always stuck to it, frequently with bitter and difficult consequences.

*   *   *

John Saunders Lewis was born in 1893, into a Liverpool Welsh family, within a community of largely Welsh-speaking, Non-conformist ex-patriates. His background was in the affluent and educated middle class section of that community. Lewis was the son of a minister and on his mother's side came from a long line of them. The clergy constituted a well-off class, and Lewis was educated privately. The language of the home was Welsh, as was that of worship. But apart from the Scriptures and the highly moralistic Welsh literature of the period, Lewis and his family tended to read the same sort of literature as their English peers. Nonconformist Wales had lost or spurned its roots in the great literary tradition of the Middle Ages, and by this time found even the fervour of the early Methodists rather immodest. Nonconformism was about to go into decline, becoming quite proscriptive, lacking in theology. The largely emotional revivals of 1904/05, looked at with hindsight, can be seen as an agonal phenomenon.

In politics, Wales had enthusiastically embraced its role as partner in the Empire; having joined Ireland in fighting for national cultural institutions, but baulking at any measure of political autonomy. Lewis was at university in Liverpool, studying English, and seemed destined for a career as an English academic or writer. The Great War proved disastrous for that old Wales, largely rural in outlook and with its religious and political life largely sentimentalised. The war was the making of Lewis, and made him a Welshman. Easter 1916 in Ireland had its effects on him also. He served in France and then in Intelligence in Athens under Compton Mackenzie. Both were later to become leaders of the new nationalist movements in their respective countries. He has described what happened to him in a radio talk, written in English. It was titled, enigmatically, 'By Way of Apology', and in it he made an interesting comparison between James Joyce and himself.

9

Like Joyce, Lewis was to be inextricably involved for the rest of his life with his native country and his religion. Whereas the Irishman chose exile in which to re-create his nation in his imagination, Lewis chose to return from exile, and even to try to re-create his nation in actuality.

In that talk he described his cultural conversion as 'piece-meal'. This applied equally to his conversion to Roman Catholicism. The process started during his late adolescence and early manhood, but it was not finally professed until 1932. In France it had been mainly the consciously Catholic authors who had aroused his interest: Jaques Rivière, Claudel, Pascal and Maritain as well as Barrès's series *Le Culte du Moi*—the latter being a strange theme for a man who was to stress the importance of the communal, the traditional, the inherited. But in that trilogy there is a young man from Lorraine who has moved to Paris, and who suffers disillusionment and moral decay. All this echoed in Lewis's mind when his father admonished him that no good would come of him until he returned to his roots. Those roots were to prove deeper than those of his father.

Lewis did return to his homeland, with many of the ideas he had taken aboard in France as well as some of those he had read about when he studied the Irish cause. What was problematic was whether he had espoused any of the romantic, militaristic, jingoistic nationalism of Maurras, Rupert Brooke and Patrick Pearse.

Unlike his close friend, David Jones, Lewis wrote next to nothing about the war. The letters he wrote to his future wife were few, and only published posthumously. He did visit Rome and wrote an intriguing little piece where he saw 'the unending glory of the Catholic Church in the indelible unity of the dead in one body . . .' and in her role as 'treasury of half the memories of civilization. And the rest are kept in memory by the artists'.

He was already flirting with the Church, but it was to literature, and then to politics, that he turned first.

\*　　\*　　\*

In 1922 his family had also returned to Wales. Lewis himself became a lecturer in Welsh at Swansea. He came to Welsh literature without any formal training in the subject. His attitude was fresh and startling, and a constant surprise or shock to his colleagues. He made a few howlers, but usually—though he was often speculative—he succeeded in casting new light on matters.

He turned to the Catholic period, before Wales was annexed by England in 1535/36, and her religion and language proscribed. At the same time he produced a series of studies of individual writers from the later, more inconsistent period. He tended to romanticise the earlier period, and to castigate much of the recent works as being moralistic and sentimental and philistine. But in all this work of criticism one could detect the exciting, dramatic elements which made him compulsive reading. The breadth of his learning and vision, the honesty and lack of cant, the interest in form as well as content, the ability to see Welsh works in the context of other literatures and other art forms, the willingness to demolish myths and sacred cows and to elevate the importance of neglected authors, all these made him an enigmatic figure, often reviled and also revered. In all of this he was in stark contrast to the other great Welshman of the time, David Lloyd George, who sentimentalised Wales, while turning his back on her. But the world statesman recognised Lewis as a man of genius, and wrote warmly of him when he was imprisoned.

Lewis's studies in the medieval period led to a famous exposition on the aesthetics of medieval Welsh poetry, which owed much to Francesco de Sanctis. Lewis, also, showed that this corpus of Welsh poetry owed a deal of its inspiration to the scholastics, to Aquinas and Aristotle, Bonaventure and Plato, and it belied Newman's dictum that one cannot have sinless literature of sinful man. This Welsh corpus of work was an edifice to compare with the great gothic cathedrals, erected *ad majorem Dei gloriam*. He also dealt with the earlier, heroic age, when Wales had come into existence from a fusion of the Celtic substratum and the post-Roman elements.

At the same time he published a major study of an eighteenth century hymn and prose writer, Williams Pantycelyn, best know outside Wales for one of his few English hymns, 'Guide Me, Oh, Thy Great Jehovah'. There is a line by a Welsh poet: 'Shakespeare, follow his example; Dante, turn to his world, but remember Pantycelyn at the same time'. Lewis went on to study Pantycelyn's works with that admonition in mind. He certainly showed his knowledge of the Divine Comedy and of Etienne Gilson's study of it. He also displayed a knowledge of that other, newly described underworld of the human unconscious mapped by Freud. The resulting book stunned Wales. Pantycelyn had been one of the founding fathers of Welsh Methodism. Here was a son and grandson of noted Methodist preachers and ministers, one who was still nominally Methodist, describing their hero as 'Europe's first romantic poet', as someone who had looked sin in the face and moved toward an experience of God which accorded with that described by a Catholic 'saint' called Bonaventure: a 'triplicate way, of purification, illumination and unification'.

This sort of stuff upset the Nonconformists, whose learning was often limited. Lewis also upset them with his reminders of how far they had moved in their practice from their old precepts. He outraged them with his flamboyant dress, his fondness for wine and good food and cigars. He was consciously an artist in Philistia. To crown it all, he published a novel, which, though highly moralistic, was akin to Madame Bovary, and dedicated it to 'Pantycelyn . . . the sole initiator of this style of writing in Welsh'.

*      *      *

Lewis's studies in the medieval world of Wales, and its more tattered traditions afterwards, had an influence on his political thought. He reflected deeply on the relationship of Wales to the rest of Europe, as part of a cultural mosaic. He eschewed the old-style romantic nationalism of most modern nation-states when he helped set up the new nationalist party in 1925. In fact, in his inaugural lecture to the party in 1936, 'Principles of Nationalism', he said that the greatest enemy Wales had ever faced was nationalism—that of the emergent nation-states in Tudor times, which had swallowed up ancient nations like Ireland, Wales, Brittany, the Basques and others. In his vision of a new European order he foresaw a continent of nations which eschewed sovereignty in favour of European unity. This was what lay behind the Treaty of Rome thirty years later.

His Europeanism, his sympathies with Catholic thought, were a drawback to his political activities. Like the Unionists in Ireland, their Welsh equivalents could use the slogan 'Home Rule equals Rome rule'. A more sophisticated version of this was made by his principal literary adversary, a poet and academic called W. J. Gruffydd. Basically, the accusation was that Lewis's thought was un-Welsh, and that he was politically and religiously dangerous in that he was said to be heavily influenced by, not only the social encyclicals, *Rerum Novarum* and *Quadragesimo Anno,* but by Maurras and the Catholic Action movement on the French right. The latter accusation was baseless, as Lewis's riposte to Gruffydd was to show. The attack and the reply were in the form of open letters published in the main literary journal, which Gruffydd edited, *Y Llenor.* That exchange still makes compulsive reading, not least because the two protagonists were destined to cross swords again, but also because of the quality of the writing, the evocation of a whole period, the very presumptuousness of the two young men. Like most of their French counterparts, both saw literature as a total way of life.

*   *   *

In 1932 he had joined the Roman Church. He had been close to it for years, and was not to reveal his action for a further five years, in order not to unduly embarrrass his father.

His claim that his conversion had taken twenty-five years was itself a theological statement for Welsh Nonconformists, whose constant talk of conversion referred to an intensely emotional experience; like a flash of lightning sent to illumine the mind. For them, conversion was not a matter of Grace building on the natural virtues, but, as one Methodist put it, of Grace 'causing a revolution in one's nature'. That man was Jonathan Edwards, the leader of the movement in New England in the eighteenth century. We are dealing with a Pauline conversion. It is probably easier for most of us to envisage a 'piecemeal Conversion', with the Holy Spirit prodding away subliminally every now and then. For in the case of Lewis, as with most converts to Methodism, and indeed Saint Paul himself, religion was already on the scene; imprinted there by baptism, circumcision or nurture.

Lewis knew a lot about those sudden, emotional conversions from his experience of the 'Revivals' of 1904/05. He also knew what had happened to another Paul, Claudel, who as Lewis says in one of his plays, 'went into Notre Dame an atheist, standing by the third column and staring at an image, suddenly believed, as one who knows, and never tasted uncertainty again'.

Saunders Lewis often talked of the super-rationality, if not the irrationality, of Faith. When taxed, in 1964, during a long and rare television interview, with his being attracted to Roman Catholicism by its social doctrine, he replied, 'I turned Catholic, not because the Catholic social philosophy appealed to me; not at all. I turned for one terribly simple reason, that I thought that it is through the Catholic Mass that God is worshipped as he ought to be by men. And that is the only reason I turned Catholic'.

That answer begged the question of how he came to believe, unless one accepts that he had remained a believer from his childhood. The change was certainly piecemeal, and partially subliminal, though, like Locke, against whom the early Methodists reacted, Lewis seems always to have been able to see God revealed in the whole Creation. And, as a poet, he has often celebrated that immanence.

On the other hand, he has always maintained that the path of Faith was an arduous one for him. His experience is, I think, well described in a play he wrote in 1940, based on a medieval legend about Amis and Amile. These two were knights sworn to filial love, who had drifted apart. Amis was by this

14

time happily married, proud of his estate and wife and two children. Amile turns up, seemingly by accident, in an advanced state of leprosy. He is given shelter, recognised and made welcome despite his affliction. In the night, he is visited by what appears to normal senses to be an angel, who tells him to ask Amis to kill his two children and wash his friend's wounds in their blood. Eventually, he does reveal this crazy message to Amis, who scoffs madly. There is talk of Abraham's predicament with Isaac and God, and the madness of Faith and faithfulness. Of course, when, honour-bound, Amis carries out the 'angel's' wishes, not only Amile but the children are restored to life and health. The children are now seen as gifts of God, rather than extensions of Amis's persona; not the 'creation of my loins'.

Lewis acknowledges in the foreword to the play a debt to Kierkegaard. And we see what he means when Amis says things like this: 'Walking as if one saw, and experiencing the night of the blind, is the perpetual life of the Faith'. Lewis, one feels, could even appreciate Amis's terrible predicament, when he talks of that 'angel's voice': 'a voice, just a voice; a tongue uttering something, like a man in his senses conversing with his kind, speaking sentences, and see: water will be wine, bread flesh, or two people one flesh, at the explosion of the words . . . Last night, there was meaning and order to life, like that of the innumerable pieces of glass which colour on a church window the image of paradise; and word came to my friend, a voice in the night speaking and then falling silent, and see the window of reason is in bits beneath my feet and life is dung'.

To be a Catholic, to have become Catholic, in the Wales of 1932, especially with Lewis's background, was not easy. He had to try to interpret Wales to the largely immigrant church he had joined, and vice versa. He did, indeed, explain and speak on behalf of the Church for years, and in the first period he faced a largely uncomprehending, often hostile and bigoted audience. But he never failed to voice his criticism of the Church also, especially at its lack of realisation that, whatever the origins of its adherents, it found itself in a country with a profoundly Christian and Catholic past; a culture in which the Faith had incarnated over a thousand years.

He remained ecumenically minded. Foreshadowing Schillebeeckx, he maintained that the movement of faith and religious experience that occurred in the eighteenth century Methodist Revival was of the Spirit, recalling an earlier order and spirituality. This was true to the extent, he felt, that when these basic new communities decided to ordain ministers from amongst themselves, the Spirit would have concurred, as the old Apostolic Order was not available at the time to them. Wales had been largely betrayed by Rome, in its concern for England, the country which had annexed Wales rather than have a Catholic flank to its west.

Lewis had little interest in matters of religious discipline, preferring the spirit of Canon Law to its letter. He rarely said anything about such matters as contraception, abortion or clerical celibacy. He did stress the importance of the family but, in his plays at least, displayed a warm tolerance towards human foibles, especially sexual ones. He only sprang to the defence of Catholicism when he felt there was some danger to the *Depositum Fideii,* and he also revealed in his work his amazing awareness of the *Mysterium Tremendum* of 'God in bread' and in his whole universe. Though passionately devoted to the old Latin Mass, and the idea of his old friend David Jones of *The Anathemata,* he remained convinced of the sacramentality of the whole of life. He did hate many of the liturgical innovations which followed Vatican II, even the few masses we had in Welsh. But he had no time for Lefebvre. He read widely in theology, but his constant spiritual reading was the Roman Daily Missal. Strangely, for a man who was so humble in his religious life, his favourite religious book of late was Kung's *On Being a Christian,* though he regretted the way Kung had reacted to the Magisterium.

As he grew older, losing virtually all his faculties except his consciousness, he still wrote, and his 'Terminal Prayer', a poem written when he was 80 years, aroused as much controversy as anything he ever wrote.

In all his poetry, and in most of his plays, there was a deal

16

of irony and paradox; the greatest ironies being, for him, *sub specie aeternitatis*. Love: agape and eros; eternity, as an absurd torture or as a sensual and intellectual fulfilment; the supreme aesthetic experience, and the frustrating, ephemeral nature of human existence on earth—all these were the matter of his poems and much of his plays. In them, paradoxes become marriages: theses and antitheses inextricably involved with each other, in creative tension.

*     *     *

However, by the early 1930s, the critic and poet had become increasingly involved in the market place. Here was no *trahison des clercs*. The twenties had been the formative years for him as a man searching for his religious and national identity. Henceforth, he was to develop, promote and defend that identity in himself and his nation, by public actions and, after he felt rejected as a political leader, by the power of his pen.

The Nationalist Party was a minority, and did not win a parliamentary seat until 1966. But it had become a powerful pressure group, and succeeded in changing the political agenda, even when Wales was wracked by the great strike and the depression. Wales moved to the left, but Lewis and the party tried to stem the tide and promote a more co-operative type of socialism. It was the tendency towards materialism and towards making men into robots that he despised in Marxist socialism. Equally, he reviled *laissez-faire* capitalism. He insisted on the primacy of the spiritual, even before Maritain published his book with that title. Lewis was a liberal Catholic owing more, finally, to Leo XIII than to the anti-modernism of Pius X. A noted critic, Dafydd Glyn Jones, has said Lewis's call to his nation was in a sense a Methodist one, 'a call to national introspection and self-knowledge; a call to cast away illusion and a call to repentance'.

For a while Lewis had flirted with the idea of an Irish-style physical force movement, but had eschewed it. However, he did want to crystallise issues for his people in a dramatic, public way. For he had a desire, 'not a small desire, but a very great one, to change the history of Wales, and make Welsh Wales into something living, strong, powerful, belonging to the modern world'.

Events were to provide him with the opportunity to do this. In 1936 Welsh public opinion had become incensed by the intention of the British Government to build an air bombing range in a remote but historic corner of north-west Wales. It was a spot renowned since the Age of Saints for its beauty, tranquillity and literary and religious associations. The project was opposed by priests and poets, scholars and patriots, pacifists and conservationists—an amalgam of disparate feelings and concepts. Welsh members of parliament, public bodies, cultural institutions and local government, the religious denominations, all united in opposition to what seemed an act of desecration. Lewis, with his former adversary W. J. Gruffydd, took a leading role in the opposition. But, as always, Welsh opposition and protest was ineffectual. Since the days of Glyndwr (Glendower) in the early fifteenth century, the Welsh had never done more than occasionally protest at what was meted out to them. There were no sanctions, except words. Lloyd George had broken down cemetery gates to allow Nonconformists to bury their dead in the parish churchyard, but they had done that in the name of their religion, not their nationality. 1936, the fourth centenary of the Act of Union, was to be different.

Lewis and his colleagues petitioned the government to receive a deputation, but in vain. Eventually Lewis, together with a well-known Baptist minister and a short story writer, set fire to what had been erected of the bombing range, having made sure that nobody was put in danger, and then gave themselves up to the police. They had committed an act of 'open, responsible violence against property', a symbolic act on behalf of Wales, an act which they wished to be judged by the Welsh people. This would be done by facing trial by their peers, as a means of 'putting their case before the bar of Welsh public opinion'. The jury at Caernarfon failed to convict them. For the first time ever a case was taken out of Wales, to England, and a new trial took place in the Old Bailey in London, a court they refused to recognise. They were convicted and sentenced to nine months in Wormwood Scrubbs. They had perpetrated the first act of defiance of England's right to override Welsh wishes since Glyndwr.

They were released to a heroes' welcome in 1937, but the enthusiasm was dissipated before long by war fever and the rumours that the nationalists were sympathetic to the German cause, as were some Breton ones. They were suspected of being in favour of following Ireland's example, where England's hour of crisis was seen as Ireland's opportunity. Lewis's speech from the dock was worthy of Emmett. He delineated the way protest against the scheme had grown, and compared the way it was responded to with the fate of simultaneous protests in England, and those were not on behalf of anything truly sacred. They had felt constrained to act, but in the open way, which laid them open to punishment, as the only way to get the government to listen.

This sort of language and action is hardly that of a fascist or anarchist, though Lewis was accused of being both. He was no clandestine arsonist or assassin. His speech from the dock reaches a high level of eloquence and human dignity, and was delivered in the first year of the Spanish Civil War, when the Axis powers were preparing to take revenge on the small nation of the Basques with their Condor Legion, and when Stalin was holding his show trials. Lewis maintained that human beings and nations had rights and duties which were dependent on a higher law than that of any state.

His reward was a bitter one. The Baptist minister returned to his pulpit; the teacher and short story writer to his classroom, and both were warmly welcomed. The senate of the university at Swansea, under duress because certain funds were being made contingent on their actions, dismissed Lewis even before he had been convicted. He was to remain in the wilderness until 1952, when he was appointed to a lectureship in Cardiff, a post he held until he retired in 1957. His action in 1936 and its aftermath became a watershed in Welsh life and letters, especially to the latter. Most writers took his side. Eminent poets were changed, utterly in some cases, as Yeats was by the events of 1916. The finest lyric poet, Robert Williams Parry, abandoned lyricism. In one poem about Lewis this is what he had to say to his compatriots:

'Dear country, if you can afford to lose the learning
Of the most learned in our midst,
You must be, of all countries,
The most blessed in its estate.

If you can afford to quench the flame
And blunt the faith of your blameless son,
You must have many a better author
Than the idle author who is in his cell.

If you wish to deny and reject him,
The most innocent beneath the heavens,
You must have many other good hearts
Who will bleed for you separately.

If you can smother with a new burden
This overloaded and tired one,
Take now your opportunity
And don't be soft-hearted like your Christ.' (trans.)

Certainly, things were never the same again, and sentimental patriotism had been dealt a mortal blow.

As the party's fortunes waned with the growth of war fever in 1938-39, and especially with the scare-mongering about alleged Nazi sympathies amongst the nationalist ranks, Lewis felt constrained to resign the presidency. He did so at the start of the war. Throughout it, and on to 1951, he wrote an extensive column in the weekly *Baner ac Amserau Cymru*. It became his main platform and source of income. The format and style were akin to those of Mauriac's bloc-notes in *L'Express*. They ranged widely in the arts and current affairs, religion and philosophy, and were almost always provocative, brilliant and unpredictable. The dramatic element in them was always compelling. He took a wide stage, and nearly every major figure in

European artistic and intellectual life down the ages was there, waiting in the wings to be summoned. He was never a name-dropper, but really did know the pedigree of any writer he quoted or discussed.

The most controversial parts of his journalism concerned the war itself. The censor in London kept a close eye on the work, in translation, and tried to have it curtailed if not prohibited. It was cut a number of times. What galled people most was Lewis's neutralism, not pacifism, and his even-handed condemnation of inhuman war methods, such as the bombing of civilians. As with his feelings about the Great War, as well as Wales's predicament in 1936, he despised dishonourable behaviour. He had little instinctive understanding of the dilemmas of the comparatively inadequate creatures, like most of us, who see most moral decisions in terms of a choice of the lesser of two evils, and who normally count the cost of any resultant actions. Another aspect of his journalistic writing which disturbed many people was the very idea of a Welsh world view; the idea of a Welsh stance on foreign affairs was unreal, if not downright treacherous.

It was while he was writing that regular column that he wrote some of his finest poems. The vagaries of his political career probably contributed to his sense of the absurdity of much of human existence. The only optimism he could contemplate was the conditional one of a Christian believer. He always remained in sympathy with disbelief though, and especially with those like Joyce and Beckett, who parodied belief. Remarkably, in most of the poems and plays there is very little bitterness or disillusion. For he had suffered a final blow to his self-esteem towards the end of the war.

In 1943, a bye-election was held for the parliamentary seat of the University of Wales. Lewis was nominated by the nationalist party, and was supported by an array of famous and distinguished people, largely from the world of letters, the arts and the churches. The seat had been held by the Liberal party, who now looked for a suitably well-known candidate. They eventually chose one from outside their ranks, in fact a former member of the Nationalist Party and a former vice-president of it. He was none other than W.J. Gruffydd. The election was bitterly fought, with Gruffydd playing on fears of anti-democratic tendencies in the nationalists, and suggesting that they were less than dedicated to the war effort. Gruffydd won comfortably, though Lewis's share of the vote, 22.5%, was easily the best result for the party to date. But the failure compounded Lewis's feeling that he was a failure as a leader and his sense of rejection. That was what finally decided him to retire from political life, apart from the odd foray in the form of a letter or an occasional lecture or interview.

He returned to his first love, literature, for the more than forty years left to him. He produced more poems, rich in Christian humanism, as well as another novel, many works of criticism, and some twenty plays, some of which achieve the greatness of his finest poetry. He gave up the bloc-notes in 1951; he retired from the second stint at the university in 1957, and then his public image dimmed. He created in his plays much of what he had failed to do in real life, and sometimes castigated his nation, explicitly or implicitly, for being spineless. Young people thought him bitter, having never met him or seen him. The picture is well described by the poet R.S. Thomas:

> And he dared them;
> Dared them to grow old and bitter
> As he. He kept his pen clean
> By burying it in their fat
> Flesh. He was ascetic and Wales
> His diet. He lived off the harsh fare
> Of her troubles, worn yet heady
> At moments with the poet's wine.
>
> A recluse, then; himself
> His hermitage? Unhabited
> He moved among us; would have led
> To rebellion. Small as he was
> He towered, the trigger of his mind
> Cocked, ready to let fly with his scorn.

Most of Lewis's plays and poems have a religious angle, be they historical works set in Wales or beyond, be they tragedies or comedies. They are also, like the works of Graham Greene and Sartre, full of real-life situations and of the profane, dealing with people's sexual as well as spiritual loves. And they usually include a deal of violence, though it is never gratuitous.

\*     \*     \*

The Nationalist Party's fortunes waned in the 1950s, but the post-1936 generation were seeking new ways of fighting for the nationalist cause. Slowly, inexorably, Lewis was drawn back into the wings of the political stage. By the late 1950s the party was faced with a dilemma akin to that of 1936, when parliamentary measures were forced through Westminster, enabling English cities to appropriate and drown Welsh valleys, dispossessing their inhabitants, in order to provide those cities with cheap water. Things came to a head in the case of a valley called Tryweryn, where there was a particularly vigorous community. There was, once more, almost unanimous, total opposition in Wales to the proposal. The nationalist leadership were under intense pressure to carry out another act of open defiance as had happened in 1936. But they baulked at the idea, and offered a compromise. Bitter disillusion set in, especially among young nationalists, and general apathy returned. In the subsequent election the Nationalist Party's fortunes slumped badly. Violence, born of frustration, broke out. Pipe lines and other installations were blown up at night. Eventually, young men were captured and imprisoned.

Then, in 1962, BBC Wales invited Saunders Lewis to deliver their annual radio lecture. He gave people a doom-laden message, in his inimitable style. The Welsh language would, 'under present trends', disappear by early in the next century. It was only by 'revolutionary methods' that it could be saved. He cast a cold eye upon the history of the language since the Act of Union, and the part played by England and by the Welsh in the process of decline. Then he proposed revolution: not a violent one, not against the person. It was to be in tune with the emerging civil rights movements in the new world, and before long in Ireland. It was reminiscent in tone of Mahatma Gandhi's passive resistance movement. It asked the people, at least the Welsh speakers, to make it impossible for government in Wales, be it central or local, to ignore the Welsh language.

It was a message for the Nationalist Party, but they ignored its central message. They were, by now, more involved with 'bread and butter' issues. He had sniped at this involvement once or twice, notably in 1958 when he attacked the slogan adopted by those in the rural heartland who were desperate for work: 'Bread before Beauty'. At that time nationalists were trying to get atomic power stations set up in their areas. They were even thinking of having such a station in the Llyn peninsula.

Lewis had no sympathy for such a slogan, which Aquinas would surely have approved of. However, a significant section of Welsh youth responded to the radio lectures, and formed *Cymdeithas yr Iaith,* The Language Society. It is still going strong, and has campaigned successfully, using militant methods with hundreds going to prison, gaining much in the way of status and making actual progress for the language. As a result, the face of Wales has been transformed. The language now has a high profile, and there's a significant growth in the numbers of young people speaking it. Welsh is becoming a normal medium of communication in the fields of education, the courts, the media and most aspects of public life. That lecture was Lewis's last intervention in politics.

\*   \*   \*

He did make one other, and most notable public appearance in 1966. He delivered a public lecture on Ann Griffiths, Wales's finest female poet and a remarkable hymn-writer. The chapel where he spoke was packed with high court judges, scholars from as far as Paris, farmers and teachers, students and preachers. Not the least of his achievements that day was to read some of the hymns with such passion that their original spiritual content became incandescent once more.

He was pleased to show how she had not described her conversion as a tempestuous process as had Pantycelyn, but as the realisation that she had a duty to honour, glorify and venerate God. But unlike Calvin, who Lewis said stressed the awe to be felt in the presence of holiness, for Ann Griffiths the emotion was love of His beauty and perfection—the beatific vision which she had written so wondrously about; looking, as she said, with the angels, not at the work of salvation, but into it. He compared this insight with that of Maritain in his chapter on Descartes and on the perception of angels. Her view was obviously in tune with Lewis's own view of the nature of worship: the 'rent' of love due to the Creator and Redeemer.

\* \* \*

Finally one comes to his very last work, a poem called 'Terminal Prayer', which he wrote in 1973 when he was eighty years old. It caused almost as much controversy as anything he ever wrote. In it he derides the inadequacy of human language to express the great truths about God and his creation, and ends by saying there is only one way of approaching the eternal and divine at the end of one's earthly life, by going 'mute to the mute'.

Critics, especially Protestant evangelical ones, saw this poem as evidence of loss of faith, or at least as an example of Homer nodding. It was couched in language reminiscent of another famous poem about man's end, by T.H. Parry-Williams. That poem speaks of 'silence, stillness and quiet', and of man's self-emptying simply revealing his nakedness 'with the night closing in about him'. It ended with this couplet,

'All we'll do, as we flee from our foolish fussing,
Is simply slip back into the great stillness.' (trans.)

On the other hand, Lewis's poem talks of the 'mute', not of abstract nouns. It reminds some of us the experience of

Christ in the garden of Gethsemane. It hardly seems a faithless poem. In a rare break with his habit of not commenting on criticism of his work, Lewis answered one of the critics, a Wittgensteinian professor of philosophy called D.Z. Phillips:

> 'I was extremely glad that he refutes the idea that it is an atheistic poem. My wish is to be counted a Christian, even if I am not a good one. I know also that it is a dangerous thing to discuss one's own poem . . .'

He goes on to show how theologically sound it is to talk of kenosis and man's inability to find words adequate to describe the reality of what we perceive through a glass darkly. Then he goes on to discuss and defend the lines about the content of the Apostles' Creed:

> 'What is sad is that it is only thus, that is through the figurative or through images, that we can portray or put before the mind's eye the faith of the Christian. For it is the Resurrection and the Ascension which are the foundation and warrant of our Hope. But what is the "Ascension"? What is it for us today? A symbol of the Unity of God the Father and God the Son and God the Holy Spirit in the salvation and guidance of the creation; our warrant that neither the universe nor the history of man nor the life of the mind nor the Parthenon nor *Fidelio* nor Aber Mawddach an hour before dawn on a fine June morning are meaningless accidents. The Ascension is not an event in time and place, but "the supreme declaration of our faith". But, as we assert things about the spiritual, the eternal, about the Trinity which is an unfathomable Unity, and which sustains every being which exists through its "Word", is not our language, our imagery, our talk of "sitting on the right hand" of necessity terribly, pitifully "comic"? How can we be adequate for the tasks with the language at our disposal? We are men, funny little creatures; there isn't that much between us and mice. Except that some of us venture to believe that God became man...

'Let us turn to the last five lines of the poem; these were the ones which offended most according to what I have read, and I am sorry for that . . . In order to curtail this discussion as much as I can, may I refer the reader to certain theologians in Germany and the Netherlands in the fourteenth century, namely Messrs Eckhart and Tauler and Henri Suso and Ruysbroek. I only know parts and excerpts from their works, and I would be ashamed to be thought learned in them. But their teachings about prayer were an eye-opener to me, and there is some of their influence and their vocabulary in these lines.'

*　　*　　*

He did, indeed, retain his faith, painfully, to the end. He died without most of his faculties, save the ability to pray. A race well run, and one which left an indelible mark on Welsh and European culture. He died to the sound of the *Pater Noster* recited, in Latin, by his friend and confessor, Bishop Daniel Mullins. The bishop detects the influence of Thomas a Kempis on that final poem, as he detected it in those final years of Lewis's life.

## Letters To His Wife-To-Be From The Front In France During The Great War

34/35. Lt. J.S. Lewis

15 December, 1916

My dear Margaret,
At present I'm submerged in mud and work. Camp comman-
dant of a camp of 4000 men left in a land that owns no coal, no
dry corner, no drinking water and roads long impossible for
traffic. It is an exciting business, and yet I like it immensely. I
go out after breakfast, take for my lunch a cheese sandwich
and watch my roads growing, my stables being built, huts
made water-proof, trees felled to provide timber and
firewood, pumps built to draw water. It is a satisfactory sort of
romance and suggests to me I should enjoy after the war going
right out to the wilds of some virgin country and building cities
and settlements—and ride home on a wild prairie horse when
dusk is advancing like an army on all sides, and the first stars
set you wondering who you are, where you are. If I were asked
what is my vividest impression in life, I answer the strangeness
of it all. It is so strange I still do not know whether all the earth
is friendly or hostile, and it never reveals itself.

Yours ever,
Saunders.

February 1917

My Dear Margaret,
. . . We are in the front line again. It is as it was before the
frost, a sort of jellatinous (sic) matter into which you sink
waist deep every time you evacuate your dug-out. In this I am
told (on fair authority I believe) that we are conducting a war.
With whom, it is difficult to tell. If you look long over the rim

of a shell-hole, in a great wood some two hundred yards off you may occasionally glimpse a man looking as wet as yourself, but a pipe in his mouth and a curious mediaeval sort of head-gear on him, who perhaps digs, perhaps carries something heavy, but is always furtive as a thief, and never anxious to be seen.

Well, he and the hawks make good game and occasionally one takes a rifle, aims slowly, caresses the trigger-guard, and presses,—and the man either staggers or makes off.

That is war in one phase and not the most picturesque. It has heaps of phases, sometimes the jellatinous (sic) matter suddenly hits you hard, you realise that this is the earth you are insulting with your howitzers and field-guns, and its muteness, its greyness and its obscure way still of pushing up a slim grass blade where it can; makes you quiet for a moment.

Well, narpoo, write me a decent folio next time, for I've a genuine hunger.

Yours ever,
Saunders.


# Principles of Nationalism

### ADDRESS TO THE FIRST ANNUAL MEETING OF THE WELSH NATIONALIST PARTY IN 1926

We meet today to begin a week of study. Most of us who have come here are nationalists, love Wales and believe that this concept of WALES is something important in our own private and public lives. My aim in this paper is not to argue for the rights of Wales in order to convince anyone of the rightness of the National Party's philosophy; but to try to face the difficult problems which claim our consideration. Our movement is a political movement. Our Party is a political Party. In politics, the foremost thing is to define aims, lest we dissipate our strength fighting for vague things. And let us remember this: extremism is a ready pitfall for every movement. I do not fear to say that there are great perils in hot-headed and unbounded nationalism. Recognizing the limits; fighting only for the indispensable, the essential, the necessary things; and then desisting not going to extremes—that is the only wisdom, the only justice.

Let us glance at the history of Wales. It is a country that was once part of the Roman Empire, that inherited the Latin civilisation of Europe, and after the fall of Rome sought to build its life on the basis of that tradition. Then it was overcome by enemies and by the thirteenth century lost all shadow of indepenedence. It was conquered. But this did Wales no great harm. It went on as before, living its own life and developing its culture, still part of Europe. Then in the sixteenth century this land was joined to England under the Tudors, and from then on the civilisation of Wales wasted away and declined. Today that civilisation is in mortal peril.

When Wales was conquered in the Middle Ages by England, no great harm came of it. When Wales was freed and made part of England under the Tudors it was dealt a mortal blow. Why?

The question is answered in many ways. People talk of the betrayal by the Tudors, of the decline of the Welsh nobility; of the disappearance of the bardic profession; of the beginnings of the middle class and wealthy merchants who saw nothing in Welsh culture; of the wrong done to the Welsh language; of the Anglicising of education.

All these are secondary causes. There was a deeper cause: the thing that destroyed the civilisation of Wales and ruined Welsh culture, that brought about the dire plight of Wales today, was—nationalism.

And now I must explain.

Have you noticed? We are by now so used to hearing things such as: Every nation should be free; no nation has the right to govern another nation; a nation must be independent; and the like sentences—that we seldom doubt or ask the meaning of these sayings. What is the meaning of 'free', 'govern', 'independence'? Certainly one can give them meanings that would justify every one of the sentences I have quoted. But they can also easily be understood in such a way that it would be quite true to say: no nation should be free; no nation has a right to independence or to govern itself. And those are the truths that most need to be emphasised today.

In medieval Europe, no one country was free, or independent or claimed that its government within its own boundaries was the supreme and only authority. Every nation and every king recognised that there was an authority higher than state authority, that there was a law higher than the king's law, and that there was a court to which appeal could be made from the State courts. That authority was the moral authority, the authority of Christianity. The Christian Church was sovereign in Europe, and Church law was the only final law. For a while Europe was one, with every part of it recognising its dependence, every country recognising that it was not free, nor had any right to govern itself as it pleased regardless of other countries. And Europe's oneness in that age, its oneness in moral principle and under one law, protected the culture of every land and region. For one of the profoundest ideas of the Middle Ages, an idea Christianity inherited from the Greeks, was the idea that unity contains variety. There was one law and one civilisation throughout Europe; but that law, that civilisation took on many forms and many colours. It did not occur to the rulers of a country to destroy the characteristics of another land's civilisation, even when they conquered that land. For beneath the numerous differences remained the oneness, the moral and spiritual oneness. And so oneness of belief, the conformity of the countries, was a protection and a cradle for every regional culture and the special qualities of every part of Europe. Hence it was Christianity and the Church that protected Welsh civilisation. Despite being conquered, being oppressed too and that quite cruelly, it grew upright and without losing the innate qualities of its culture. No doubt Wales often yearned for freedom, but did not fear losing its heritage, nor did it. Because there was one law and one authority throughout Europe, Welsh civilisation was safe, and the Welsh language and the special Welsh way of life and society. The idea of independence did not exist in Europe nor

31

the idea of nationalism, and so no one thought that the civilisation of one part was a threat to that of another, nor that multiplicity of languages was inimical to unity. And that was so—I would like to emphasise this—because that unity was moral, based on a moral law and a common creed.

Man's intellect is a feeble and uncertain thing. When he has truth and the roots of a good life, he easily loses them. So it was in Europe. In the sixteenth century, the age of Luther of Germany, Machiavelli in Italy and the Tudors in Britain, the moral unity of Christendom was destroyed, and instead of Christianity another principle came to rule, i.e. nationalism. The basis of this doctrine was that the final authority in life and the final law was State authority and the king's law. The authority of the Church and the moral principle of political life were denied. State government, so it was said, was supreme, and the king's law above all conscience and all morality. Every country had the right to complete and unconditional independence. The government was supreme in all—religion, conscience, the whole of human life. The king, not the Pope, was the Head of the Church, and the king's law could change creed and theology and standards of morality, if he pleased. Any revolt against the State authority, the Government, was a crime against God, said Luther. So, instead of there being one authority in Europe, tens arose; instead of one law, many; instead of unity, confusion. Naturally every authority was a danger to its neighbour, and every government strove to grow stronger, expand, and plunder. One civilisation was the enemy of another. Variety could not be imagined other than as a weakness, as division. Dictatorship demanded uniformity, one law, one language, monotony. If one government was against another, it was also the enemy of every difference of tradition, culture and language within its own boundaries. Since material strength was the main basis of authority, uniformity was essential. In the political philosophy of the Middle Ages all oppression was condemned, all tyranny, all laws that violated that precious thing: man's personality. But in the political philosophy of the age of Luther, and from then on, government was exalted, oppression changed into justice and violence into rightness. Because it was by oppression that uniformity and strength of government and kingdom might be achieved. There, very broadly, you have the principles of sixteenth century nationalism. Those were the ideas of the Tudors in Britain. And those were the principles that destroyed Welsh civilisation. Every difference between Wales and England was obliterated. In the two countries there was one government, one language, one State law, one culture, one system of education, one religion, that is, government religion, government language, government education, government culture. Sixteenth century nationalism was nothing but the triumph of materialism over spirituality, of paganism over Christianity. And it was this materialistic and pagan triumph that destroyed our Wales.

I remind you of these things as a warning. Let us not argue for Wales's rights on the basis of this nationalist philosophy. For it is a materialistic argument; and in a materialistic argument, might is right. Our nationalism must be different. We must appeal not to material rights but to spiritual principles. We must approach the English government with a moral argument, and believe the day will come when once again the value of the principles of morality will be recognised. For the day of materialistic philosophy has come to an end. Imperialism is a natural effect of this paganism. But one result of the last war is the realisation that imperialism is something to be ashamed of, and that every attempt at uniformity in political life leads to war and destruction. What is called the League of Nations, but which I would prefer to call by the more Welsh name of the Society of Nations *(Soceite des Nations)*, is an attempt to loosen the hard chains of material nationalism. I will return to the problem of the Society of Nations. Here I merely suggest that the creation of this institution, and its recognition by Great Britain, are a sign that European opinion is beginning to be uneasy, and that there is now a chance for our party's argument on behalf of Welsh civilisation to be heard.

What, then, is our nationalism? This: a return to the

medieval principle; a denial of the benefits of political uniformity, and a demonstration of its ill-effects; thereby arguing in favour of the principle of unity and variety. Not a fight for Wales's independence but for Wales's civilisation. A claim for freedom for Wales, not independence. A claim that she should have a seat in the Society of Nations and European society by virtue of the value of her civilisation.

First of all, let us not ask for independence for Wales. Not because it is impractical, but because it is not worth having. I have already shown that it is materialistic and cruel, leading to violence, oppression and ideas already proved to be bad. The age of empires is fast passing, and afterwards there will be no meaning or value in independence. Europe will return to its place when the countries recognise they are all subjects and dependent. If this does not come to be, Wales for her part may be content to recognise the supremacy of England. That is not the greatest evil. Let us recall what it was like between the thirteenth and sixteenth centuries. Today we too can build a Welsh civilisation without independence.

So let us insist on having, not independence, but freedom. And freedom in this affair means responsibility. We who are Welsh claim that we are responsible for civilisation and social ways of life in our part of Europe. That is the political ambition of the National Party.

What basis is there for this claim, and what does it mean? It is based on historical facts and their value. It is a fact, we believe, that social life in Wales through the ages created a way of thinking, of experiencing life and of expressing the human spirit, which is especially peculiar to us; and it is true also that the precious things in Welsh history and Welsh life today are the things that are consistent with this Welsh tradition. Now, every thinker knows well enough that it is very difficult to name the characteristics of a nation, and claim that a nation has special qualities that another nation cannot foster. But however difficult it may be, yet I believe it can be shown to every fair-minded man that Welsh civilisation is essentially different from English civilisation. To prove this, let us peruse this August's Welsh and English newspapers. The English newspapers are filled above all by two kinds of affairs—economical and political, especially the matter of the coal strike, and sports affairs, especially tennis and the England-Australia cricket match. On the other hand, this month's Welsh papers are filled by a number of lengthy, extensive and detailed adjudications of goodness knows how many eisteddfod competitions in poetry, prose, singing and composition. It is in its main and most characteristic meeting that the nature of a nation may be recognised. Three weeks ago many of us were at the Swansea Eisteddfod. For a whole week, about twenty thousand Welsh people spent day after day following a feast of song and instrumental music, of poetry and criticism, and talk of criticism and of the arts. The remaining Welsh people in all parts of the country, who could not be there, followed the accounts of the sessions and argued about them, with amazing unanimity. This is Wales's annual festival. Here is where Wales shows the things she especially values. That is to say, the eisteddfod is a fair symbol of the concept of Welsh civilisation. It is also consistent with Welsh history, consistent with the tradition of a country that set such a high value on the arts in the difficult times of the Middle Ages and insisted on keeping poetry and music as the pursuits of gentlemen despite all hardship. I do not say that these are the only characteristics of Welsh history. No, unfortunately. But undoubtedly here is a Wales that exists, and exists in the face of a thousand difficulties and the weight of other ways of life and of very different models that are doing all in their power to poison her best aspirations.

I will go further and say that the success and furtherance of this Welsh concept depends on the Welsh language. It is always in the Welsh-speaking parts of Wales that eisteddfod succeeds best. Where Welsh is alive and vigorous, there you will find flourishing local eisteddfodau, literary meetings, reading classes, singing schools and an admirable interest in literature and music. And wherever Welsh declines, and the English way of life and language replace it, these things degenerate, and one finds football matches, races, billiards clubs, and the cinema, and if there is any class at all held under the aegis of the colleges, it will more than likely be a class in economics:

*"Y llwybrau gynt lle bu'r gan*
*Yw lleoedd y dylluan".*

("What were once the pathways of song, Are now the haunts of the owl.")

Yes, all this is familiar to everyone. And I am sure there are profound and more philosophical arguments for the preservation of Welsh. But it is on simple, down to earth things that I would like to base my argument today. For this is the essence of politics. The idea is too commonly held that the real stuff of politics consists of arguments about great, abstract and imperialistic topics. That is a deplorable idea. I can take no interest in politics at all other than the politics touching the everyday life of my neighbours and compatriots. This should be the main task of politics in Wales: the safeguarding of the Welsh culture that I have described; the ordering of life in Wales so that these things, the best we have, the concept of the eisteddfod and the literary pavilion and the art exhibition and the reading class, may be increasingly safeguarded and encouraged and elevated and improved. All Welsh life should be ordered so as to ensure the priority and success of these things.

Some people used to say that this was something for the home to do. I believe that argument is dead by now. It was always the argument of the timorous and the craven, those who learned to give the front seats in life to the English, and to keep Welsh civilisation in rags like a little Cinderella by the ashes of the humble hearth at home. I repeat: these matters are political matters, the best things in the life of our country. And Welsh political life must be arranged so as to protect these things from the doom that threatens them today. That is the main reason why we formed our Nationalist Party. I will not now attempt to prove the error of the 'home' argument, but I comment on one thing only. If Welsh, and the Welsh culture are kept only on the hearths of Welsh-speaking Welshmen, then the language and the culture will be dead long before the end of this century. For outsiders come increasingly to the countryside in the North and to the populous t͏ villages in the South; and by their intrusion and their the current of Welsh life is rapidly being anglicised. Only a political movement can save us. We must turn the out-siders—if I were Greek, I would say the barbarians—we must turn them into Welshmen, and give them the Welsh mind, the Welsh culture, and the Welsh language. That is what will safeguard the only civilisation that is traditional in Wales.

(May I here add a word in parentheses. You will see, ac-cording to this argument, that every poet and writer and artist and scholar who enriches the literature and art of our country, is doing work of unequalled political value, is strengthening the cause of Welsh freedom. They can do nothing more valuable. Do not, therefore, try to get every artist and scholar to do other work, that is to say, political propaganda, speeches and arguments. Not every artist, poet or writer is capable of it. Do not be vexed with them if it so happens that they have no in-terest in practical politics.)

But to resume. In order to ensure the safety of the Welsh concept and culture, political authority is therefore essential. Wales must be planned in a Welsh way, and her whole life made Welsh. More freedom must be given to Welsh culture to work like a leaven through the whole of Wales. Welsh educa-tion must be made Welsh in spirit and in language. Priority must be given in the schools' syllabus to Welsh literature and Welsh should be made the sole medium of education from the elementary school to the university. Thus, every child in Wales, whatever his mother-tongue, will inherit Welsh culture and language which is the only key to that culture. That language must be Wales' only official language, the language of Government in Wales, the language of every county, town and district council, of the council of workers themselves and of the lawcourts. Every public medium that broadcasts infor-mation, that teaches or entertains the country, such as the wireless, must also be in Welsh, and used to strengthen and elevate the Welsh concept. In a word, the whole of Welsh social life and every instrument of social life, must be constantly and unswervingly adapted towards one aim: a Welsh civilisation for Wales. Only thus will the chain of history and culture and civilised life be kept unbroken in this part of the world, linking us with the past, and giving us nobility, tradition, stability and beneficial development.

Society cannot exist at all without government, without a central authority; and that central authority must act mainly to foster the best concept of the society. That is, the government of Wales must be Welsh in spirit and language.

That being so, we must have self-government. Not independence. Not even unconditional freedom. But just as much freedom as may be necessary to establish and safeguard civilisation in Wales; and that is a freedom that will be not only beneficial to Wales but also an advantage and safeguard for England and every other neighbouring country. For instability and lack of tradition in any country is a danger to the peace of every other country. Leaving Wales as it is today, full of disorder and uncertainty and without a firm tradition, would very soon be likely to cause rebellion and turmoil throughout the whole of Britain. I do not know whether the English government understood during the coal strike how indebted it was to Welsh culture and the National Eisteddfod for the calm and order there was in South Wales during all the weeks of the dispute. If Welsh culture is capable of this today, at a time when it is weak, what could it not do when it is installed and fittingly crowned? That is what the aim of self-government will be. That too is a condition of self-government. The Welsh civilising concept is the only worthwhile argument for self-government. One could not, for instance, claim self-government all for an English Wales, except on the basis of the old materialistic nationalism,—a basis which to me is odious. But we lay claim to self-government, because without it we cannot definitely ensure the furtherance of Welsh culture. And the idea that lies beneath our Party's policy. We must be able to turn all public institutions into Welsh ones, especially our schools and colleges, our councils and local authorities and law-courts equally so, and that is in practice impossible without self-government. So let us start on this work in Wales, starting with the local authorities within our reach; and as we do have as much power over the law-courts, let us study the plan Mr. O'Sheil will be describing for us on Thursday, and let us try to get up our own Welsh law courts, and take our cases there. In every way and in everything let us try to make a Welsh Wales a fact. Then, when it exists and is a fact, we can go to the English government and ask it to recognise the fact, and recognise the value of the fact—recognise it with a generous measure of self-government.

That cannot be done while Wales considers itself part of England, sharing in England's political life, and admitting that London and the London Parliament are the focus of its life. That is why the National Party insists that its members break their connection with English parties, and refuse to send representatives to the English Parliament. While we are thus a politicial part of England it is folly to argue for Welsh education for Wales. For 'political part' means 'social part', that is, part of English civilisation. And if that is what Wales is, then education in Wales should be English in spirit and language, and Welsh schools should discipline the children (as do the majority today) to forget the Welsh concept and adopt the Englishman's concept and the English type of civilisation. Henry VIII was totally consistent: he made Wales a part of England and made English the official language of Wales. I know that this is a stumbling-block to many of middle-aged Welshmen who are patriotic enough, but have grown accustomed to a compromise between their patriotism and their loyalty to the Liberal Party. But in fact, the story of those Welshmen and of that Party confirm our belief. For from its beginning to its expiry today, the Liberal Party has done nothing for Welsh civilisation, except corrupt the Welsh concept with English ideas and ambitions. Let us therefore hold firmly to this: that the Welsh concept needs a central Welsh authority in Wales. You cannot serve God and Mammon. You cannot either serve England and Wales. Another proverb that shows this situation effectively is: No-one sews a patch of new stuff on old clothing; otherwise the patch will tear free from the old, and the tear will be worse. If the Party's policy appears harsh in this, the reason is so that the tear may not be worse. Only the Welsh concept can save Wales, not the English material.

One more word. What will crown this movement to build Welsh civilisation in Wales? This: that Britain and Europe and every country recognise the value and importance of that civilisation, concede that it has a part in a contribution to the life of the world, and so give it a seat in the Society of Nations. It is strange and funny how popular the Society of Nations is in Wales. It is surprising to see the Society of Nations flourish best in a nation that no other nation recognises to be a nation at all. There is another criticism to be made of the Society of Nations. Although there are branches of its association in so many Welsh churches, yet hitherto the Society of Nations is a pagan and materialistic thing. Not one of the Great Powers in it has offered to foreswear the principle of independence and when it was proposed to put the British Fleet under the authority of the Society, England soon raised her voice against it, claiming freedom and independence. Therefore, let us Welshmen be very cautious before allowing this Society to steal our hearts. Wales as it is today cannot influence the Society of Nations at all. That is the truth, despite all that is said to the contrary. But when Wales gets self-government, one of the conditions of that Act will be that England recognises our rights to a seat in the Society of Nations: that it recognises Welsh civilisation and its special role in the modern world. Then, Wales and the Welsh concept can influence Europe and the world, and our membership of the Society of Nations will crown the effort that was begun not in a materialistic spirit of narrow and godless nationalism, but in a generous spirit of love for civilisation and tradition and the best things of mankind.

(translation by Bruce Griffiths)

# Letter About Catholicism

*This open letter was addressed to W. J. Gruffydd, professor of Welsh in Cardiff, and editor of a prestigious literary magazine,* **Y Llenor***. It was published in the summer of 1927. In it Lewis complained that the editor had been attacking him, and what Gruffydd called the Neo-Catholic movement in Wales. This, it was claimed, was evidence of the influence of Charles Maurras and the* **Action Française** *on Lewis, and it had narrowed his sights. In fact, as Lewis pointed out at the start of the letter, it was another Welsh writer, called Bebb, who was a disciple of Maurras, following a period in Paris. Lewis went on thus:*

If I owed Maurras a debt, it would not be today, when his work is under a cloud, that I would deny that...I have read three or four of his books, especially his work in literary criticism, for he is an important critic. But I must state the fact that his political ideas have had almost no influence on me...If you will be patient enough to look again at my pamphlet on *Principles of Nationalism*, you will see straight away that the gist of my argument, my plea for a European and anti-state way of thinking in political matters, is completely at odds with all Maurras's teaching...To the *Action Français* France exists against Europe. For *Y Ddraig Goch* (the party journal, edited by Lewis) Wales does not exist except as a part of Europe.

Maurras and his school are not the only teachers of Catholic thought in France today. The truth is that a strong Christian renewal is one of the principal features of French literature in our day. I admit a heavy debt to the Christian poet and dramatist, Paul Claudel, to the novelist François Mauriac, and to the literary critic who died so young and suddenly, Jacques Rivière. I also learnt everything I know about the Christian philosophy of the Middle Ages from that great scholar, Etienne Gilson. If you wish to know the sources of much of my thought, I implore you to read these authors. Then, I think, you will understand better why I have no sympathy with the modernist tendencies of Welsh Nonconformism today, nor with the sentimental Christianity of books such as *The Life of Jesus* by Middleton Murry.

41

The great loss to Welsh literature in our day is that we have no anti-Christian writers. We have no one (with the exception, perhaps, of one great poet) who denies Christ, who denies Christ his claims, who understands exactly what is involved in the Christian call, and who says "No" to him. I would have nothing but total admiration for the strength of mind and honesty of such an author. Many of the great authors of France in this day are such men. André Gide is such a man. So is the finest literary critic Europe has seen since the war, Ramon Fernandez. In Wales we do not find this strength or honesty. We only have heretics. Our literateurs boast that they are "Nonconformists", and each nonconforms to everyone else. But they all claim to be Christians. They do not deny Christ as gentlemen would or should. They heap on him an insult a hundred time worse than denying him; they distort him. Christ has become clay in their hands, and he is turned into a seer, a man of genius, a prophet, an artist, a lover, a humanitarian, an "Aunt Sally" in the poets' fairground.

*He goes on to attack Modernism in the Nonconformists, and then to talk of a study in which he is engaged on one of the great eighteenth century poets and hymn-writers, William Williams, Pantycelyn, in one of whose works a character could not accept a certain doctrine because he had realised he was a "sinner." And this, Lewis, said,*

when Rousseau had realised he was "a child of God." It is Rousseau who is the source of the latest thinking in Wales...None of the modernists and the romantic mystics are psychologists, and because they know nothing of psychology and self-inquiry, they know nothing about sin either.

This is a pity. Losing sin is a loss to literature. Without sin all that we get is lyric poetry such as we have in Wales today, and which is to be had, I hear, in heaven also, another country which is short of sinners. But here on earth we should respect our heritage and make the most of sin. It is the stuff of the best tragedies in the world, the works of Shakespeare and

Racine. Sin is the substance of classical novels, and the passionate consciousness of it is what gives Dostoevsky his incomparable power...

A religion which does not give sin an important place in its system is a religion of "the Prophet". That religion may put great emphasis on communion with God and on following Christ, but will not cheat any learned person into believing that it is anything but the opposite to Christianity. The mark of Christianity, always, has been that it laid such emphasis on sin, elevating sin to such glory and importance that it was necessary for Christ to be nothing less than God, and he dying as a man, in order to disenthrone sin. And to the Christian mind, sin is the special attribute of man, the most human thing in existence and thus essential to poetry and literature. The constant tendency of prophetic religion is to deify man, turning every man into a little christ—that is, losing his rich, comprehensive humanity, and impoverishing the theatre and the novel, and destroying psychological literature. I am not arguing now on behalf of religious literature, but for the retention in literature of the great rich ideas that exist in Christianity. That is what makes the works of those novelists in Italy and France who reject Christianity worthwhile. André Gide is not a Christian. But Gide does not deny that sin exists. Rather, he chooses sin. And lest anyone thinks that that statement is presumptuous and terrible, let it be remembered that that would have been the fate of Pantycelyn as well if God had not overcome him: "I preferred to retain my sin,/How sweet is hidden bread,/Against my will/You brought my faults under my feet." And my sympathies are thoroughly with authors such as these, and my admiration for their works is immense.

The result of losing the consciousness of sin is Christian Modernism, and because of that I detest it. And it is the same sentimental blindness—the effect of the sick tendencies of Rousseau spreading throughout Europe—which is shown in hatred for dogma and sacrament and definitions in religion. It is natural for those who deprecate sin to hate definition. Once one accepts defining as a principle in life, it will have to be applied to the spirit of man, to the ecstasy of the prophet and the magic of romance, and that would lead to the discovery of sin—that which has been denied. The religion of the prophet cannot stand definition.

## The Blessed Sacrament

(On the occasion of a visit by a number of my anti-Catholic friends to a Catholic church)

They came into your house
And sat somewhat nervous and rather bold
Without bowing to the Host nor bending knee,
O, Master of Hosts, do not be annoyed
At their lack of courtesy;
For in your Hall there is only
An altar with its flowers and candlesticks higgledy-piggledy all
    over the place
Like a loaded dresser in an antique shop,
Funny, pathetic pictures of your Passion and Crucifixion,
With images of Joseph and Mary in Brummagem plaster
Standing like Aunt Sallies in a fair,
And St. Teresa like a fashion plate in Vogue.

These came under your roof
As if to the Rouges' Gallery in Madame Tussaud's;
How could they comprehend your strangely tender
    mischievousness?
Your solemn faced children
With their sober zeal for your ungraveness,
Here amidst the bric-a-brac of our puny rituals,
Receive, underiding Father
Their harsh derision as true worship.

For who in his right mind,
Without another candle
(O, Father of the lights)
Would ever find you playing hide and seek, with your home
In the guise
Of wheat
An insignificant particle amongst all the chaos?
It's no wonder the children do not kneel to their missing Lord.

But when the day comes
When these tread your Heaven without scorn
And kneel in amazement there to Your human guise,
Let us, your poor captives
Whom you penalised here with the biting knot of Faith,
Give us a share, with your children, of their wonder.

1936

## Why We Burnt The Bombing School

(The Caernarfon Court Speech)
13th October 1936

*Inside the courtroom, after making his protest against the way in which the address of one of the other defendants had been destroyed by its having to be translated in bits and pieces, Mr. Lewis then started to address the jury in English.*

The fact that we set fire to the buildings and building materials at the Penrhos bombing range is not in dispute. We ourselves were the first to give the authorities warning of the fire, and we proclaimed to them our responsibility. Yet we hold the conviction that our action was in no wise criminal, and that it was an act forced upon us, that it was done in obedience to conscience and to the moral law, and that the responsibility for any loss due to our act is the responsibility of the English Government.

We are professional men who hold positions of trust, of honour, and of security. I must speak now with reluctance for myself. I profess the literature of Wales in the University College of Wales at Swansea. That is my professional duty. It is also my pride and delight. Welsh literature is one of the great literatures of Europe. It is the direct heir in the British Isles of the literary discipline of classical Greece and Rome. And it is a living, growing literature, and draws its sustenance from a living language and a traditional social life. It was my sense of the inestimable value of this tremendous heirloom of the Welsh nation that first led me from purely literary work to public affairs and to the establishment of the Welsh Nationalist Party. It was the terrible knowledge that the English Government's bombing range, once it was established in Lleyn, would endanger and in all likelihood destroy an essential focus of this Welsh culture, the most aristocratic spiritual heritage of Wales, that made me think my own career, the security even of my family, things that must be sacrificed in order to prevent so appalling a calamity. For in the University lecture-rooms I have not professed a dead literature of antiquarian interest. I have professed the living literature of this nation. So that this literature has claims on me as a man as well as a teacher. I hold that my action at Penrhos aerodrome on September the eighth saves the honour of the University of Wales, for the language and literature of Wales are the very *raison d'être* of this University.

And now for my part in Welsh public life. I speak briefly about it. I have been for ten years President of the Welsh Nationalist Party, and editor of its organ *Y Ddraig Goch (The Red Dragon)*. I have been a member of the Advisory Committee of the University of Wales on Broadcasting, the chairman of which has been the Pro-Chancellor of the University, the Bishop of Monmouth. I have made a special study of the economic problems of Welsh unemployment and reconstruction, and was the originator of the Welsh National Industrial Development Council. In South Wales I have been in constant touch with my unemployed fellow-countrymen, and have successfully founded a club, the membership of which is growing and spreading over Wales, whereby on Thursday of every week a man whose position in life is comfortable gives up his dinner and sends the price of it to provide a three-course dinner for an unemployed fellow-Welshman whose larder on Thursday is empty.

Now, if you examine these activities and if you examine our record, you will find that our works, our programme, our propaganda have been entirely constructive and peaceful. There has never been any appeal to mob instincts. In fact, our leadership has been accused of being too highbrow and academic. I have repeatedly and publicly declared that the Welsh nation must gain its political freedom without resort to violence or to physical force. It is a point I wish to re-affirm today. And I submit to you that our action in burning the Penrhos aerodrome proves the sincerity of this affirmation. Had we wished to follow the methods of violence with which national minority movements are sometimes taunted, and into which they are often driven, nothing could have been easier than for us to ask some of the generous and spirited young men of the Welsh Nationalist Party to set fire to the aerodrome and get away undiscovered. It would be the beginning of methods of sabotage and guerilla turmoil. Mr. Valentine, Mr. D. J. Williams and I determined to prevent any such development. When all democratic and peaceful methods of persuasion had failed to obtain even a hearing for our case against the bombing range, and when we saw clearly the whole future of Welsh tradition threatened as never before in history, we determined that even then we would invoke only the process of law, and that a jury from the Welsh people should pronounce on the right and wrong of our behaviour.

*The Judge interrupted: 'You are telling the jury—and I say this in your own interests—the reasons why you took the steps you did and burnt down the aerodrome; and I tell you that that is no exuse in law, and that the more you persist in telling the jury your ideas about Welsh nationalism and Welsh culture, the less excuse there is for having committed this act. So far your argument has been totally irrelevant to the charge.'*

*Mr. Lewis answered:* I thought I was speaking on it the whole time. I am sorry. *And he continued with his address:* We ourselves, public men in Wales and leaders of the Welsh Nationalist Party, fired these buildings and timbers. We ourselves reported the fire to the police. We have given the police all the help we could to prepare the case against us. Is that the conduct of men acting 'feloniously and maliciously'? I submit that we are in this dock of our own will, not only for the sake of Wales, but also for the sake of peace and unviolent, charitable relations now and in the future between Wales and England.

It is charged against us that our action was 'unlawful.' I propose to meet that charge by developing an argument in four stages. First, I shall show with what horror the building of a bombing range was regarded by us and by a great number of Welsh people in every part of Wales. Secondly, how patiently and with what labour and at what sacrifice we tried and exhausted every possible legitimate persuasion to prevent the building of the bombing range. Thirdly, how differently the protests and remonstrances of Wales and Welsh public men were treated by the English Government, compared with similar protests, though less seriously grounded protests, made in England in the same period. Fourthly, I shall try to put before you the dilemma and the conflict of obedience in which the Government's cruelty placed the leaders of the crusade against the bombing range, and the limits to the rights of the English State when it transgresses the moral law and acts in violation of the rights of the Welsh nation.

In an English pamphlet stating the case against the bombing school in Lleyn, Professor Daniel has expressed with pregnant brevity the heart-felt fear of all thoughtful Welshmen.

*The Judge again interrupted: 'What Professor Daniel said has no bearing on the case. I only say this in your own interest, that if you go on addressing the jury as you have done, you are—so far from putting up any defence—making the case against you worse.'*

*Mr. Lewis continued:* It is the plain historical fact that, from the fifth century on, Lleyn has been Welsh of the Welsh, and that so long as Lleyn remained unanglicized, Welsh life and culture were secure. If once the forces of anglicization are securely established behind as well as in front of the mountains of Snowdonia, the day when Welsh language and culture will be crushed between the iron jaws of these pincers cannot be long delayed. For Wales, the preservation of the Lleyn Peninsula from this anglicization is a matter of life and death.

That, we are convinced, is the simple truth. So that the preservation of the harmonious continuity of the rural Welsh tradition of Lleyn, unbroken for fourteen hundred years, is for us 'a matter of life and death.' I have said that my professional duty is the teaching of Welsh literature. My maternal grandfather was a minister of religion and a Welsh scholar and a man of letters. He began his ministerial career in Pwllheli. He wrote the greatest Welsh prose work of the nineteenth century, *Cofiant John Jones Talsarn (The Biography of John Jones of Talsarn)*. One of the most brilliant chapters in that book is in the seventh chapter, which is a description of the religious leaders of Lleyn and Eifionydd in the middle of the nineteenth century. It is impossible for one who has blood in his veins not to care passionately when he sees this terrible vandal bombing range in this very home of Welsh culture. On the desk before me is an anthology of the works of the Welsh poets of Lleyn, *Cynfeirdd Lleyn, 1500-1800 (Early Poets of Lleyn, 1500-1800)*, by Myrddin Fardd. On page 176 of this book there is a poem, a *cywydd,* written in Penyberth farmhouse in the middle of the sixteenth century. That house was one of the most historic in Lleyn. It was a resting-place for the Welsh pilgrims to the Isle of Saints, Ynys Enlli, in the Middle Ages. It had associations with Owen Glendower. It belonged to the story of Welsh literature. It was a thing of hallowed and secular majesty. It was taken down and utterly destroyed a week before we burnt on its fields the timbers of the vandals who destroyed. And I claim that if the moral law counts for anything, the people who ought to be in this dock are the people responsible for the destruction of Penyberth farmhouse.

*At this, applause was heard in the court, and the Judge ordered everyone to be quiet, and the officers to take anyone who made such a commotion again outside. Mr. Lewis continued:* Moreover that destruction of Penyberth House is, in the view of the most competent of Welsh observers, typical and symbolic. The development of the bombing range in Lleyn into the inevitable arsenal it will become will destroy this essential home of Welsh culture, idiom and literature. It will shatter the spiritual basis of the Welsh nation.

It was the knowledge of the catastrophe that the proposed bombing range would bring to Welsh culture and tradition in this, one of the few unspoilt homes of that culture, which led to thousands of Welshmen not normally interested in political affairs to protest vigorously against such an outrage. I have to show now that these protests were on a national scale, that they were representative of the Welsh nation, that nothing was neglected or left undone to convince the English Government of the seriousness of the occasion, and that efforts of peaceful, legitimate persuasion were exhausted in our endeavour to prevent the catastrophe. I shall summarize the story of the protests as briefly as possible.

It was in June 1935 that the Air Ministry's proposal to establish a bombing range in Lleyn was first announced. Immediately the Caernarfonshire branches of the Welsh Nationalist Party held a delegate committee and sent to the Ministry a statement of their unanimous objection to the plan.

In January 1936 the campaign against the bombing range was renewed with urgency, and from that time on it ceased to be a matter of local interest. It was taken up throughout Wales and became a national concern. Protest meetings were organized generally in Lleyn and Caernarfonshire. Resolutions of protest were passed by Welsh churches and representative meetings of the religious bodies throughout Wales.

Protests were equally general from all the Welsh secular societies and institutions, the University of Wales Guild of Graduates and the Welsh national youth movement (Urdd Gobaith Cymru), as well as Welsh Cymmrodorion societies in Cardiff, Swansea, Llanelli, Aberystwyth, and representative meetings of Welshmen living outside Wales, in London, in Liverpool, Manchester, Birmingham. Before the first day of

May more than 600 Welsh societies and religious bodies had passed unanimous resolutions demanding the withdrawal of the bombing range. These resolutions were sent on to the Air Ministry, and the agitation in the Welsh press was a sign of the widespread approval of the protests.

We kept the Prime Minister and the English Air Ministry fully informed of our opposition. On March the thirty-first I wrote to the Prime Minister, begging, in view of the gravity of the affair, for an interview. I said in my letter: 'An important body of Welsh people read this proposal as one to prevent which even liberty, even life itself, might properly be thrown away.' The Prime Minister declined to grant an interview, and sent in answer a stereotyped statement exactly similar to that sent to all other protesters.

On May the first I broadcast a talk through the national wave-length of the British Broadcasting Corporation, on Welsh Nationalism. I took the opportunity to make an urgent appeal for the saving of Lleyn from this bombing range. The Government continued to ignore every appeal.

We organized a plebiscite of the people of Lleyn. It was conducted entirely by voluntary workers giving their spare time to tramping the scattered villages and farmhouses of the peninsula and paying their own expenses in food and bus fares. Over five thousand of the electors of Lleyn signed the petition to Parliament and to the Prime Minister asking for the cessation of the bombing range. Our workers were welcomed everywhere. They met with a practically unanimous sympathy, and with time they would have obtained the signatures of almost the entire rural population of Lleyn. Similar plebiscites were conducted in Llanberis and among the Welsh of Liverpool, where five thousand adult Welsh men and women also signed petitions. Before the end of May well over one thousand Welsh churches and lay bodies, representing over a quarter of a million Welsh people, had passed resolutions of protest.

On May the twenty-third we held a final national demonstration at Pwllheli. It was attended by seven or eight thousand people, and they had come in motor buses from all parts of Wales, as well as from centres outside Wales. The meeting received much notice in the English newspapers everywhere because of the attempt of a gang of some fifty drunken roughs in Pwllheli to prevent the speeches from the platform.

The platform represented the whole of Wales, leaders of religion, of scholarship and public life. The chairman was the most eminent literary man in Wales, Professor W.J. Gruffydd. Professor Gruffydd put the resolution calling on the Government to withdraw their plans for Lleyn and inviting the Prime Minster to receive a deputation on the subject. A show of hands revealed an overwhelming majority in favour of the resolution. The negative did not exceed fifty.

On June the fourth the request was sent to the Prime Minister to receive a Welsh national deputation. It was sent on behalf of the five thousand petitioners of Lleyn, the thousands of petitioners outside Lleyn, and the fifteen hundred bodies representing nearly half a million Welshmen who had resolved to protest against the Lleyn bombing range. The letter requesting the Prime Minister to receive a deputation was signed by over twenty eminent Welsh leaders. They included the principals of Aberystwyth and of Bala and of Bala-Bangor theological colleges, the secretary of the Honourable Society of Cymmrodorion, the Bishop of Menevia, moderators of the Presbyterian Church of Wales and the chairman of the Congregational Union of Wales, and the professors of Welsh Language and of Welsh Literature at the University Colleges of Bangor and of Aberystwyth.

A secretary to the Prime Minister replied that 'the Prime Minister does not feel that any useful purpose would be served by his acceding to the request that he should receive a deputation.'

On June the fifteenth, the English newspapers circulating in Wales reported thus: 'More than 200 acres at Penyberth Farm have been cleared and levelled for an aerodrome site. The contractors are beginning to erect an aerodrome today.' Thus ended peaceful persuasion along legitimate democratic lines. There only remained now the way of sacrifice.

But the effect of the English Government's contemptuous rejection of this nation-wide protest from Wales, both on Welsh national sentiment in general and on the Reverend Lewis Valentine, Mr. D.J. Williams and myself as the accepted leaders of the crusade, cannot be properly gauged without considering also the contrast between the Government's treatment of Wales and their treatment of England.

Let me recount briefly the story of bombing range sites proposed to be set up in England at the same time as the Lleyn establishment. One was at Abbotsbury in Dorsetshire. It is a well-known breeding place for swans. Because of that, and because English writers and poets were allowed space in *The Times* newspaper and generally in the English press to express their passion for swans and natural beauty of scene, the Dorsetshire site was moved.

Then came Holy Island in English Northumberland. Mr. G.M. Trevelyan wrote a letter to the press to explain that Holy Island was a sacred region: it was a holiday resort for city workers; it had historical associations with Lindisfarne and St. Cuthbert; it was the most important home of wild birds in England. He argued that Northumberland duck were no less sacred than Dorset swans. He was supported by leaders of English scholarship and letters. The Air Ministry summoned a public conference to consider the matter, and the bombing range was withdrawn.

Will you try to undersand our feelings when we saw the foremost scholars and literary men of England talking of the 'sacredness' of ducks and swans, and succeeding on that argument in compelling the Air Ministry to withdraw its bombing range, while here in Wales, at the very same time, we were organizing a nationwide protest on behalf of the truly sacred things in Creation—a nation, its language, its literature, its separate traditions and immemorial ways of Christian life—and we could not get the Government even to receive a deputation to discuss the matter with us? The irony of the contrast is the irony of blasphemy.

On June the twenty-second, at the Union of the Congregational Churches of Wales at Bangor, the chairman, the newly appointed Archdruid of Wales, the Reverend J.J. Williams, speaking to a resolution condemning the Lleyn bombing range, said: 'It is our intention to prevent the establishment of this bombing school by every legitimate means possible. But if legitimate means finally fail, I believe there is enough resolution in the Welsh nation to remove the bombing camp by other means.'

He spoke for Wales. But—and I come now to a crucial point in my argument—he spoke also for the universal moral law (what we call in Welsh *y ddeddf foesol*) which is an essential part of Christian tradition and is recognized by moral theologians to be binding on all men. 'Remember that God who created men ordained nations,' said Emrys ap Iwan, and the moral law recognizes the family and the nation to be moral persons. They have the qualities and the natural rights of persons. And by the law of God the essential rights of the family and the nation, and especially their right to live, are prior to the rights of any state. It is part also of the moral law that no state has the right to use any other national entity merely as a means to its own profit, and no state has a right to seek national advantages which would mean genuine harm to any other nation. All that is universal Christian tradition.

It is also Christian tradition that men should obey the moral law rather than the law of a state whenever the two should clash.

*The Judge said: 'I have to administer the law of the land, and you are making statements which are inaccurate.'*

*Mr. Lewis continued:* It is universal Christian tradition that it is the duty of members of a family and of a nation to defend the essential rights of the family and of the nation, especially it is a duty to preserve the life of a nation, or to defend it from any mortal blow, by all means possible short of taking human life unjustly or breaking the moral law. That is the Christian tradition.

It was in the clear light of this fundamental principle of Christendom that Lewis Valentine, D.J. Williams and I resolved to act at Lleyn. The responsibility of leadership was ours. We could not shirk it. We saw the English state preparing mortal danger to the moral person of the Welsh nation. We had exercised the greatest patience in attempting every possible means of persuasion and appeal to prevent the wrong. We had the unanimous voice of all the religious leaders of Wales with us. The English Government took no heed at all. The bombing range was begun. Building was proceeding.

We resolved to act. We determined on an action that would proclaim our conviction that the building of this bombing range in Lleyn is by all Christian principles wrong and unlawful. We resolved on an act that would compel the English Government to take action at law against us. We went and gave ourselves up to the police authorities and compelled them to take action against us. We made absolutely sure that no human life would be endangered. You have heard the pitiful story of the night-watchman. The only true statement in all his story is that he suffered no harm at all.

We damaged property. It is valued at some two thousand pounds odd. Exactly by that action we have compelled the English state to put us in this dock. Only by appearing in this dock on a charge sufficiently serious to allow a maximum sentence on us of penal servitude for life could we bring the action of the English state to the bar of conscience and of Christian morality. Every other means had failed. But we have put our lives in the balance against this act of Government iniquity. It was in preparation for this day and this hour, when we should appear before you twelve, our fellow-Christians and fellow-countrymen, and should explain all our action to you and the meaning and significance of that action, and should ask your judgement on us—it was for this and in the belief that we could prove the moral justice, the absolute justice, of our act, that we have lived and hoped from the moment that our decision was made.

It is perhaps necessary to say something about the amount of the damage we caused by our fire. It exceeds two thousand pounds, we are told. It is obvious that the damage caused is frivolous compared to the harm that the successful establishment of this bombing range in Lleyn will cause. Actually, if it were practicable to estimate in terms of money the cost to us of the efforts we all expended in our crusade to persuade the Government to withdraw the bombing range, the cost of the time and labour freely given by all our fellow-workers and by Welsh religious leaders who travelled to and fro addressing protest meetings, it could be shown that the bombing range has already cost us very many hundreds of pounds.

But the loss that this bombing range, if it be not withdrawn, will cause to Wales is not a loss that can be estimated in thousands of pounds. You cannot calculate in figures the irreparable loss of a language, of purity of idiom, of a home of literature, of a tradition of rural Welsh civilisation stretching back fourteen hundred years. These things have no price. You cannot pay compensation for them. It is only in Eternity that the destruction of these things can be valued. We were compelled, therefore, to do serious damage to the bombing school buildings. Only serious damage could ensure that we should appear before a jury of our fellow-countrymen in a last desperate and vital effort to bring the immorality of the Government's action before the judgement of Christian Wales.

You, gentlemen of the jury, are our judges in this matter, and you have to give a verdict on a case that is not only exceptional but a case that is of momentous importance. I suppose there is no previous example of the leaders of a struggle for the defence of a nation's culture against an alien and heedless state staking their freedom, their livelihood, their reputation and almost their lives, and putting themselves in the dock in order that a jury of their countrymen should judge between them and the brute power of the state. To do this is to show our trust not only in your justice as the jury, but also in your courage. We ask you to have no fear at all. The terminology of the law calls this bombing range 'the property of the King.' That means the English Government. It means these bureaucrats in the Air Ministry to whom Wales is a region on the map, who know nothing at all of the culture and language they are seeking to destroy.[1]

But there is another aspect to this trial that gives it special importance. We have said from the beginning, and it was the point we emphasized in our letter to the Chief Constable of Caernarfonshire, that our action was a protest against the ruthless refusal of the English state even to discuss the rights of the Welsh nation in Lleyn. Now, everywhere in Europe today we see governments asserting that they are above the moral law of God, that they recognise no other power but the power of the state. These governments claim absolute powers; they deny the rights of persons and of moral persons. They deny that they can be challenged by any code of morals, and they demand the absolute obedience of men. Now that is Atheism. It is the denial of God, of God's law. It is the repudiation of the entire Christian tradition of Europe, and it is the beginning of the reign of chaos.

The English Government's behaviour in the matter of the Lleyn bombing range is exactly the behaviour of this new Anti-Christ throughout Europe. And in this assize-court in Caernarfon today we, the accused in this dock, are challenging Anti-Christ. We deny the absolute power of the State-God. Here in Wales, a land that has no tradition except Christian tradition, a land that has never in all its history been pagan or atheist, we stand for the preservation of that Christian tradition and for the supremacy of the moral law over the power of materialistic bureaucracy. So that whether you find us guilty or not guilty is of importance today to the future of Christian civilisation and Christian liberty and Christian justice in Europe.

If you find us guilty the world will understand that here also in Wales an English government may destroy the moral person of a nation—

*The Judge said: 'That is absolutely untrue.'*

1 In the copy of the address duplicated before the Trial (and afterwards published) the sentence ended like this: '...who know nothing at all of the culture and language of Wales, but will desecrate our sanctuaries like a dog raising its hind leg at an altar.' This copy was in front of Mr. Miles and Mr. Edmund Davies: they saw these words shortly before Mr. Lewis arrived at them, and started to become restless. He didn't see their signs, but he passed the words without reading them.

*Mr.Lewis continued:* You declare that the Government may shatter the spiritual basis of that nation's life, may refuse to consider or give heed to any appeal even from the united religious leaders of the whole country, and then may use the law to punish with imprisonment the men who put those monstrous claims of Anti-Christ to the test. If you find us guilty—

*The Judge said: 'That is untrue. Will you stop? I am not going to allow you to make statements which are not only untrue but almost blasphemous.'*

If you find us guilty—

*'You are not to say that again!'*

I wasn't going to. If you find us guilty, you proclaim that the will of the Government may not be challenged by any person whatsoever, and that there is no appeal possible to morality as Christians have always understood it. If you find us guilty you proclaim the effective end of Christian principles governing the life of Wales.

On the other hand, if you find us not guilty you declare your conviction as judges in this matter that the moral law is supreme; you declare that the moral law is binding on governments just as it is on private citizens. You declare that 'necessity of state' gives no right to set morality aside, and you declare that justice, not material force, must rule in the affairs of nations.

We hold with unshakable conviction that the burning of the monstrous bombing range in Lleyn was an act forced on us for the defence of Welsh civilisation, for the defence of Christian principles, for the maintenance of the Law of God in Wales. Nothing else was possible for us. It was the Government itself that created the situation in which we were placed, so that we had to choose either the way of cowards and slink out of the defence of Christian tradition and morality, or we had to act as we have acted, and trust to a jury of our countrymen to declare that the Law of God is superior to every other law, and that by the law our act is just.

We ask you to be fearless. We ask you to bring in a verdict that will restore Christian principles in the realm of law, and open a new period in the history of nations and governments. We ask you to say that we are Not Guilty.

Thank you, my Lord.

*[The Caernarfon jury failed to agree on a verdict.]*

## The Life Of Saint German—A Radio Play (1936)

In the interval between the two trials, a brave high official in the British Broadcasting Corporation in Wales offered Lewis a commission to write a radio play set in the Age of Saints. It was a way of giving him a platform, if not a pulpit, and the Age of Saints should have been safe enough. Lewis wrote the work remarkably quickly, as if inspired. It was titled *Buchedd Garmon (The Life of Saint German [of Auxerre])*, and dealt with that period in the fifth century when the emergent post-Roman Welsh civilisation was under threat from without and within. From without, the barbarian hordes; from within, the Pelagian heresy.

The work was in verse, and was full of 'strange' Roman Catholic ritual and language, some of it avowedly anachronistic. But the stress was on the two-fold nature of the *pietas* demanded of the Welsh leader, *Emrys Wledig*, Ambrosius Maximus, once he had been enlightened by St. German. The high point of the drama is reached with two speeches by German and Ambrose, which are worth quoting:

ST. GERMAN:

The ramparts of civilisation are tottering,
Nearer and nearer from the east the torches of the
Barbarians flash from forest to forest,
And far off in sandy Africa
Hordes of vandals rush to lay siege to the walls of
  Hippo,
While there, to the background of sounding shields,
Augustine, sick hero,
Old man, bishop of the city,
Fills his last vellum with the errors of the Pelagians
And the secure articles of the Faith.
For on us has fallen the day for defending,
The day of the two-fold defending,

59

The day for building Christianity, and maintaining
the frontier.
And how will the city be defended?
What dwelling shall we create,
What co-building in love and what co-guarding,
Are we not one in Adam, one in Christ?
And this is the error of the Pelagians,
The shattering of the unity of our nature,
And our new unity through Grace,
So that a man of letters is not of the same nation
as the poor man,
But, rather, wins for himself his own heaven
In unremitting self-indulgence,
In the days of the triumph of the Goth.

*Ambrose is moved, eventually, to respond:*

God's Prince,
A man planted a vineyard on a fertile hill,
Dug it and planted it with the noblest vines,
Enclosed it and raised a tower in the middle,
And gave it to his son as an inheritance
To maintain his name from generation to
generation.
But a herd of swine rushed into the vineyard
Smashing its enclosure, to trample on the vines and
devour them.
Is it not right for the son to stand in the opening
And summon his friends to him,


So that the breach may be closed and his
inheritance saved?

German, German,
Wales, my country, is a vineyard given into my
care,
To be passed on to my children
And my children's children
As an eternal inheritance;
And see the swine rushing upon her to despoil
her.
I, now, call on my friends,
Lay and scholarly,
Join me in the gap,
Stand with me in the breach,
So that we may retain for the ages to come the
beauty that has been.

60

And this, my Lord, is the vineyard of your
  beloved too;
The glade of Faith, from Llanfair to Llanfair.*
Will you come to lead my host beyond in
  Powys?

ST. GERMAN:      In the name of the Lord of Hosts,
I will come, o King.

# Amis And Amile

(A verse play, translated by H. Idris Bell, written for radio in 1939)

Mr. Saunders Lewis's play was written to be broadcast in the
B.B.C.'s Welsh service at Christmas, 1939, but the outbreak of
war prevented this. It is founded on a medieval French story,
of which there is a fifteenth-century Welsh translation. The
story may be read in English in the Everyman volume,
*Aucassin and Nicolette and other Mediaeval Romances.* In
translating the play I have followed the metre and rhythmical
movement of the Welsh as closely as is possible in a different
language and have also rhymed wherever rhyme occurs in the
Welsh. Only in two or three short passages where native Welsh
metres, not reproducible in English, are employed, have I
departed from my model, imitating the effect as nearly as I
could.—H. Idris Bell.

### THE HALL OF THE CASTLE. CHRISTMAS EVE

AMILE:      Is the door shut, Porter?

PORTER:      Yes, my lord Amile.

AMILE:      The tables are empty; no sound comes from the
  kitchen.

BELISENT:      Light to-night, my lords, is our supper.

FOOL:      What we have in meat and drink
Would all go under my nail, I think.

AMILE:      It is but short time now to the mid-night office.
It is not meet that we go full-fed to greet the
  baby Christ.

(*Llan = settlement, and Mair is the Welsh for Mary. The name Llanfair is very common in Wales up to this day.)

61

| | |
|---|---|
| FOOL: | My curse on the Pope—before Christmas with fasting to grieve us! |
| | Why must we die ere Paradise ope to receive us? |
| BELISENT: | Yet I will keep, my Amile, provision of food and wine, |
| | Lest some late traveller chance to come |
| | And knock, like Joseph and Mary on the doors of Bethlehem. |
| AMILE: | Belisent, best of women, wise is your word. |
| | You now, candles upon our altar, |
| | My two small sons, who are your mother's two eyes. |
| | You will rise early to-morrow to bring your praise to the manger, |
| | And sing carols to Christ in the hay: |
| | And so—to bed, you rogues. |
| FOOL: | Off with wine, off with food, |
| | Off with children and Advent mood. |
| BELISENT: | Husband, it is the custom that children, on the eve of Christmas, |
| | Should light a candle and set it in the window of the house; |
| | For to-night, who knows but He may come, as once to Bethlehem of Judah, |
| | A babe seeking for shelter, or in guise of a beggar, |
| | And inasmuch as ye did it to one of these little ones |
| | Ye did it unto Me: wherefore, |
| | These two before they go to sleep |
| | Would light their candle to guide the Babe and his mother through the night. |
| | And you two, gentles, |
| | Join with us in the custom: |
| | While the children bring their candle to lighten Mary's path |
| | Do you now sing the Christmas Carol, greeting the Mother of the Word. |
| MEN: | Mary, say, for our relieving |
| | When gat Jesus his conceiving? |
| WOMEN: | I beheld, God's message bringing, |
| | Face to face, an angel singing. |
| MEN: | Say, what sang he when before thee |
| | Gabriel bowed him to adore thee? |

| | |
|---|---|
| WOMEN | "Ave, vial of compassion<br>Merciful to man's transgression." |
| MEN: | Say, what force did on you come,<br>Thus to bear God in your womb? |
| WOMEN: | Free did God create us all;<br>Blame on Him can never fall. |
| ALL TOGETHER: | Hail, in meekness all-transcendent,<br>Joy of angel hosts resplendent,<br>Maid and mother, fount and portal,<br>Thou the light of every mortal. |
| AMILE: | See, the candle is lighted.<br>Bright as a ray of starlight is the taper;<br>Who knows what pilgrim<br>Seeing its flame through the night's fatigue,<br>Will bring on this eve a blessing on you, my<br>    sweet babes,<br>And on my house and the household, for<br>    payment. |
| BELISENT: | My darlings, good-night.<br>The angels of the manger to-night are round<br>    you.<br>To-night no spirits walk nor devil<br>Nor daunting perils;<br>Your waking will be happy to-morrow, the<br>    children's feast,<br>To the wondrous birth and smile of Christmas.<br>And now, ask your father's blessing as you go. |
| AMILE: | This night and in the hour of death,<br>May the Father above us keep you, my<br>    children. Amen. |
| ALL: | Good-night, dear children, a Merry Christmas. |
| AMILE: | Five years ago to-day, Belisent, do you<br>    remember the day? |
| BELISENT: | How could I forget it? Can I forget Amis, our<br>    friend,<br>Who for your sake and mine put his life at<br>    hazard? |
| FOOL: | If hither he come I'll give him a present. |
| BELISENT: | Why, fool, what present for Amis? |
| FOOL: | I'll give him my cap and my bells, my place and<br>    whate'er on my plate is:<br>For I am a fool but for money; a bigger fool<br>    he, and all gratis.<br>Just think that a man should imperil his skin,<br>    acquiring an Empress's daughter, |

|  |  |
|---|---|
|  | And after should give her, though nothing he win, to his friend—yet his own peril bought her! |
| BELISENT: | But, fool, he was married already. |
| FOOL: | Then the greater fool he that he kept not the maid: |
|  | For the wife that befalls to a fool at his wedding |
|  | Is a surly she-bear in the breeches arrayed. |
| AMILE: | Peace, fool, you know not how idle is your rhyming. |
|  | Some way from Paris, by the river Seine, |
|  | In the fields of clover, |
|  | Is the church and monastery of St. Germain; |
|  | There, one eve, with our hands on the high altar and its relics, |
|  | We swore an oath before the Sacrament, Amis and I— |
|  | Never will I forget the oath. |

*   *   *

*A strain of music: its memory brings to his mind the sound of horses' hooves*

|  |  |
|---|---|
| AMIS: | Here is the church. Let us enter. |
|  | Stoutly have you fought, Amile. |
| AMILE: | And you, you were like to be my death. |
|  | Know, Amis, I have wandered all France to seek you. |
| AMIS: | And I have roamed the wide world lamenting for Amile. |
|  | And lo, when we met, armed the two of us like this, |
|  | Each held the other for a robber of the wayside, |
|  | And we fought till our lives were in peril. |
| AMILE: | Never again must this happen. |
|  | From henceforth, yea, though it may be in purgatory I find you, |
|  | And in whatever strange shape, Amis my friend, |
|  | My soul will leap to give you greeting. |
|  | Let us kneel. Let us ascend to the altar. |
|  | Let us lay each one his hands on the relics: |

| | |
|---|---|
| | I swear to God and to you, Amis, I swear it— |
| AMIS: | I swear to God and to you, Amile, I swear it— |
| THE TWO: | I will never fail in love nor in counsel |
| | Nor ought that to friend for friend is fitting, |
| AMILE: | And between me and you falsehood shall never be. |
| AMIS: | And between me and you falsehood shall never be. |

*　*　*

| | |
|---|---|
| AMILE: | Never will I forget the oath. |
| BELISENT: | Would that Amis were with us this Christmas. |
| | What feast, what jubilation |
| | Would we not have with our two sons. |
| AMILE: | And I, if he came, |
| | I would fill this goblet of mine and his goblet too, |
| | And long would be the drinking. |
| BARD: | Fair is your goblet, my lord. |
| | Pardon a poet's curiosity, intent on craftsmanship; |
| | A vial of goldsmith's work is this, glorious in gold and silver, |
| | And precious stones adorn it. Its like I never saw. |
| AMILE: | Nor are you like to see. You have judged with discernment, poet. |
| | It was Pope Constantine gave it me in Rome; |
| | He baptized Amis and me together, |
| | Two babes brought to him to St. Peter's church, |
| | And he gave to us two goblets, of one colour both, |
| | Of one size, the work of one goldsmith; part either from other |
| | And no man could tell which is which. |
| BARD: | Even as this goblet is your life, Earl, |
| | Rounded, sufficing, |
| | Without blemish or dint: |
| | To you Heaven has given a heaven below here, |
| | As in the lake's bosom the sun beholds his own shape; |
| | All lands are loud with your praises, |
| | And your wife and your two comely heirs: |

|  |  |
|---|---|
|  | A lovely dance through golden griefless hours, |
|  | Your wealth and your children, with fortune at your side. |
| FOOL: | The cup has gone to your head, you old fogy; |
|  | Laudation's for rhymesters; in prose 'tis bogy. |
| BELISENT: | Never mind him, fool. It is yours to speak truth in its harshness. |
| FOOL: | 'Twixt bard and fool men reach the very truth. |
| AMILE: | Let the bard sing, if he will. |
| BARD: | I will sing praise to the Earl of Normandy |
|  | And his wife, Belisent, the Emperor's daughter of France. |
| FOOL: | And for my part, as fool, to me falls the burden. |

*The bard sings; the company take up the refrain.*

|  |  |
|---|---|
| BARD: | For the gem of the Normans with the Muse I will grapple, |
|  | In the midst of the holly trees praising the apple, |
|  | My one lord, my only, our bulwark and shield |
|  | The giver of gladness to township and field. |
|  | A health to our lord, our buckler and sword, |
|  | The fountain and fullness of peace accord. |
| FOOL: | A verse for the Countess now. |
| BARD: | My string I will strike in praise of her tresses, |
|  | The Emperor's daughter, the flower of Princesses; |
|  | Like reddest berries her lips are to see, |
|  | The glory of Summer, Spring's brightness is she. |
|  | To the wife of our lord, our mistress adored, |
|  | The fountain and fullness of peace accord. |
| FOOL: | To the children now; theirs is the feast to-morrow. |
| BARD: | To my princes' two children my praise now be given, |
|  | Bright wheat of their harvest-field, loved of high heaven, |
|  | Those blossoms most perfect, what babes could you meet, |
|  | Where'er the sun shineth, so lovely, so sweet? |

To the heirs of our lord, the light of our
board,
To the fountain and fullness of peace and
accord.

*Loud knocking is heard on the door*

PORTER:          Whose summons is that
                 With its knocking on the door
                 That breaks the peace of the night?

*Knocking again*

FOOL:            The children be praised, an early fish has risen
                 to their candle.
                 Yon knocking is like the knocking of death
                 himself.

AMILE:           Open to him, my porter. No man to-night must
                 meet with refusal.

*The door is heard opening, and is immediately followed by the
sound of a clapper like that carried by lepers*

BELISENT:        Sancta Maria! It is the bell of the leper.
MANY:            Leprosy!... A leper!... God help us all.
PORTER:          What seek you here, Sir?
AMIS:            Refuge and alms for affliction.
PORTER:          Here is no spital,
                 But a houseful waiting for Christmas;
                 Go to the monastery, half a mile further.
AMIS:            The night is fearful; entreat the lord of the
                 castle.
                 To give me shelter in his stable for the night.
FOOL:            Ha! Ha! "Because there was no room for him
                 in the inn."
BELISENT:        My lord, on the night of His birth can we turn
                 affliction from the door?
AMILE:           But the leper? What of the children and the
                 household?
BELISENT:        Christ will bring sorrow to none to-night
                 If you put your trust in His name.
FOOL:            No bringer of peace upon earth was the Lord,
                 And queer tricks at times He'd play with the
                 sword.
BELISENT:        To-night be there no talk of swords among us.

67

| | |
|---|---|
| AMILE: | Of what like is this man, porter? |
| PORTER: | There is dignity in his voice. I have not seen his face. |
| AMILE: | Bring him in that we may question him<br>And keep this side of the table, all of you. |

*The clapping is heard approaching*

| | |
|---|---|
| AMIS: | A blessing on the house and this compassionate family. |
| AMILE: | Whence come you, fair Sir; tell us who you are. |
| AMIS: | An exile from afar under God's heavy hand. |
| BARD: | See, his face. Do you see? It is all gnawed away—<br>Even to his mother he would be unknown. |
| AMILE: | Why do you wander thus at Christmas? |
| AMIS: | I have a friend; if he but knew of my affliction<br>I should have from him shelter and protection,<br>And to reach him is my aim. |
| AMILE: | Have you no family to protect you? |
| AMIS: | I had a wife once. Now I am worse than a widower. |
| FOOL: | Every married man is worse than a widower. |
| AMILE: | Gentle, fair Sir, are your answers,<br>And sad though your lot is, you are not without courtesy.<br>If you would abide here to-night, you shall have a roof and a pillow;<br>Yourself know well what care befits a leper. |
| AMIS: | May God, my Lord, repay you;<br>Here too I find tears for the lot of man,<br>And men's fortunes touch the heart of mortals. |
| BELISENT: | Will you take food, my friend? |
| AMIS: | May I have from you a drink of wine? |
| BELISENT: | You shall have it and welcome. |
| AMIS: | Nay, Lady, not in goblet of yours,<br>Lest it harm some maid in the washing.<br>I have my own goblet; pour the wine into this. |
| BELISENT: | The goblet! Oh, the goblet! Holy Mary! |
| BARD: | Of one hue, of one shape with the goblet here;<br>There is no man living could say which is which. |
| FOOL: | 'Tis Benjamin's story of old:<br>If goblet there is in the sack<br>A goblet comes out, alack! |

68

| | |
|---|---|
| AMILE: | Say, you leprous stranger, |
| | Are you robber or murderer? Is it for that is your chastisement? |
| | The goblet there in your hand, its owner gave it not of free will; |
| | Know you whom you have slain? And to whom you come for vengeance? |
| AMIS: | In fair fight, in tournament, and for friend's sake, |
| | So only have I despoiled any man's life. |
| | If it is for that I am punished, I do not know. |
| BARD: | In tournament? O God, was he too a knight once? |
| AMILE: | Answer me, man, nor keep me waiting longer, |
| | How came yon goblet to your possession? |
| AMIS: | Pope Constantine give it me in Rome. |
| AMILE: | Amis? Never, not Amis? |
| AMIS: | Touch me not, Amile. Keep away. |
| AMILE: | Forgive my blindness. My brother, Amis. |
| AMIS: | It is yours to forgive me that I come as unclean leper, |
| | Hideous with leprosy, under your roof-tree. |
| BELISENT: | Let there be no talk of pardon. Your coming, Amis, |
| | Is the Christmas of our hearthstone. |
| AMIS: | It was you, Belisent, first knew me. |
| BELISENT: | As I poured out the wine. |
| | At the shock of the goblet I gazed deep into your eyes. |
| | The leprosy that gnawed your flesh has not darkened your mind's candles; |
| | In them shone the flame of tranquility that I saw in the tournament at Paris. |
| | But I stood mute, the pang like an arrow in my throat. |
| | Amis, how has it gone with you? |
| AMIS: | Like a ship flung into the monstrous fury of the tempest |
| | Which shakes it like a bone, bare and white. |
| BELISENT: | To-night you have steered your bark to haven: |
| | Here you shall find peace and the hearth's protection, |
| | Hands to appease pain, children's laughter— |
| AMIS: | You have children? For that thanks to God in Heaven. |

69

| | |
|---|---|
| BARD: | Two three-year-old babes. You shall hear them to-morrow |
| | Calling you for Christmas. |
| | It was their candle guided you hither but now. |
| AMILE: | Fair Belisent, let us question him no further. |
| | Look, pain and weariness have bowed his neck. |
| | To-morrow you shall tell us your story, Amis, my brother. |
| | And all the turns of fortune on your rough journey; |
| | But to-night rest and sleep are best. |
| | Let us prepare him a royal bed in my room. |
| | Do you, Belisent, and the household go to the midnight office |
| | To give your thanks to the Babe on His altar. |
| | For me, I will stay here to do my friend service, |
| | And at dawn we will go together churchward |
| | To renew the oath made in the monastery of St. Germain, |
| | That I will never fail in love nor in counsel |
| | Nor ought that to friend from friend is fitting— |
| AMIS: | And between you and me falsehood shall never be. |
| AMILE: | Never will I forget the oath. |

*Music. A choir singing*

Stars of night, why blaze ye thus,
Pleiades and Sirius?
*Christus natus hodie,*
In little span God's self in man
    concealed.
For whom does ocean chant his round,
Zephyr sing with lulling sound?
*Ex Maria Virgine.*
For Heaven's own child in Bethlem mild
    revealed.
    Noel. Noel. Noel.
    In the hid and starry midnight
    With no cry nor pain of labour
    Glided Jesus, pearl of heaven, from Mary's
        womb.
    Noel. Noel.

Seraphim and Cherubim,
Say, what wonders now begin?
*Ecce qui creavit nos,*
All Heaven's a psalm, in earth is balm
    excelling.
Zabulon and Naphtali,
All your mourning now lay by,
*Lux fulgebit super vos,*
Comes radiance new like heavenly dew
    distilling.
    Noel. Noel. Noel.
In the hid and starry midnight
With no cry nor pain of labour
Glided Jesus, pearl of heaven, from Mary's
    womb.
Noel. Noel.

# ACT II

## AMILE'S BEDROOM
## THE NIGHT BETWEEN CHRISTMAS EVE AND CHRISTMAS DAY

RAPHAEL: Are you asleep, Amis?

AMIS: I am not asleep, my friend, Amile.

RAPHAEL: You have answered rightly. It is a friend calls
you.
But it is not Amile.

AMIS: Who, my Lord, are you?
And how came you to me like this at midnight?

RAPHAEL: I am an angel of God, and my name is
Raphael.

AMIS: From the depths of my nothingness,
Welcome to you, my Lord Raphael,
If you come to claim my soul.

RAPHAEL: Nay, friend, it is not death who asks his prey.
You have won to yourself for friends the angels
on high,
Who sang your praise to God seeing that you
alway,
Like Job, endure your woe without a cry.
Me now the Lord has sent, this night,
To His saint, to make him whole.

71

| | |
|---|---|
| AMIS: | How, Lord, shall I win healing?<br>God's will be done. But I fear, I<br>tremble.<br>Lead me not, for I am weak, into temptation,<br>But deliver me from evil. |
| RAPHAEL: | Two little sons he hath, your friend, Amile:<br>Bid him slay with his sword those children dear<br>And with their blood, so shed, your body<br>    smear.<br>Thereby, saith God, shall he your sickness heal. |
| AMIS: | O Raphael, Angel, it is not God that asks this? |
| RAPHAEL: | I bring a message, Amis. To Him belongs the<br>    way. |
| AMIS: | Ask my heart's brother<br>To kill his two sons with his own hand<br>That my sickness may be healed? |
| RAPHAEL: | I said not that. Not to right body's shame<br>Doth He send down archangels to your afflic-<br>    tion.<br>With more tremendous aim as a weak babe He<br>    came<br>And trod the road from manger to crucifixion. |
| AMIS: | Is it then for the sake of Amile's soul that this<br>    shall be? |
| RAPHAEL: | It is easier for a camel to go through the eye of<br>    a needle<br>Than for a rich man to enter into the<br>    kingdom of heaven. |
| AMIS: | My Lord Raphael, to me was given once<br>The honour to venture my body for his.<br>Listen now to my supplication:<br>If his world is too rich,<br>And his prayer to heaven grown half forgetful,<br>If he is too strong, with his wife and children,<br>If, on feast days, he comes near to<br>    sinning<br>With mere lip service to God.<br>Be it mine to pay for pardon to him,<br>Deepen my affliction, be your hand heavy on<br>    me,<br>Drive me once more into exile,<br>And receive on his behalf all my<br>    sufferings. |
| RAPHAEL: | Sweet and comely it is to suffer for the need<br>Of a soul that we hold dear; |

|   |   |
|---|---|
|   | But if God lays sorrow on his children |
|   | Their pitiful crying shall be turned to glory. |
|   | There is but one |
|   | Wound that is for ever foul, |
|   | To lose the name of saint. |
|   | Is it this that you wish for Amile? |
| AMILE:*(from his bed)* | Amis, Amis, who is here? |
| AMIS: | There is no one here, my friend. |
| AMILE: | I woke. I heard voices talking. |
| AMIS: | It was I saying my prayers. |
|   | Forgive me that I woke you. |
| AMILE: | No, someone was with you in the chamber... |
|   | Is the door open? |

*He is heard crossing the room in the darkness*

No. The door is closed.

*Approaching the bed of Amis*

|   |   |
|---|---|
|   | Amis, who was with you? |
| AMIS: | My friend, there was no man living |
|   | But I myself praying and supplicating God. |
| AMILE: | I felt his presence. Some other, not you. |
|   | I will swear he pronounced my name. |
| AMIS *(alarmed):* | How? What did you hear? |
| AMILE: | Ha, you are afraid. Then someone was with you. |
| AMIS: | More often is your name in my prayers than any man's, |
|   | But for the ear of heaven was my intercession. |
| AMILE: | It was not you named me. It was another's voice. |
| AMIS: | My friend, I have said it: no living man was here. |
| AMILE: | Why do you fear, Amis? Where is your wonted boldness? |
|   | If you have servant or escort, as befitted your former state, |
|   | What use to conceal them or send them away by night? |
|   | There is freedom here to your servants as to me and my household, |
|   | And it is Belisent's prerogative to maintain them. |

73

| | |
|---|---|
| AMIS *(laughing)*: | My escort is safely beneath your root-tree. |
| | The leprosy is the only servant that keeps his allegiance. |
| | Go, my Lord, to your bed, and sleep, for here is Christmas. |
| AMILE: | No, on my oath. |
| | I know that a stranger came to my house and to this room. |
| | My truest of friends, abuse no longer my welcome. |
| | By the love there was between us, by the kindness of Belisent, my wife, |
| | Who prepared with her own hands this royal bed, |
| | Say! who was here talking with you? |
| AMIS: | Have I not said there was no living man? |
| AMILE: | What, then, was with you? |
| AMIS: | Ask me not, Amile, for God's sake. |
| | Ask me not. |
| AMILE: | It is right I should know it. |
| AMIS: | Your bliss hangs on your not knowing. |
| AMILE: | I must know it. |
| AMIS: | There is nothing harder for me than to say it. |
| | For if I say it, |
| | I know I shall have neither your love nor your fellowship |
| | For ever and ever. |
| AMILE: | I make to God my avowal, |
| | Whatever you say, I will never be wroth with you. |
| AMIS: | You cannot make that promise. You know not, you do not imagine |
| | The gulf that will open between us if I tell you. |
| AMILE: | Do you doubt the word I have given? |
| AMIS: | Raphael, the archangel, came to me from God. |

*A pause*

| | |
|---|---|
| AMILE: | Nor is it strange. Among the angels of heaven |
| | Has been your conversation this long time. |
| | What will the angel have from me? |
| AMIS: | Why from you? Why do you rush into the lake of affliction? |
| | It was to me the angel gave his commandment. |
| | On me be the punishment if I disobey it. |

74

| | |
|---|---|
| AMILE: | To me was the message. I have a right to know it. |
| AMIS: | Every man has a right to his pain. Man has no other right. |
| | But to give to man his right, that is for God's grace to accomplish. |
| | Amile, do not ask of me your right. |
| | Question me no further. |
| AMILE: | I have given my word. You must confess it. |
| | If the message is God's, God cannot promise evil. |
| AMIS: | These were his words: |
| | Two little sons he hath, your friend, Amile, |
| | Bid him slay with his sword those children dear |
| | And with their blood, so shed, your body smear. |
| | Thereby, saith God, shall he your sickness heal. |

*After a moment of silence, Amile breaks out into*
*unnatural laughter*

| | |
|---|---|
| AMILE: | I deserve this. You have caught me fairly, like a rat in a trap. |
| | But, friend, your jesting to-night is bitter. |
| | Is it the leprosy that has changed your nature? |
| AMIS: | Go, my Lord, to your bed. The sport is ended now. |
| | I am free, and you too. To-morrow, I will resume my journey. |
| AMILE: | Free, but how? |
| AMIS: | From your commands and from the angel's bidding. |
| AMILE: | Was it the angel's bidding that I provide two coffins for my children |
| | To grace the Christmas table for me and their mother? |
| | They are strange folk, archangels. |
| AMIS: | Yes, unhonoured, like every suppliant. |
| AMILE: | And their names are Falsehood and Envy. |
| | When you came hither, Amis, joyful was your welcome, |
| | Honour, respect and love were your portion, you a leper, a homeless outcast. |
| | You saw the sunshine of my home, the beauty of Belisent, |

You heard of my two sons, two heirs of my
    greatness,
The spur by which the gods prick men on to
    excellence,
To establish the glory of a lineage from sire to
    son and to
You, the childless one, you saw this and you
    were consumed
In your weakness by the venom of envy and
    evil malice.
Here in your bed you planned it, you shaped
    your vengeance
To bring upon me, at Christmas, the whirlwind
    and winter of destruction.
Leprosy has made you cruel, Amis, to pay good
    with evil like this.

AMIS:    My Lord, not like tidings of great joy
Did I hasten to tell my tale,
And not without urging did I avow it.

AMILE:    I did not know the jealousy gathering within
    you.

AMIS:    Not my invention was the angel whose voice
    you swore you heard.

AMILE:    But it was you devised the hideous murder of
    his message.

AMIS:    Would God you were right.

AMILE:    Do you not fear to lay on God the cruelty of
    Herod?

AMIS:    Ah, miserable me, that fear the face of man
More than God to whom face is nothing.

AMILE:    Why then were you not afraid in presence of
    your angel?

AMIS:    Because it was my death I thought to welcome.

AMILE:    How knew you that he was an angel?

AMIS:    He said it.

AMILE:    Did you see him?

AMIS:    No, but heard his voice.

AMILE:    What sort of voice has an archangel
That you should know it?

AMIS:    You heard him, Amile.

AMILE:    It was a man's voice I heard, a man's voice
    pronouncing my name.

AMIS:    It was a man's voice that called me, a voice like
    yours.

AMILE:    Would an angel come in such sorry fashion?

| | |
|---|---|
| AMIS: | Was it not as a man that the Son of Man came to mortals? |
| | We cannot hear an angel save as a man. |
| AMILE: | Have you ever before this heard an angel's utterance? |
| AMIS: | Never at all. |
| AMILE: | Can you prove to me that it was Raphael? |
| AMIS: | How can I prove it? Nor could Joseph |
| | When he heard in a dream, "Fear not to take Mary." |
| AMILE: | Tell me, Amis, if it came into the Devil's mind |
| | To tempt you to damn a hated soul |
| | And drive it to blaspheme God, |
| | Would it not be with a man's voice he would speak also? |
| AMIS: | May Heaven preserve me from him. |
| AMILE: | Answer me. Would it not be with a voice like your friend's voice. |
| | The Devil would call your name in the darkness? |
| AMIS: | Yes, even so would he call me. |
| AMILE: | What think you? Would he call in your ear |
| | That he was your soul's fowler? |
| AMIS: | No. Not in his own shape does a fiend appear before us. |
| AMILE: | Would it not rather be as an archangel of Heaven |
| | Charging you to put your friend's faith to trial |
| | That the Devil would exalt your heart's hidden longing |
| | Into the dreadful summons of God in the night? |
| AMIS: | Who knows? More deceitful than aught else is the heart |
| | And evil beyond hope. Who shall know it? |
| AMILE: | Will you swear to me that it was an angel? |
| AMIS: | I will not swear, for I know not. But I will say that I believe |
| | It was Raphael; I will put my reliance on God |
| | That he will not leave me to be the Devil's prey. |
| | To walk as one who sees, and to know the night of the sightless |
| | Is the daily life of faith. |

God asks of you nothing but to judge as your
    light serves,
And if for fear of devils or malice of my heart
You judge my message vain, then rest your
    spirit in quietness,
And put to-night's ill dream from memory.
When the dawn comes I will betake me
    churchward,
Through the lepers' window I will follow the
    Christmas office
And will leave my blessing on you and your
    household for ever.

**AMILE:** Amis, I am a carnal man,
Sudden of temper, wild in passion, as you
    remember of old.
But now it is for my children that I fight;
The children who are dearer to me than my
    own existence;
A hundred times they were on my breast, here
    in my arms—
I could not, I cannot kill them.

**AMIS:** Nor could I, Amile. You have suffered enough
    already,
I strove with the angel only that I might avoid
The pain of this talk. And thought in my
    passion
It was for you I was pleading; thus in his prayer
    to God
Does a man's heart deceive him.
You too, have done what you could. God's
    ways are dark to man.
Go, my friend, to your bed now.

**AMILE:** To my bed? How could I rest there?
You have sprinkled on my pillow a venom that
    has devoured sleep.
Oh, that I were an angel or it might be a devil
To creep into your soul's recesses and tear out
    the truth or the lie.
If it is the truth to-night you have spoken, then
    malice sits on the throne of creation
Playing with us fools of men as a cat by a
    barn-door;
If there is deceit in your heart, how can I live
    longer

|  | When the half of my soul—my proof that baptism avails me— |
|---|---|
|  | Nurses the suppuration of his fury in a corrupted heart? |
|  | To-night, this night of Christmas, the world has become to me a dunghill. |
|  | I have filled my barns with puff-balls. |
|  | Yes, well-nigh could I kill my children lest their life be made bitter with the name of a friend. |
| AMIS: | There is no true friend but One. |
| AMILE: | Amis, too black is the night for me to see your face or your eyes; |
|  | Here in this blackness you are but a voice, like an angel, |
|  | But a voice like death's own. |
|  | Awhile ago there was a man I counted my friend, |
|  | He bore the same name as yours; |
|  | On the relics of a saint, on the altar of the sacrament, |
|  | He gave his word to God and his word to me; |
|  | My Lord Amis, |
|  | Do you remember the oath that was sworn at St. Germain? |
| AMIS: | "Let us kneel down. Let us ascend to the altar; |
|  | Let us lay each one his hands on the relics. |
|  | I swear to God and to you, Amile, I swear it— |
| AMILE: | "I swear to God and to you, Amis, I swear it— |
| THE TWO: | "I will never fail in love nor in counsel |
|  | Nor aught that to friend for friend is fitting—is fitting. |
| AMIS: | "And between me and you falsehood shall never be." |
| AMILE: | I adjure you by the oath, |
|  | And as you hope for salvation, |
|  | Is it true that he who came to you |
|  | Spoke as you say? |
| AMIS: | As I hope for salvation |
|  | It is true, Lord, too true. |
| AMILE (returning to his bed): | Never will I forget the oath. |

*     *     *

Calm the night, holy the night,
Mounded snows, roses white,
Shroud the roof, and Mary there
Kneels amid the hay in prayer:
See, in a manger lies God.

Calm the night, holy the night,
Lake and rill still and white;
'Tis Love's hour, the early lambs
Snuggle voiceless by their dams.
See, he is born Lamb of God.

## ACT III

### THE PORCH OF THE CASTLE. CHRISTMAS MORNING

| | |
|---|---|
| 1ST WOMAN: | Good morning, Porter. |
| 2ND WOMAN: | A Merry Christmas, Porter. |
| PORTER: | Good afternoon, lasses. |
| 1ST WOMAN: | Just hear the old grumbler; he blames us Because he was up a quarter hour before us. |
| 2ND WOMAN: | And that too when we all went to the midnight office. And it's not yet light either. |
| PORTER: | Hurry, maids, to deck the tables: Bring the goblets and the bottles; The household, when they come home, will be thirsty. |
| 2ND WOMAN: | What's to be seen from the door, Porter? Let me see. The mist is rising from the meadow. I can see even to the church-door. |
| 1ST WOMAN: | I wonder, did Amile go to the morning Office? The door of his room was shut. |
| PORTER: | I saw the leper making his way towards it. Like a bramble walking. |
| 2ND WOMAN: | The Countess was with us at midnight. |
| 1ST WOMAN: | She did not sleep long. She went again to the morning Office. I will join in the offering for the children, she said. |

| | |
|---|---|
| PORTER: | There are people coming out of the church. |
| | Heap up the fire to blaze in welcome. |
| | What ails them that they are dancing and carolling? |
| 2ND WOMAN: | Let me see. Ha, ha. Like drunken folk embracing each other, |
| | And their merry legs out of sight in the mist. |
| | Christmas is here, tra, la, la. |
| | Dance with me, Porter, and I will give you a kiss. |
| PORTER: | Better a box on the ear. 'Twould hurt less. |
| 1ST WOMAN: | Here is Earl Amile... A Merry Christmas, my Lord. |
| | The children are not up yet. |
| AMILE: | No? Let them sleep. It is still early. |
| 1ST WOMAN: | They'll grumble no end when they find everyone down. |
| | Their candle has burned to the stump. |
| PORTER: | There's a strange jollity at the church door, my Earl. |
| 1ST WOMAN: | My lord is shivering with cold. |
| | Stand by the fire, my Earl. |
| | Will you take wine to warm you? |
| PORTER: | There's something afoot, my Lord. |
| | Here comes the Fool, dancing towards us. |
| 2ND WOMAN: | Let me see, fatty. |
| PORTER: | The Countess is following and the household. |
| 2ND WOMAN: | Yonder's a strange knight walking with the Countess. |
| | Tall, stately, and slender he is. |
| 1ST WOMAN: | What became of the leper, I wonder? |
| AMILE: | Has he departed? |
| PORTER: | He went to the Office, my Earl. |
| AMILE: | Look if you can see him with the household returning. |
| 2ND WOMAN: | Let me see. No, he is not, my Lord. |
| AMILE: | That is all the better. |
| 1ST WOMAN: | Shall I wake the children to greet their mother, my Lord? |
| | It is but an hour to the last Office. |
| AMILE: | Let them sleep awhile. |
| | It will be trouble enough to wake them. |
| PORTER: | The Countess is walking on the strange knight's arm. |

|  |  |
|---|---|
|  | If you were not by the fire, my Earl, I would swear he was Amile. |
| FOOL *(from afar)*: | Oyez! Oyez! Oyez! |
| 1ST WOMAN: | You are still cold, my Earl. Here is a cupful of wine. |
| AMILE: | Let it be. I want no liquor. |
| 1ST WOMAN: | Are you bound for communion then? I would not advise it. |
|  | Your fingers are dead white. |
| AMILE: | They were red enough just now. Two hands, two corpses. |
| BELISENT: | Bear me along with you, Amis. |
|  | My feet cannot keep pace with my longing. |
|  | It is true, is it not? It is you? Say it is. |
| AMIS: | I myself, Belisent. |
| BELISENT: | Come, let us run again, both. |
|  | A foolish thing is a woman's eagerness. |
|  | I am laughing and crying by turns and I trip in my running. |
|  | Let us hurry to Amile, let us hurry. |
| PORTER: | It was a strange communion at church. They are drunk, the whole congregation. |
| 2ND WOMAN: | Let me see, let me see. I don't know why, but I too am giddy by now. |
| FOOL *(nearer)*: | Oyez! Oyez! Oyez! |
| 1ST WOMAN: | A pity I can't call the children to see the merry-making. |
|  | Is the Earl in a fever, think you? Has he touched the leper? |
| BELISENT: | Let us walk again for a while, Amis. I have lost my breath dancing. |
|  | To-day you are like a lad, who yesterday was sick and a cripple. |
| FOOL *(arriving)*: | Oyez! Oyez! Good news for Christmas. |
| PORTER: | What is the matter? |
| FOOL: | Aren't I telling you? A wonder! A miracle. |
| 2ND WOMAN: | Let me see, let me see. What is it, Fool? |
| FOOL: | Haven't I told you already? Let a man get his breath again. |
| 2ND WOMAN: | What have you told? What is it? |
| FOOL: | I've said it again and again. Why won't you believe, you stupids? |
| PORTER: | To-day is Christmas Day. It is New Year's Day a week hence. |

|  |  |
|---|---|
|  | That's the Fool's wonder. |
|  | He lost his wind running to tell us the news. |
| BARD *(arriving)*: | Has the Earl heard? Where is he? |
| 1ST WOMAN: | Yonder by the fire. Go to him, Bard, and let us hear the story. |
| BARD: | My Lord, have you heard the tidings? |
| FOOL: | Of Amis, Amile, of Amis, |
|  | That has set us all stammering. |
| BARD: | Who is now like a twin to you. |
| FOOL: | No wonder he could take your place in the tournament at Paris. |
| BARD: | Your two gold goblets are not more like each other. |
| FOOL: | But easier to steal, what? |
| AMILE: | What is all this? Are you all mad like me, |
|  | Have you lost your senses last night? |
| FOOL: | His leprosy is lost and he's whole, |
|  | And my wind is all broken to bits, |
|  | Here's too much that is lost, on my soul, |
|  | For you to go losing your wits. |
| 2ND WOMAN: | Here they are. The Countess on the arm of Amis. |
|  | Come here, Porter, I must give a kiss to something. |
| PORTER: | Yonder's the door. It's no wider than your mouth is. |
|  | My Lord, the Countess. |
| BELISENT: | O Amile, too long was the short road from church |
|  | For my joy's heavy burden. |
|  | Heaven has given us a gift for Christmas! |
|  | See, Amis, your friend, is whole. |
| ALL SINGING: | Sun and moon and stars, now sing ye |
|  | Praise, praise to God, |
|  | Firmamental waters, bring ye |
|  | Praise, praise to God; |
|  | Ice and snow and rain downpouring, |
|  | Summer, winter, tempests roaring, |
|  | Lightning, thunder, shout in wonder |
|  | Praise, praise to God. |
| BELISENT: | Let us all drink to Amis, health and long gladness. |
| ALL: | To Amis...A blessed Christmas to Amis. |
| BARD: | Behold he comes, from death's grim gripe set free; |

|               | Our welling tears were choked ere they were shed— |
|---------------|---|
| FOOL:         | And for his leprosy, why, let it flee<br>To lousy lounger and to scabby head! |
| BELISENT:     | You do not drink, my Amile. Are you going to the last communion? |
| AMILE:        | I have made offering enough to God.<br>He asks of me nothing further.<br>Is this Amis or a wraith? |
| BELISENT:     | Husband, why do you doubt it? |
| AMILE:        | How was he healed then? |
| BELISENT:     | There was peace in the congregation, kneeling in the darkness of the church,<br>Intent as the two candles kindled on the stone of the altar,<br>While the Light of the World in the midst made strong our hearts<br>Outstretched on the arms of the candlestick, His cross.<br>O sweet, daily adoration of the humble mass<br>Satisfying with its wonted rite the birthday of the Word;<br>Out in the mist knelt Amis peering through the lepers' window,<br>An outcast from the choir,<br>But he was wrapt on the wings of our prayer and the unsullied hands of an angel.<br>With the sacrifice to the presence of the Lord.<br>Profound was the joy of communion.<br>The ardent doves of the parish by the table of the Seraphim<br>With wide open beaks devoured the heavenly grain;<br>And when I saw Amis there in our midst, I felt no wonder nor alarm,<br>For holy in the eyes of angels was his company this long while— |
| AMILE:        | The Devil choke you, wife. |
| BELISENT:     | My Amile, what is this? |
| AMILE:        | Nothing, nothing.<br>I am sick of the conversation of angels.<br>I have not heard yet how the knight was healed of his sickness. |
| BELISENT:     | You, Amis, tell him. |

| | |
|---|---|
| AMIS: | I was leaning on the lepers' window |
| | Like one in Hades peering at an opening in Heaven. |
| | And I heard a voice that called me— |
| AMILE: | A voice? Still a voice? You burn to pile up falsehoods, |
| | You know it was no voice that healed you. |
| BELISENT: | My Lord husband, you are like one beside himself. |
| | The summons of angels from Heaven was ever the grace of Christmas; |
| | They came to Mary and the wise men from the East, |
| | They sang across the acres of the shepherds; |
| | They draw near to us too this hour. |
| | Ever since the children kindled last night their flame in the window |
| | And opened the door to receive Christ in the unclean leper, |
| | The whisper of wings is about us |
| | Shaping the miracles of Grace. |
| | A Christmas gift from the Heavens is the new health of Amis. |
| AMILE: | No giver is Heaven but a huckster, |
| | And bitter is its merchandise. |
| BELISENT: | O Amile, no blasphemy to-day. |
| | I know the cause of your strangeness. |
| | The children who should sweeten our Christmas still slumber. |
| | And empty would be the feast of the Birth and the miracle of our friend's healing |
| | Without their laughter and prattle. |
| | I will go and wake them early. |
| AMILE: | Wife, see my sword here; |
| | If you seek the children it shall pierce your heart. |
| BELISENT: | God preserve you, husband. |
| | There is blood on your sword-blade. |
| AMILE: | It was two pigeons I killed but now; foolish ones that fled not from me. |
| | But that is nothing. Look to your own throat. |
| AMIS: | Belisent, do not fear. The cause of your Lord's agitation |
| | Is a father's care for his sons, his fear of terrors to come. |

But, Amile, God who is slow to anger has dealt
    with us more largely than our merits;
He proved last night that we are but worms, in
    good or ill fortune:
He burdened us even to the limit of our powers
    to endure.
To-day he has pardoned unworthiness, he has
    absolved me from my promise,
He has turned away my uncleaness in token of
    his great mercy.
The test has gone by, and your sacrifice also,
    Earl.
And the dawn is here. Go to the children; have
    no fear.

BELISENT:    What is all this, my Lords?

AMILE:    Tell her, Amis, and the price that was paid for
    your healing.

AMIS:    Last night, when all was silence and peace
And the night in midst of its rapid course,
A voice came to me, Countess, as of an angry
    warrior,
And filled the place with death.

AMILE:    A voice, only a voice.
A tongue saying something, like a man in his
    right mind,
Holding a converse with his fellow,
Pronouncing sentences,
And behold, water will be wine, or bread flesh,
Or two beings one flesh,
On the words' detonation.
O word immutable,
O arrow that left the bow-string.
Last night for me life had meaning and system.
Like a myriad quarries of glass
In a church window tinting the image of
    paradise;
And a word came to my friend,
A voice in the night speaking and then falling
    silent,
And lo! the window of reason is fragments
    under my feet
And life is a dunghill.

BELISENT:    At what hour was this?

AMIS:    At midnight.

| | |
|---|---|
| BELISENT: | The hour of the angels of the manger. |
| | What said your voice? |
| AMIS: | "Two little sons he hath, your friend, Amile; |
| | Bid him slay with his sword those children dear |
| | And with their blood, so shed, your body smear: |
| | Thereby, saith God, will he your sickness heal." |
| BELISENT *(faintly):* | Yes...And what followed? |
| AMIS: | Long tears and hesitation, |
| | And farewells said and lamentation: |
| | Ice where two hearts had been; |
| | Then at dawn this wonder seen. |
| AMILE: | And then you slept, Amis? |
| AMIS: | My fatigue overcame me. |
| AMILE: | I never saw sleep that was sounder. |
| | Like the sleep of a corpse that is washed for burial. |
| AMIS: | Forgive me, Amile. |
| AMILE: | What need of forgiveness? Sleep was fitting for you. |
| | It was I, not you, was bidden to kill his children. |
| | Would not your deep sleep be handy for pouring the blood into your sores, |
| | As I tossed and turned the unclean carcase to wash it throughly? |
| BELISENT: | My soul, you have been in Purgatory. |
| | I will go to fetch the children. |
| | You will see Heaven takes no vengeance of man's impotence. |
| AMILE: | Softly, softly. My sword is not yet in the sheath; |
| | You approach them at risk of your life. |
| | My friend, you slept soundly, |
| | Through the prayerless hours not broken by the voice of any angel— |
| BELISENT: | Hours of the shepherds and the Babe— |
| AMILE: | The hours of a murderer's nightmares. |
| | I swore in the grip of their dark talons it was not God who prompted to murder, |
| | That reason and law and need were a shield to my sons in the night. |
| | But when this knight called on my knightly oath— |

87

| | |
|---|---|
| AMIS: | You fill me with fear, Amile, I called you not, no, never. |
| AMILE: | You know, when our quarrel ceased the oath lay like a glove before me. |

Listen to me for a while: I never believed in your angel:

I believe now and tremble in my lost soul.

Last night, when I heard you sleeping

I rose in the dark to look on your perjured slumber.

If you had feared death in my house, would you not have fled into the darkness,

Not rested yonder in peace under my care?

I looked on the shape of your sickness, and easy it was to have choked you,

But the quiet of your slumber stood like a surly watcher about you.

Not as believing your word or the prayer you babbled,

Not for the honour of glorious friendship,

Not to submit to your angel,

Did I walk the road that was mine.

'Twas the oath alone that held me, a knight's oath, hand on the relics,

Held me bound to my doom, though Heaven itself were untrue.

And so, without God, without faith, without hope, without love,

I drew my sword from the sheath.

My Lady, mother of my sons,

'Tis you I have smitten so harshly,

Short will be my farewell.

It is time that I fled from your presence, a vagabond shamed.

Henceforth when my shadow is seen, with finger on lip every mother

Will hush her infant to sleep, not baring her breast.

Know this and understand it: under the judgement of Heaven

I lifted my hand to my sword-hilt, I challenged Raphael to stay me,

For one cold minute I waited; no sound nor sign was given:

And the sword fell.

| | |
|---|---|
| AMIS: | You have killed the children? |
| AMILE<br>*(as if to himself)*: | Two comely corpses to-day for burial, |

Weak babes; love for me filled them;
Woe to my hand that killed them...
Two comely corpses to-day for burial,
Bone of my bone, they two:
It was my sword pierced them through.
O God, I ask no burial from you.

BELISENT: Clear the tables, women.
Make here two litters.
I go to fetch the children.

*The church bells are heard playing a slow dirge,*
*while the bard sings*

BARD
*(singing softly)*:

What lamentation
 Is heard in Rama,
Grief, tribulation,
 And salt tears shed?
What sorrow unsleeping
 In Bethlem of Judah,
Rachel weeping
 For children dead?

O ye, who yonder
 With harps victorious
Uplift, like thunder,
 The Lamb's own strain,
Twelve times twelve thousand
 In raiment glorious,
Firstfruits of the Gospel—
 Look on our pain.

O Jesu, hear us,
 *Kyrie eleison,*
And now draw near us
 In mercy, Lord—
We make confession,
 *Christe eleison,*
Of our transgression;
 Be thou adored.

*Suddenly the dirge changes to triumphant carols;*
*the laughter of the children is heard approaching,*
*and then their voices calling*

| | |
|---|---|
| CHILDREN: | A Merry Christmas, Mummy. |
| | Daddy, may we go now to the manger? |
| BELISENT: | Behold me and the children the Lord has given to me |
| | For signs and for wonders. |
| | I found them in their bed playing. |
| | See the little red line like a gold ribbon round their throats |
| | Where the sword struck them.... |
| | Stand not astonished, my dear ones, lest you frighten the children. |
| | They know but of sleep beneath the sheltering wings of angels. |
| | It is the wonted mercy of the Saviour wrought all this. |
| AMIS: | In dust and ashes I bow me, |
| | For my eyes have seen Thy salvation. |
| AMILE: | Mine eyes have seen the Lord; |
| | And hateful to myself am I. |
| | O Amis, without cry or birth-pang was born the Babe of Mary; |
| | But a pang more bitter than death was His birth in my heart. |
| | These children I never saw until now; |
| | It was my own pride that I fondled, my life's continuance and promise, |
| | The joy and the strength of my seed, the splendour of my wife's loins; |
| | I loved myself in them more than I loved my own living; |
| | And in them I was slain by God with my own right hand. |
| | Now to God they belong, not to me. |
| | And God in them will I worship; |
| | The Babe Jesus has turned every babe to a sacrament now. |
| | Come, Belisent and Amis, let us follow these two to the manger |
| | And lay them at Mary's feet in gold and frankincense and myrrh. |

*The choir sings as they go towards the manger*

*Adeste, fideles,*
*Laeti triumphantes,*
*Venite, venite in Bethlehem,*
*Natum videte Regem angelorum,*
*Venite adoremus,*
*Venite adoremus,*
*Venite adoremus Dominum...*

## THE END

# Against Purgatory

Don't slay me like a dog, Death, when you come,
In an instant, with rifle shot or bomb,
Nor in my sleep, in case I slip into your clutches
Without a shiver, summons, shout or scare;
Nor wait for the winter of exhaustion
When no desire or passion can be aroused,
The sap of old emotions asleep beneath my witheredness,
Waiting to re-awake in the new spring of a new world;
But, rather, as a stout forester selecting his tree,
Come to me, sound with your axe a grave warning,
Strike once, twice until the layers
Fly off, the branches quake, bend under their weight;
Uproot me from the earth, before
The charcoal burners over there arrive.

1941

# The Carpenter

From day-break to evening the carpenter,
In the shade of his workshop, had worn a frown;
He knew his hand was trembling
Sometimes from the anguished joy of the
Mute song nestling
In his full heart.

When sunset came
She would come too, his betrothed,
A pitcher in each hand,
She'd come, the bright one, the beloved,
From the well, and through the gardens,
And stand a moment
On that threshold there.

The song in his heart could never tell him,
Ever, how undefiled
Was the virgin Mary;
The sweet looks of
The pure maiden
Were still, deep pools
Reflecting unseen stars.

Her modest stride
As luminous as the early primrose,
April dew on violets;
Like heaven's banner blinding
Any wanton looks, her steps;
Everyone would be pure from looking
At the blameless maid.

He closed his eyelids,
And awaited her like a prayer;
He recognised her steps;
He stared: between the pitchers,
Between his beloved's arms
He discovered the outline
Of a mother.

Mary stood on the threshold,
"Joseph." He moaned.
'Are you a virgin, you?'
Gently and calmly,
The living Christ between her loins,
The immaculate answered
"I am a virgin."

What stabbing doubts,
What bitter hours of torment,
Did he not suffer;
The wild onslaughts of fiends,
Stunned disappointment and morose despair
Attacking his heart to blaspheme
Heaven's heir.

It was night for his soul;
There was no prayer nor the light
Of a star or a dawn;
Mutely, without a groan
He tottered on his knees
Until the demons threw him
To the ground as if dead.

And he heard in his dream
An angel say: "Do not be afraid
To take Mary as your wife,
For the son she has conceived
Is of the Holy Spirit
And through him it has been promised
The Dragon's head shall be bruised."

And on the dew there was sunshine
When the carpenter went into his workshop
From his mute dream.
He sawed a length of beautiful cedarwood,
Planed it and polished it,
And on the fine plank
He drew the plan of a cradle.

1941

# The Good Thief

You did not see him on the Mount of the Transfiguration
Nor the night walking the waves,
You never saw corpses blush when his invocation
Touched their biers or their graves.

It was when he was bleeding you saw him, callously whipped,
A crown of thorns upon his head; standing there stripped;
Then nailed on a pole like a sack of bones,
Outside the Pale, like a scarecrow...

You never heard him fashion Parables, a Parthenon of words,
Nor his tone when He talked of his Father.
You never heard the secrets of the Upstairs Room
Nor the prayer before Cedron and the betrayal.

It was amidst an orgy of sadists revelling in woe,
With their screeches, howls, screams and cries,
That you heard the heart-break cry of their prey:
'Why hast thou forsaken me?'

You on his right hand, your colleague on his left,
Writhing like skinned frogs;
Flea-ridden robbers as a retinue to his shame;
Courtiers for a mock king in his agony.

Oh, master of courtesy and manners, who revealed to you
Your part in this cruel parody?
'Lord, when you come into your kingdom, remember me' —
The kingdom conquered by dying.

*Rex Judaeorum:* you were the first to realise
That that blasphemy was a living oracle;
The first to believe the Latin, Hebrew and Greek
That a gibbet was the throne of God.

Oh, thief who stole Paradise off the gibbet's nails,
Fore-runner of the nobility of Heaven,
Pray that we too, before the hour of our demise,
May encounter and experience Him.

1942


## Mary Magdalen

No one can know about women. There are some,
Like this one, whose pain is a sealed tomb;
Their pain is buried in them, there is no fleeing
From it, nor deliverance. There is no ebb
Nor flow to their pain, a dead sea without
Movement in its depth. Who—is there anyone—
Can roll away the stone from the tomb?

See the dust on the path dragging itself lamely:
No, let her be, it's Mary, going to her peace,
Depth calling unto depth, grave unto grave,
Corpse drawing towards corpse in the hateful morn;
She's been in a grave for three days, in a world which had
    ended
In that resounding afternoon, the words—'It is finished'—
The cry which bled her heart like a sword-point.

It is finished; finished. Mary fell from the hillock
Into the cavity of the last Pasch, into the pit of a world
That was but a grave, with its breath in a mute grave,
Mary fell into the death of perdition, stunned,
A world without a living Christ, the terrifying Sabbath of the
    creation,
Pit of the hundred thousand centuries and of their deletion,
Mary lay in the tomb of the quivering universe,
In the trough of the night of the senses, in the cauldron of the
    smoke,
The great tresses that had wiped his feet turned white,

95

All the flowers of memory withered except that of the shower
    of blood;
Cloud upon cloud enveloped her, with their evil stench
An ember in her gorge, destroying her vision
Until they extinguished God with their piercing terror,
In the co-dying, the joint burial beneath a frown.

See her, Christ's Niobe, dragging to the brow of the hill
The rock of her pain following her from the leaden Pasch
Through the black dawn, the cold dew, the heavy dust
To where there is a stone heavier than her broken heart;
With difficulty, the clumsy feet stagger over thorns
The troublesome tears doubling the mist before her,
Her hands reaching out towards him in barren yearning.

Only one luxury is left her beneath the heavens,
One farewell caress, reminiscent tenderness, one
Last carnality, sad consolation, sublime,
Weeping again over his legs,
Anointing the feet and washing the savage wounds,
Kissing the ankles and drying them with her hair,
Being able to touch you, Rabboni, O Son of Man.

Let us pity her. He did not.
The pure, incandescent love which steels
The saint through blow upon blow,
Which pursues the flesh to its fort in the soul, its home
In the heavenly spirit, and its lair in the most holy,
Which burns and kills and devours up to the final skirmish,
Until it has stripped and embraced its victim with its steel claw.

Little did she know, six days before the Pasch,
As she poured the moist, precious nard over him, bountifully,
That indeed 'she kept this for my burial';
She didn't imagine, so loving his praise for her act,
That she would never, ever touch his feet and hands again;
Thomas would be allowed to put his hand in his side; but she,
    despite her tears,

96

Only in the pity of the Bread would she henceforth meet the
bruised flesh.

There she is, in the garden at the break of day;
She makes herself look towards the cave; runs,
Runs to the remains of her bliss. Oh, can she believe it,
Believe her eyes? The stone on the ground,
The grave empty; mute and bare;
The first lark rising over the bare hill-top,
And the nest of her heart empty and bereft.

As plaintive as a pigeon's is her cry,
Like Orpheus lamenting Euridice
She stands amidst the roses wailing without surfeit
'They have taken my Lord...taken him,'
To disciple and angel alike,
'And I do not know where they have laid him,'
And to the gardener the same utterance.

She was stupified, shattered, subsiding in her woe.
The mind reeling, the reason scattered, unless
Some person comes who will snatch her out of her flesh to
crown her—
Suddenly, like an Alpine eagle falling on its prey—
With the love that moves the stars, the power that is a Word
To raise and restore: 'and he said to her, "Mary,"
And she turned and said to him, "Rabboni".'

1944


## Emmaus

No one will find it now,
Its history only lasted an hour;
Rocks and path, utterly lost
Is trafficless Emmaus.

But there lives on in its chronicle
The Paschal sun-day of the Universe,
The bounteous argument and sweet invitation,
The bread-wafer of Emmaus.

What apparition is that in the distance,
Burrowing in the sand, at the late hour of the stars,
For a city by Salem with its gate,
For a road to Emmaus?

Is it a phantom Arab or Rabbi?
Or, increasing woe! is it me
Awaiting the dawn of that short hour
Of Emmaus which exists no longer.

1946

## Ode To His Grace The Archbishop Of Cardiff

*This ode was to his friend Dr. McGrath, a noted linguist and scholar. He was an Irishman who had learnt Welsh. When Lewis was in prison, he visited him there in his 'full canonicals'!*

The days of the odes of Faith have flown—no respect
Is paid to the Archbishop of Teilo's land;
God in bread, ha-ha, ho!
After Freud, the instruments of radio;
The Lord's Mass, what for?—The race
Is but a troop of cinema-addicts,
From film to film, till they tire
Of pleasuring their existence at one bound

In the obliging, city night—
Catholic its family
A tribe, like a fairground, grows silent
At the jerk of a bell, the strident summons of the servant is
    powerful,

98

And the soul from its enormous dissipation
From the vale of illusion awakens,
Naked, belated, from the great defiling,
To a tomorrow-less hour
Where there will be fervent, quiet clinging to the hidden,
      bruised
Calvaries of Wales
And the sweet force of memorial offering
Of the infinite intercession which occured;
There your Ecclesiastic sacrifice
On the chalice of Jesus will be appreciated,
The unity of the mediation of Christ above—in heaven
And here beneath the sky above.

You will provide an altar and a door—bringing
Goodness to Wales;
'Neath the bang, clap and stop-tap, zing and buzz,
The muster of the waltz, frets and roars,
Bringing the Richness of Heaven to be treasured
And placing the Lamb of God in his house;
Putting on Patrick's Breastplate against the decay in the
      ancient shrine,
The gifts of Ann's daughter to keep it bright.

1946

## The Essence Of Welsh Poetry

During the wars of Napoleon there was a country squire of the
name of Lloyd living in the old house of Cwmgloyn, inland a
little from Trefdraeth (or Newport on the English maps) on the
north coast of Pembrokeshire. He was a justice of the peace.
His father had been high sheriff of the county in 1771. The
family had been much concerned with the sea, and squire
Lloyd had ships built for him at Trefdraeth and at
Aberystwyth. One of these, the *Hawk*, was a fifty-ton
schooner made from his own woods at Trefdraeth, partly for

trade, partly for his pleasure voyages. It was later sunk by the French. At its launching a local poet, one Ioan Siencyn, wrote a poem to greet it and its captain, and its squire-owner. After a finely imaged description of the *Hawk* breasting the sea, the poet visualises squire Lloyd on board, travelling to England and Ireland, but especially visiting his friends in North and South Wales. There the gentry and local poets come to meet him, and one verse describes their welcome to him:

> Around their tables laden with steaming dishes,
> He shall hear histories of those good men, our
>     ancestors,
> And *cywydd* and *englyn* and odes of Taliesin,
> And he shall drink his fill of golden barley beer.

That poem was written close to the beginning of the nineteenth century. It speaks simply and naturally of odes of Taliesin and *cywydd* and *englyn* as part of the pertinent welcome to squire Lloyd of Cwmgloyn. Taliesin was a poet of the sixth century. *Cywydd* and *englyn* were metrical forms of the Welsh Middle Ages. But for Ioan Siencyn at the very end of the eighteenth century they were all necessary for the proper entertainment of the Welsh squire in any Welsh country house. Poetry was part of the tradition of hospitality.

Now will you imagine with me that a poet of the fifteenth century, some great figure such as Tudur Aled, had been released to revisit Pembrokeshire at the launching of the *Hawk*, and had listened to the reading of Ioan Siencyn's verses to squire Lloyd. What would our fifteenth-century master have thought or said? He would note with warm approval the occasion of the poem. Just such an event, the completion of a new house or a new ship had in his time also been the appropriate moment for a complimentary poem to the head of a family. And Tudur Aled would have relished Ioan Siencyn's development of the image of the *Hawk* as it was launched on the water:

> Spread now your wings, forget the green woodlands,
> Learn to live mid the mouthing of seas.

When Siencyn calls on Neptune and Triton to protect the schooner, Tudur Aled would remember that he, in the early sixteenth century, was beginning to learn the use of those Greek gods from his friends in the circle of Cardinal Wolsey; and then when the poet returns to his bird-schooner and describes the *Hawk*:

> Your wings playing high as the clouds,
> Your breasts cleaving the salt billows,
> Let your beak pierce the waves, your belly furrow
>     them,
> Your rudder scatter them in spray-suds.

the fifteenth-century poet would have recognised it as just that serious playing with image that was part of the technique of poems inspired by manual craft in his own day. And as the poem grew to the final eulogy of squire Lloyd and his society, to the reference to Taliesin and talk of the deeds of his forefathers storied over the yellow beer on the laden dining table, Tudur Aled might well exclaim: 'My art still survives in this last decade of the eighteenth century and the great technique and the old mastery are not all forgotten. This country poet, this Ioan Siencyn, is truly an heir of our ancient discipline; he also sings the immemorial ideals and the pattern of behaviour of the leaders of the Welsh people, and I recognise him as a poet of the long line that began with Taliesin in the North.'

There, I think, we capture something essential in the progress of Welsh poesy. We call it the literary tradition of Wales. It means you cannot pluck a flower of song off a headland of Dyfed (South-West Wales) in the late eighteenth century without stirring a great northern star of the sixth century. And all the intermediaries are involved. The fourteenth century gave the technique of *dyfalu* or image-making, the sixteenth century brought in the Virgilian echoes, the seventeenth gave the measure. The whole body of Welsh poetry from the sixth century onward has contributed directly to Ioan Siencyn's verses. And, mark you, the poem I am discussing is an obscure piece of work by a little known poet whose name is in no history of Welsh literature nor in any anthology. It was last published in a forgotten volume at Aberystwyth in 1842. Why do I use it as a peg for this talk? Because it reveals the nature and continuity of the Welsh poetic tradition and because it reveals its quality and creative virtue: for the virtue of that tradition is that it may enable a quite minor poet to write a major poem.

Sir Idris Bell has written recently that 'the unique contribution of Wales to the world's literature, the poetry which, because it *is* unique, most obviously deserves and requires interpretation, is the classical great tradition of the Mediaeval bards.' I accept that, save that I hold that the tradition remained the main Welsh literary tradition down to the nineteenth century. But the Middle Ages are the ages of its energy and splendour. Up to the death of Llywelyn, Prince of Wales, in 1282, that tradition was Taliesinic. It was heroic verse, and its matter was praise of God and the saints and the king or prince. Poetic praise, as with the Greeks, is the portrayal of an ideal which is the body of unity of tribe or society or nation. That is the function of eulogy in heroic poetry and in primitive society. It is in that sense that heroic poetry is the main educational factor in primitive, aristocratic communities. It was so in Wales. But with the death of the last Llywelyn, the Welsh poetic tradition faced a crisis in its development. What now, without the Prince, was to be the theme of heroic verse? Had the tradition of Taliesin to be abandoned?

The crisis was resolved by two clerics. For simplicity's sake let me talk only of Einion the Priest as the teacher and saviour of the tradition and author of the first text-book of the master-poets that has been preserved for us. Today it is easier for us to understand Einion's contribution to Welsh poetic thought than it was fifteen years ago when I first dealt with this matter. The close connection of medieval philosophy with poetry is now widely recognised. In 1936 Arthur Lovejoy published an important book in America on the Great Chain of Being. Then, inspired by Lovejoy, Dr. Tillyard of Cambridge published in 1943 *The Elizabethan World Picture*. I think that the chapters on the Chain of Being in Tillyard's book are the best available English introduction to the matter of the great classical poetry of medieval Wales from the time of Einion Offeiriad. Tillyard shows that the idea of order in the Creation was basic to all medieval thought, and it was considered under the image of a great chain or ladder of degrees of being, starting from the very throne of God. 'The idea,' says Tillyard, 'began with Plato's Timaeus, was developed by Aristotle, adopted by the Alexandrian Jews, spread by the Neo-Platonists, and from the Middle Ages till the eighteenth century was one of those accepted commonplaces more often hinted at or taken for granted than set forth.' Then Tillyard quotes from some of the medieval exponents of this conception, and finally shows how profoundly the doctrine affected the poetry of Spenser and Shakespeare and Milton.

Now it is this Great Chain of Being that is the main content of Welsh poetry from the fourteenth century to the sixteenth. It is a logical enlargement of the Taliesin tradtion. It is set forth in those chapters of the grammar-book of the poets which discuss *How all Reality is to be praised in poetry*. And there is a sixteenth-century treatise called the *Graduelys* which is the fullest Welsh discussion we possess of the Chain of Being. The Chain starts with the Trinity and descends through Our Lady and the Saints and down all the celestial hierarchies. Then we find described the corresponding orders of the Church Militant on earth, from Pope and Cardinal down to parish priest and beggar friar. There follow the hierarchies of the laity, the emperor, the kings, the Princes of Wales, dukes, lords, knights, esquires, freemen. The grammar books tell what are the appropriate excellencies of each grade and how they are to be praised. It is this universal order, this graded plurality of God's creation, that is the theme of the classic poets of Welsh *cywydd* and *awdl*. It accounts for the confidence and grandeur of their song. It is the explanation of almost all their imagery. For their comparisons and metaphors come also from the philosophy of the Chain of Being. Medieval natural philosophers held that as each grade of men had its peculiar excellence, so also in the natural world. The lion is king of beasts for his might, the stag has primacy of speed and pride, the eagle is king of birds as the oak tree is of the forest and salmon of fish; air is higher than water which in its turn is above the land. All nature is linked thus in the Great Chain and there are correspondences in all the orders...

Poetry is great and classical when a high seriousness of function in society and profound philosophic content meet with a form that is unique and subtle and richly expressive. That is true of the great centuries of the *awdl* and *cywydd*. If this classical poetry of the Welsh bards is, as has been claimed, unique, the explanation is that their matter, their explicit and implicit theme, is the philosophic conception of an integrated Christendom taking its place in the great realm of divine order, and that the *cywyddd* and *awdl* were shaped by fearless artificers into bright mirrors of that order. There is in European poetry only one thing that can compare with it, and that is *The Divine Comedy* of Dante.

1947


## Ascension Thursday

What is abroad on the hills, on a May morn?
Look at them, the gold of the broom and laburnum,
The incandescent surplice on the shoulders of the hawthorn,
The devout emerald of the grass and the still calves.

The chestnut tree's candelabra are lit,
The hedgerows kneeling and the birch a mute nun,
The cuckoo's two-notes over the polished hush of the brook,
The mist an apparition bent over the thurible of the dales:

Come out, men, from your council houses
Before the rabbits scatter, come with the weasel
To see the earth elevate an immaculate wafer
And the Father kiss the Son in the blessed dew.

1950

# A Meditation On The Assumption

(First published in Welsh in 1951, in *Baner ac Amserau Cymu.*)

I listened last night to the broadcast of an anthology of Christmas poems and carols. The narrator remarked that they were scarce. He suggested that the explanation lay in the fact that the Nativity celebrations gave the Mother too prominent a place, the Mother of Our Lord, and that the Protestant poets of Wales would beware of that. A sad suggestion.

I thought afterwards about the fervent protests that were made in Wales in November against the declaring of the Assumption of the body of Mary into heaven as a dogma by the Pope. Two things surprised me: firstly, that the Welsh denominational newspapers without exception held this to be a new doctrine; secondly, that the general criticism of the editors was that the declaration was a sign or proof of an increase in superstition. "This in 1950!" said one editor. Stranger, perhaps, than those two things was that so many editors were harshly condemning without knowing anything of the doctrine. Mary, Mother of the Lord, died a natural death. Her body was buried, but it did not experience putrefaction. The Lord Jesus Christ took her body and assumed it into heaven to be united with her soul. Or, as the poet Bleddyn Ddu said in his ode to be found in the Red Book of Hergest:

| | |
|---|---|
| *O'r byd pan aeth,* | When from the world went, |
| *Mawr ddewiniaeth,* | by wondrous power, |
| *Mair ddiwenydd,* | Joyful Mary, |
| *Daeth nifer cain* | A fine host came |
| *I gael arwain* | to be allowed to carry |
| *Ei gelorwydd—* | her bier— |
| *Duw a'i deulu* | God and his family, |
| *I gyfleu* | to take, |
| *Yn gyfluydd* | as a host, |
| *Corff bendigaid* | the blessed body |
| *A hy enaid* | and the brave soul |
| *Mair huenydd.* | of radiant Mary. |

I am no theologian; my knowledge of theology is childish. Therefore I shall not try to demonstrate the validity of this doctrine about Our Lady. For me to try to understand the mind of anti-Catholic Welshmen is a proper and, in some measure, a useful thing to do. When I hear this doctrine declared to be superstition, then I think two questions arise.

Do Welsh Christians accept the Apostles' Creed? If not, why do they call themselves Christians? The Apostles' Creed states apropos the Second Person of the Trinity, One God, "that He rose again the third day from the dead, that He ascended into Heaven"—in His body of flesh. Is this superstition?

Now, whether it be right or not, be it superstition or truth, the belief held by Christians since the day the Holy Ghost descended on the apostles in Jerusalem up to today is that what happened to the body of the Lord Jesus in its Ascension will happen also to the body of each and every man since the beginning of the world who is saved through His death. And that for one body, namely the undefiled body of the Virgin in whose womb the body of God Himself was formed, that ascension, that comes to all who are saved, has already occurred. Her dust is not in the earth. There is a piece of matter that God created already in heaven. That is our guarantee that the others who believe in Him will also be taken into heaven. The golden chain connects our bodies with that of Mary; and though our flesh may go—as Hamlet says—to stop the hole in a beer barrel, yet it will be collected in the form and the image of the body of God Himself and the body of His mother in the final glory. The Christian faith is wondrous and terrible, and its hope lies beyond human reason and imagination. It is more supernatural than we can conceive. And yet we get pitiful little half-baked humans like myself to call it "superstition." "And this is 1950!" If they were Communists or atheists I would not complain. But ministers and preachers and editors of denominational papers!

God help us, Welshmen. How bleak is our society! We have neither the manners nor the memory of a human family or a nation. We have neither the manners nor the traditions of a divine family or a church. For us the respect paid by centuries of generations of Christianity to the maid whose delivery we are remembering this Christmas is superstition, or worse, idolatry. We have lost the family feeling for her. And the result is that it is only somewhat, and insecurely, that we hold the family conviction even about the Child she gave to the world. We do not stand with the whole family to declare our conviction that he is the *"Filium Dei unigenitum, et ex patre natum ante omnia saecula. Deum de Deo; Lumen de Lumine; Deum verum de Deo vero....*

We find contemporary Welsh historians and theologians afraid of these names, supposing them to be heretical, and condemning Williams Pant-y-Celyn for mentioning the blood of God and the cross of God, and dreading the mention of the Mother of God. We have lost the tradition of family, the tradition of Antioch and Nicea. As Joshua Thomas testified in his *Hanes y Bedyddwyr* in 1778 ("The History of the Baptists"): "There were many old popish fables amongst the old people. I remember well the following words and ones like them: God's Cross, God and Mary, etc."

Yes, the Apostles' Creed and the Nicene Creed are amongst the popish fables that we lost. And when we celebrate Christmas it is not the Holy Family that we see, but rather the birth of the founder of the Welfare State and the forerunner of Mr. Aneurin Bevan—"true God from true God." We hold the belief that Mary's body was assumed to be united with her soul to be superstition and blasphemy for the simple reason that we do not seriously, from real intellectual conviction, believe in the incarnation of God. It was not the flesh and bones of God that were nourished in her womb, by her blood; it was not God that sucked her breasts—no, no, no, if we believed that we would be terrified of suggesting that the same body suffered the revenge of sin, the infection and corruption, the consuming by vermin, the derision of dirt on the dust of the sanctuary of the Godhead. But no, the Incarnation is no more than an old people's popish fable. For us, what is real is the Father Christmas of the chain-store and the non-alcoholic wine of the pop-bottle and the radio sermon on the brotherhood of the world.

"No one can see God and live." "Who has seen me, has seen the Father also." The dreadful contradictions of the faith. The first is easier to believe than the second. The paradox of the manger, "God and His family." Of course in Bleddyn Ddu's poem the meaning of "God and His family" is the old meaning, namely God and His retinue of saints. But at Christmas we are celebrating the coming of God into the family, into a union of blood, of humanity. There was a man who is God. And because of that there will be, and already is, soil from the earth in God's heaven, outside space and time. I myself am writing these lines quite quietly between two pipefuls of Edgeworth tobacco: if I understood what I am writing every particle of my constitution would be blown beyond the reach of the smoke of an atom bomb. Christmas is beyond all human reason. That is why we in this epoch can only belittle it, empty it of its content, pull it down to earth as a nice sentimental story; and our instincts are correct in insisting on pulling the body of Mary out of heaven. For in doing that we are pulling God out of the Babe and then some form of "agreed syllabus" will be sufficient religious education for a Catholic and a Unitarian: the history and geography of Palestine; the folklore of Bethlehem; the contribution of the Jews to the civilisation of the West; modern humanism.

Why then did the Pope choose the exact mid-point of the twentieth century to declare the dogma of the final glorification of the Mother of God? It is the battle between two materialisms that has given rise to the crisis of this century. It is an earthly materialistic paradise that is promised us alike by Hollywood and Moscow, and it is with material weapons that the battle will be decided. Never before in the whole history of man has materialism been held forth as an ideal, a religion, as an object of worship for humanity, as blatantly as is done today. Industrialism is offered as a Messiah to the continents of Africa and Asia. "Technical" education, learning to master gear and the forces of matter, that is the humanism of the twentieth century in Russia and Wales. We insist on trying to pull down the thousand-years-old forests of Africa, the temples of the druid altars of the negro, to feed margarine factories. By now every piece of the material creation is something "that can be used" for our wants. The sanctity of the flesh has disappeared and in the factories of Dachau it was proved that human skin could be converted into plastic material to become bookcovers and membrane for lamp-shades. All the material, all the matter of the universe is something "that can be used" by men, and it is nothing more. Looking, looking and worshipping, looking without desiring anything—the aesthetic experience and energy that is the essence of religion and the supreme purpose of the existence of rational beings—that has nearly been lost from the face of the earth. The sanctity of matter and the flesh has gone into oblivion.

And so, while the engineers of Moscow and Washington and London are excavating in the underworld of Siberia and Alaska and Merioneth for uranium for the atom bomb—in the belly of the whirlpool of the night of the twentieth century—at the moment of the wildest dread and hysteria of humanity—see the Chief-bishop of God on earth calling on men to look, to look beyond the furthest stars, to look beyond time and place, to look at a body, a body such as those that became ashes in Hiroshima, there undefiled and immaculate, there with the Son, there with the expectant spirits of the saints, there in the Safety as a forerunner and a promise: "Why are you afraid, O you of little faith....Do you not know that your bodies are temples of the Holy Ghost?" That is the message of 1950 in the crisis of the world. There is some value in a Pope: when the scientists are proclaiming to the Pleiades "It is we who control the fate of matter," the voice of Rome answers "God married the soil."

(translated by Harri Pritchard Jones)

# A Note On David Jones

(Translated from the Welsh. Originally printed "by way of Preface" to the catalogue of the retrospective exhibition of 1954-5 at the Tate Gallery.)

It is a grief for David Jones that he has no Welsh. He reads what he can get of competent English translation of early Welsh verse and prose. He corresponds with scholars about the Ancient Books and old tales and the myth and Matter of Wales, and he treasures the grains thus garnered. He feeds his meditation and his imagination on the Welsh past; it is a key to his work as English poet and as painter.

Another key is the Faith. Observe the inscriptions, phrases from Introit or Gospel, shown here with the pictures. It would be a blunder to pass them by with merely a glance. The artist worked long at them, praying them to their shape on the paper, building them up with brush-work around and within them, even as pious Welsh mothers used once to embroider the Promises into samplers on cottage walls.

There's a passage in Part 4 of *In Parenthesis* where Dai boasts in the trenches of France; it borrows its plan from a poem in the *Book of Taliesin*:

> This Dai adjusts slipping shoulder straps, wraps close
> his misfit outsize greatcoat—he articulates his English
> with an alien care.
> My fathers were with Black Prince of Wales
> at the passion of
> The blind Bohemian king.
> They served in these fields,
> it is in the histories that you can read it, Cor-
> poral—boys
> Gower, they were—it is writ down—yes.
> Wot about Methuselum, Taffy?
> I was with Abel when his brother found him,
> under the green tree.

That is how David Jones, poet and painter, sees things and paints them. Doric and Ionic and Corinthian columns, all the age of Greece and Rome, are a background to the parenthetic travail of Aphrodite. The past is all a now, the eternal in the petal, tree branches in the clay of the teapot and in the brittleness of glass. The earth herself in her alert pain dreams of the hand that has shaped her. Nor man nor place stands alone. The scapegoat of Israel is caught in the barbed wire of 1915 and the trees of the field walk in through the windows of your house. David Jones is an artist who affirms that the vision in the final canto of Dante's *Paradiso* is an ever-contemporary fact.

## Students And The Mass

(from *Efrydiau Catholig*, a Catholic magazine he edited.)

Probably, most readers of this magazine are students in Welsh colleges. Hardly any one of them will be a Catholic in name and from conviction. Many may well be Catholics in their hearts and by inclination. Perhaps the time has come for us to say something about the position of university students in the circumstances prevailing in the world of today.

'The Great Ruler has placed us at the end of the Ages of Time.' That appears more probable today than in 1701. The third world war is quite likely to come upon us before the middle aged grow into old age. When it comes, two enemies will use hydrogen bombs or worse. That can happen in any year ahead. According to all the information available to us from the experts, that will mean the end of the world. In spite of that, we see men and women aged about eighteen years embarking on university courses. And the ordered, leisurely lectures!

No doubt students in the Science Department have some excuse and can enjoy some degree of comfort. Science has tended to become more and more technical and applied in recent years. This means that the science student can at least have the experience, and the presumptuous pleasure, of learning to understand the developments which put in the hands of man the ability to destroy the world. From the natural, human, present standpoint there is some intoxicating, narcotic pride involved in the understanding, the amazement, the mastery of the principles governing powers which are so stunningly explosive. The science student of today can enjoy something of the thrill which Prometheus experienced before he was struck down by Jove. That can give him a sense of the order of things, some sort of explanation, some degree of control over events. Enough, perhaps, to give tragic meaning and worth to scientific studies before we reap the final fruits of the last laboratory.

What shall we say of the Arts Department? Can we justify in this day and age spending weeks to comprehend the poetic jousting of Gruffydd Gryg and Dafydd ap Gwilym? Or Jane Austen's technique with dialogue? Or the topography of Hell in Dante's poem? Are we not fiddling while Rome burns? Should we not hang our fiddle in the rafters? [Welsh idiom for giving up.] Students have a right to ask such questions. It is our duty to try to answer them. It is not good enough to carry on in the same old ruts simply because they are ruts and to carry on in them is easier than breaking out of them, or because scholarship provides a temporary refuge from life and from the contemplation of death. The end of the world, or the end of our world, is near at hand. It is useless to talk about transmitting learning and tradition to the ages to come. There's a good chance that they won't come. 'The black-clawed Destiny which is nigh will snatch away the whole Body of Time from us bit by bit,' and we worry about the disappearance of dialects. The old humanist answers won't do any longer, either. Nor the modern feckless answer: that man cannot but attempt to entertain himself while he continues to exist, and perhaps the odes of the fourteenth century are a more snobbish form of vanity than filling in Littlewoods football coupons. Well, if that be the only defence of our vocation, there remains one other thing we could do which would be a greater favour to our students: we could shoot ourselves or drive our cars into the waters off the docks. Put an end to ourselves, not at the moment of the bomb, but through an act of will. At the most, we should only lose about twenty years; twenty years in which our existence as university people would become increasingly meaningless. Is not the *raison d'être* of humanistic scholarship disappearing? Let us consider another proposition. It is possible that God exists. It is possible for the 'Christian revelation' to be true.

If it were true, what then, young student? Then, there would be meaning and purpose to each and every hour of history. The last twenty years of civilisation would be as important as the year when Abraham went out of Ur of the Chaldees. The ending of the world by a hydrogen bomb would not destroy or delete anything. To learn how the Latin element came into the Welsh language and what changes occurred in long and short vowels would be as meaningful five minutes before the bomb exploded above Cardiff as when the principle of the thing first dawned on the mind of Gruffydd Robert in Milan. Reading the first chapter of *Pride and Prejudice* or listening to the Alfredo Wang quartet playing a work by Mozart five minutes before the Day of Judgement would be a fitting and wise act of preparation. For, according to the Christian revelation, all that is is the Creation of God. Therefore the whole history of the universe is in praise of God ...*etiam peccata*; even the dialogue of Myrddin and Taliesin. And if it is so, then, for the Chrstian, every science and art is in worship of God. Worship is the *raison d'être* of scholarship; because of that the value of scholarship lies beyond accidents and is independent of the after-effects of any hydrogen bombs.

Therefore, if this be true, it follows that a student who is a Christian has to relate his studies and scholarship to Calvary. For without Calvary there can be no worship. Puleston Jones once asked, 'What is the Cross but a revelation?' The Catholic answer is: worship. The sacrifice of the Cross is the only sufficient worship on behalf of the whole of humanity. Apart from it, there is no worship. All other worship exists only by being in it and through it.

In more leisured and safer times, less in crisis than ours, there is always a dangerous pride threatening any Faustian, unworshipping scholar or scholarship. Today, in worship alone does scholarship find purpose and meaning. There is only one normal sacramental, Catholic means of connecting the everyday life of men and women with the Sacrifice of Calvary; that is the Mass. It is also through the Mass, and only through the Mass, that a connection can be established between the college lectures of the Catholic students, their hours of reading and their leisure hours of talking, drinking, playing and dancing, and the Sacrifice of the Cross. For the Catholic believer the Mass has always been an obvious necessity in university life, for it is from the Mass that the university originated. But today, in these years at the end of the ages, the years of the hydrogen bomb, with these students, young men and women, hesitantly groping for some foundation, some rock to stand on, for something which could give meaning and worth to their studies under the shadows of the cobalt clouds—how can they do without the worship of the Sacrifice of God's Son at the centre of their academic life and as a focus for it?

1955

# By Way Of Apology

(A radio talk, 1955)

Some people today seem to think that modern English poetic drama began with Mr. T.S. Eliot. I was born and brought up in Liverpool. I went to Liverpool University three years before the first world war broke out. At that time the Liverpool Repertory Company had close links with the University, and it was the Repertory Theatre that stirred my interest in plays and play-acting. I remember being overwhelmed by young Miss Sybil Thorndike's performance in the Gilbert Murray translation of *Medea*. I thought on and off for some years about that revelation of Euripides. It was Miss Thorndike's Medea that gave me my first idea of a kindred character in Welsh legend; later on I wrote the first two acts of my own play *Blodeuwedd* in the hope that some day and some where there might be a Welsh-speaking Sybil Thorndike.

The war broke into my university course, and when I got back to Brownlow Hill after the war, Lascelles Abercrombie was on the staff of the English school. I used to meet him for lunch at the Central Station Restaurant sometimes on Mondays. He had a train to catch at five o'clock for Colwyn Bay, where he had a tutorial class. So from one to half past four we lunched and sat on and talked.

He had been writing plays in verse for some years. They are neglected now, unwisely as I think. I have a memory of a one act play of his, *The End of the World*, acted by the Liverpool Repertory. It was quick poetry and exciting drama, and that is, I believe, true of one or two of his longer plays also. Three or four of the English "Georgian poets" wrote verse plays; Flecker and Drinkwater had some commercial success; but Gordon Bottomley and Lascelles Abercrombie were the only two who really needed a theatre for their poetry. There's a spate of power in Gordon Bottomley's imaginative plays that triumphs over or through his stiff diction and narrow range of rhythms. But Abercrombie was concerned to make his speech and speech-rhythms living, likely, dramatic talk—the poetry should be in the energy of the speech. His characters put more of themselves into every statement just because they speak in verse. That was a thing we discussed over the Central Station lunch table.

But the home of English poetic drama in the first quarter of this century was across the water in Dublin. It was the Abbey Theatre that really and truly married poetry and the stage just at the time when the Ibsen of William Archer was the established canon in London. The Abbey Theatre poets had an advantage that was widely discussed outside Ireland—they had around them a country people speaking an English that seemed to be constantly and unconsciously the very stuff of poetry. Let me quote what Synge said about this in 1907 in his preface to *The Playboy of the Western World*:

"In the modern literature of towns, richness is found only in sonnets or prose poems or in one or two elaborate books that are far away from the profound and common interests of life...

...One has...Ibsen and Zola dealing with the reality of life in joyless and pallid words. On the stage one must have reality and one must have joy: and that is why the intellectual modern drama has failed, and people have grown sick of the false joy of the musical comedy. In a good play every speech should be as fully flavoured as an apple, and such speeches cannot be written by anyone who works among people who have shut their lips on poetry."

This was what many poet-dramatists in England also were searching for in the first quarter of this century. It wasn't merely the Anglo-Irish poets. Thomas Hardy was an influence both in prose and in verse and George Bourne's Bettesworth books had sent many poets and writers to live in Gloucestershire. Lascelles Abercrombie went there for a time and I hope I'm correct in saying that his play *The End of the World* was given a Cotswold setting. Poetry and poetic drama needed roots in a community. Everybody was agreed about that. Yeats and Synge and Lady Gregory and Padric Colum had found their need in the Irish peasantry, Hardy in Wessex, Moorman in the Yorkshire dales and their rich dialect. Poetic speech and regionalism and nationalism were an answer to the all-invading industrialism of the time. Let me quote Synge again:

"In Ireland, for a few years more—(how right that sad foreboding was)—we have a popular imagination that is fiery and magnificent and tender; so that those of us who wish to write start with a chance that is not given to writers in places where the spring-time of the local life has been forgotten."

This search for places and communities where the spring-time of the local life flourished, and the defence of such places and communities, were very much a concern of poets both before and immediately after the first world war. It is an interest that links Yeats and Synge with D.H. Lawrence, just as it links them also with the Maurice Barrès of *La Colline Inspiree*. I should like to suggest that *The Waste Land* when it came was not in theme and matter a new departure, but rather a restatement and culmination.

I had seen the Abbey Theatre players once in Liverpool before 1914. It was in London late in 1919 that I saw them in the *Playboy of the Western World*. Do you remember a saying of James Joyce in his first novel:

> "When the soul of a man is born in this country, there
> are nets flung at it to hold it back from flight. You
> talk to me of nationality, language, religion. I shall try
> to fly by those nets."

It was in that spirit and that intention that I went to the war. But it happened in France that I stumbled on the work of Maurice Barrès. I read a lot of him in the wet trenches of 1916, and when I was sent back to England with a "blighty" in 1917 I was inevitably a nationalist in literature. Barrès had convinced me that Wales for me was not a net but a root.

All conversions are slow and piecemeal. I still hoped to write in English and even to make a living at it, verse and prose and plays. But my stuff now would be the matter of Wales. How then could one find an English diction that would interpret the native speech of the Welsh? Synge seemed to me to be a classic. I delighted in his profound poetic irony, so central and un-eccentric, especially in the *Well of the Saints* and in the *Playboy of the Western World*.

I thought that the prose rhythms of those plays and of Lady Gregory's and Padric Colum's were close enough to the rhythms and grammatical patterns of Welsh to provide a possible and plausible English for my purpose. I spoke of it as an Anglo-Celtic convention, and it was in that convention that I wrote *The Eve of Saint John.* This was my first play, and so far my last in English. I couldn't be satisfied with its diction and I settled the issue by turning and learning to write in Welsh. It was the logical thing to do. Didn't someone say that logic is the very devil?

## Excerpts From *Blodeuwedd* (1948) And *Siwan* (1956): Variations On A Single Theme

*Two plays, arguably Lewis's greatest, are very similar in theme. One,* **Blodeuwedd** *(Fashioned of Flowers), is based on a Welsh medieval tale from the* **Mabinogi***. The other,* **Siwan,** *is about the marriage of Siwan, daughter of the English King John, and wife of Prince Llywelyn, Prince of Wales, when his dynasty was at its height in the thirteenth century. She was used to French courtly manners, and was astounded when her husband executed a lover whom he had discovered in adultery with her. The lover was Norman and an important political ally. Siwan herself was banished from Llywelyn's table and bed for a year.*

*Both plays are about Eros and Agape, about grace and evil, about violence and the altruistic in love, and about the instinctive and the arranged in marriage. In* **Blodeuwedd** *we have a prince, Lleu, cursed by his mother never to find a wife from among humankind, for whom his magician of an uncle creates a woman out of flowers. She is a prototype sex object, without kith or kin except amongst the beasts. She entices a young man to her bed, and eventually persuades him to slay her husband. But the magician restores him to life, and he returns to wreak his revenge. The lover, having had his surfeit of her lust, welcomes death with open arms, and poor Blodeuwedd is 'exiled' back to the forest as an owl.*

### BLODEUWEDD

*This is how Lleu described his first sight of the maid created for him:*

118

'Never, never shall I forget the blessed morn
I first saw Blodeuwedd:
Yourself and Math coming across the lawn,
And there, between you, naked as the flowers at dawn,
The dew still moist upon her cold breasts,
Undefiled breasts like the heart of a lily
When night bows its head into her bosom, she walks
The soul of greenest springtime in a human form.
I looked at her, and she at me,
And dressed her nakedness with ardent kisses.
And these arms, the lustful arms of youth—
My arms which had been so empty—her girdle of
    steel.'

*Later Blodeuwedd tells her maid how she feels captive in that
very human form:*

'Oh, you will never understand,
Never, never, my woe; you nor anyone else.
You do not know what it is to be lonely.
Your world is full, you have a home,
Kith, kin, father, mother, brothers,
So that you cannot be a stranger in this world.
Wherever men have trodden is habitation,
And all Gwynedd, where your forefathers lived,
Your hearth, a roof erected
By generations of your ancestors;
You are at home in your own country
As if in a bed made for you
By loving hands which had long awaited you;
For me, I have no habitat
Amongst all the ways of men; search throughout
    Gwynedd,
And all Britain, there is no grave
Belongs to me, and the world is cold,
Alien, without ties of love
Or nationhood. That is the nature of my fear—
Afraid of my freedom, like a rudderless ship

On the sea of humanity...Hark! What horn is that in
   the distance?'

*It is that of the man fated to be her lover, enticed, trapped by*
*her naked passion. She is excited by the prospect, like a hunts-*
*man:*

'Be still, uneasy bosom, your hour has come...
Though I've bent under courtly customs
And men's rituals this twelve months, they'll hold me
   no longer.
My elements are excitement and freedom,
And my law is lust, the lust that drives the seed
To shatter the soil that keeps it from the sun.
There is in me too that which reaches for that light and
   warmth
To grow to fulness, branching out above the grove
Without a knife to prune it. And I know
This knight to be a herald of passion.
I am familiar with the huntsman's horn; it was not my
   husband's
Thin lips that blew that lively note;
These lips are full, red, greedy, merry,
And worthy mates for mine.'

*She asks the lover, Gronw, what attracted him to her. He*
*replies:*

'Who can ever tell? Your features, form, your gait,
Your body burning like a flame out through your
   dress.'

'And nothing else? Did you not realise
The strangeness of my birth? Before you came to me
This body was a prison wall,
Like a lethal web about a butterfly,
And you came like springtime to where I lay
And gave my body wings, made my blood dance.

I shall no longer be lonely among families;
Your smiles are my pedigree and rights
Among mankind. There is but one will
In plants and men; no puny ritual
Nor custom or judgment can incarcerate the heart that
    feels
The rays of love upon it. Come, beloved,
Life belongs to us, and to love is to be free.'

*That love or lust drives Gronw to murder, to sacrifice his fami-*
*ly, household and all responsibilities to kith and kin. It excites*
*him beyond all reason. It drives him later, though, to welcome*
*death:*

'I cannot escape from you except through death,
The poison of your kisses is in my blood.
What should I live for? To taste again for years
What I have already tasted, the surfeit that's in the
    flesh,
The woe and shame of countless surfeiting in vain?
Your love is a tomorrow-less grave; no baby
Laughs on your bosom, there is no cradle in your hall;
But at night there was the sound of a crazed wretch
Baying on lusty bosom in the dark,
Biting filth, and the derisive laughter of an owl.
I lost the path of men to follow a torch
And the enchanting pipes of the marsh, and sank in it,
Embraced a star, a bat at my lips;
Today a bolt struck me and I woke;
I see my home, my youth in Penllyn,
And myself now: oh, loathsome; and your looks at
me—
I'd rather than your kiss your husband's sword.'

*Lewis treats Blodeuwedd very sympathetically. Eros has her*
*say and her rights. His idea of the virtues of Agape, his* **pietas,**
*can be gleaned from a speech by unsuspecting Lleu to his wife.*

121

'Many a time, Blodeuwedd,
I have wished to die. But now
Living has a taste, like biting an apple,
And your love is the chair in Caer Siddi*
Whose occupant no plague or age can strike,
And I there, a king;
Whom no one can usurp,
Neither fear nor longing nor even death itself;
For the kingship of love is unchangeable.'
'Is anything unchangeable with men?'
'Infatuation dies, because it is fragile
And quick like youth. But love
Grows like an oak throughout life's storms,
And in its shelter a home is made, a family,
And the aristocracy and government of the land.
Our love, pure lady,
Will be the security and roof of Ardudwy,
The pattern for the people, nurture of our tribe,
And we shall be blessed by princes
For our firm concord now.'

## SIWAN

*This is what Prince Llywelyn tells his wife, Siwan, when she agrees to return to his bed and council chamber a year after her lover's execution:*

'Our marriage was a political one, my lady,
And between us a gap of a quarter-century.
Well, that is the custom, it is the foundation of alliance
And concordance between nations, mutual tolerance
    and construction.
But four years later, when you arrived
A virgin to Snowdonia, like a sapling silver birch,
My heart turned over suddenly as if I had seen the
    Grail;

(*One of the halls in the Celtic Other World.)

For me there was light wherever you trod.
But I suppressed my amazement rather than frighten
    you
And when I felt you quivering here in my arms
I didn't bruise you with clumsy kisses
Nor nauseating sweaty embraces; I disciplined myself
    severely
So that you would not find me loathsome; I was
    reticent,
Courteous, formal;
And you stopped trembling; this hall became your
    home
And I a not too distasteful part of the furniture.
That was how I worshipped you, my flame, from afar
    and silently,
Holding back from trespass with fondling words;
But I drew you into my life's work,
I arranged my household, my kin, my kingdom accord-
    ing to your word,
And gave to your splendid mind the freedom of office.
I remember the afternoon you returned from your
    father,
From your first embassy; my life was in danger that
    time.
You were but fifteen,
And Dafydd your son barely two months old. You
    came home
With my life and Dafydd's kingdom
Intact under your girdle. And that night
It was you who embraced me. I had no words to
    express
My enchantment; I conquered the tremor of my
    body;—
But after that night I was terrible to my foes;
I gathered Ceredigion, Powys and the South
And plaited them into your son's crown, for him in
    primogeniture
In spite of the Welsh custom, in spite of the split in my
    house;

I demanded that the Pope and King of England
    recognise him,
And the Pope proclaim his immaculate royal lineage;
This all I planned and erected for you, you were my
    temple,
My worship of you—


## Letter To His Friend, David Jones, The Writer And Painter

(Lewis discusses his play-writing.)

158, Westbourne Rd., Penarth, Glamorgan.

25 March 1959

My Dear David,

It was nice to hear from you. I think the publication of your essays would itself justify my coming to London to celebrate, so when I hear from Harman Grisewood (whose name is of course very familiar to me) I'll say a cordial yes and try to fix a date.

Yesterday I was with Sian Phillips (They are rehearsing a television performance of *Treason* at Cardiff), I gave her your compliments which was to give her much pleasure, and she remembers Valerie Price very well ("danced exquisitely" she said) so will you tell her to phone me anytime she comes to Cardiff?

I am at this time writing a play on the very hackneyed theme of Esther, the Old Testament and Apocrypha story. But I write or I build up a play painfully slowly and I envy the fertile facility of the successful playwriters. All my plays are myths, even when they seem (like *Brad*) realistic. I am really very old-fashioned and have a nasty suspicion that I'll be found a fraud! Even so, Esther is a lovely theme, and I'll have Sian Phillips for the radio interpretation.

I hope you'll have a happy Easter feast and no more Lent for a year.

Cofion Cu,
Saunders.

# Esther

*It is a recurring theme in Lewis's work that man and woman can not only venture to fall in love with God, but that His involvement with fallen, flawed humanity is also a matter of being madly, unrelentingly in love.*

*In two cases Lewis dealt with love and marriage in a Welsh setting. His second novel,* **Merch Gwern Hywel,** *(The Daughter of Gwern Hywel), was based on the true story of an ancestor of his who, though a Methodist minister, eloped with a well-off farmer's daughter in the years after the battle of Waterloo. It was adapted as a successful television play. During the period dealt with, the Methodists were leaving the established church, before they themselves became an establishment. Once again we see Lewis's insistence that tradition and rebellion are necessary for each other; that tradition becomes stifling, becomes a dead hand, without creative acts of renewal which give things a new impetus and, possibly, a new direction. The second Welsh-based work also dealt with the question of love and marriage in the mixed, mid-nineteenth century world of Episcopalians and Presbyterians (Calvinistic Methodists) in rural Wales. The question was whether one was free to choose one's spouse, or had to have one's marriage arranged. It is typical of Lewis that, while making his characters and situations totally convincing in themselves, he also succeeds in revealing the interface between the old duality of free will and predestination, which had exercised the minds of Calvinists so much, and between the Catholic and Calvinist views on salvation.*

*In the play, also based on historical fact, a parlour maid is married twice: once to an Anglican squire, and, subsequent to* his death, to a Methodist preacher. Early on in the play the two men meet, and discuss the problem of marrying below one's station. The minister points out to Sir John that 'if marriage be a voluntary act on both sides...then there is no inequality.' That, again, said something of how Lewis saw our relationship with God. And he delights in making the Calvinist espouse what he regarded as a Catholic viewpoint.

**Eros** and **Agape** feature in the play **Esther** also. Though it deals with the age-old problem of anti-semitism, with revenge, and the whole problem of being a despised but 'chosen' people, it is also an intensely personal drama between lovers. Esther ventures all, at Mordecai's behest, to save her people from genocide. But her greatest fear is, not that the king will refuse to extend the royal sceptre towards her, thus saving her life, but that he, her beloved, might not love her. We have an allegory of the relationship between God and man, be they seen as individuals, or as corporate men, Israel or the Church. We also have echoes of Pascal's gamble, as Esther ventures all on the belief that her Omnipotent Emperor loves her. Hers is a leap of love, and it reveals that, not only is her 'god' lonely, but he also craves her love.

### ESTHER
(1959)

*[This play is based on the two Biblical books about Esther. It has been translated and broadcast in English on television, as have many of Lewis's other works, and has also been translated into Hebrew and broadcast in Israel.]*

*The action in the first act takes place in the Court of King Ahasuerus (Xerxes) in Susa. A marble staircase rises from the floor to the entrance. Out of sight on stage-right a crowd of messengers listen to a proclamation being read by the servant Harbona, while behind him, in the shadows on the left, stands Haman, the Agagite, the Chief Minister. He has a table beside him, with cups on it. Trumpets sound as the curtain rises for Act I.*

| | |
|---|---|
| MESSENGERS: | Silence! Silence for the King's messenger. |
| HARBONA: | *(reading the proclamation)* The great King Ahasuerus to the Princes, Rulers and Governors |

|  |  |
|---|---|
|  | who rule beneath him on the the hundred and twenty seven provinces from India as far as Ethiopia. |
| THE CROWD: | Silence! |
| HARBONA: | As I, Ahasuerus, am Lord of many nations and ruler of the whole world, I have always wished to govern gently, securing for my subjects a tranquil existence, and maintaining peace throughout the far-flung empire. |
| CROWD: | Peace! |
| HARBONA: | But Haman has made known to me; Haman who is second in honour in the realm. Haman our Prime Minister and Chief Officer, who excels in wisdom and unfailing good will. |
| THE CROWD: | Haman! Haman the good! Haman the Agagite! |
| HARBONA: | Haman has made known to me that a despicable nation has mingled and mixed with all the tribes of the world; a nation whose laws are in opposition to all other nations; a nation which regularly transgresses against our royal commands, so that the unity of our realm cannot stand secure. |
| CROWD: | Treason! Treason! Which nation? Treason! |
| HARBONA: | The Jewish nation. |
| CROWD: | The Jews! The Jews!...Silence! |
| HARBONA: | We, therefore, now, knowing how this nation has constantly attacked and opposed every man, resisting those things we have commanded, committing every evil that they can, we hereby proclaim and command, through letters to all the dukes and princes and governors of each and every province of our empire: |
|  | On the thirteenth day of the twelfth month of this year, that the whole Jewish nation shall be destroyed and killed by the sword and by hanging, the old and the young, both men and women, children and sucklings, without pity or mercy, so that each and every Jewish soul may descend into hell, without a single member of their race left alive on earth. In the name of Ahasuerus the King. |
| CROWD: | Death to the Jews!...To the grave with the Star of David! *(Trumpets sound. The messengers go their separate ways. Then Haman is heard laughing heartily.)* |

| | |
|---|---|
| HAMAN: | Wonderful, Harbona! Superb! Superb! Come here and have a glass of wine. You deserve it. |
| HARBONA: | Thank you, sir...Long life to Haman the Agagite! Yes, reading a proclamation is thirsty work. |
| HAMAN: | Thirsty work? It makes my mouth water. |
| HARBONA: | Water? Hardly? Blood, rather; a pretty bloody proclamation in my opinion...Your work, sir? |
| HAMAN: | The King's seal, but my work. |
| HARBONA: | As I'd thought. Our Persian style isn't quite so apocalyptic. |
| HAMAN: | What does that mean? |
| HARBONA: | "The old and the young, both men and women, children and sucklings, so that each and every Jewish soul may descend into hell!" *(He laughs for a while.)*...Rather semitic for my taste, as a Persian, if I may venture to say so, sir. |
| HAMAN: | You're nearer the mark than you thought, young man. The words belong to a Jew. |
| HARBONA: | A Jew? |
| HAMAN: | Yes, a Jew. A blood-thirsty tiger named Samuel. One of their prophets. |
| HARBONA: | And how did you get hold of them? |
| HAMAN: | It was with those words that Samuel ordered the destruction of my nation, and her king, Agag. He, himself, with his own hand killed Agag when he was an unarmed prisoner, standing innocently before him. |
| HARBONA: | Please, sir. |
| HAMAN: | You can see now why I remember those words, remembering the blood-letting; remember the massacre. Only a few of my people escaped. |
| HARBONA: | And you now seek your revenge. |
| HAMAN: | Each and every Jew will have to pay for what happened. |
| HARBONA: | Haman the Agagite! |
| HAMAN: | I am of the house of Agag. |
| HARBONA: | Did you witness the massacre? Were you there? |
| HAMAN: | No, I was not there...at least not in the usual sense of being there. |
| HARBONA: | When did it happen—when Samuel killed Agag? |
| HAMAN: | Five centuries ago. |
| HARBONA: | What? |
| HAMAN: | Five centuries ago. |

| | |
|---|---|
| HARBONA: | *(Laughs long, and somewhat derisively.)* Good gracious, sir, nobody seeks his revenge for something that happened five hundred years ago. Nobody remembers anything over five centuries. Five centuries ago the Persian Empire didn't exist. Nor the city of Susa. |
| HAMAN: | Agag existed. Samuel existed. The Jews exist today. And I exist. |
| HARBONA: | Do the Jews remember all this? |
| HAMAN: | When Samuel killed Agag, he too was seeking revenge for something which had happened five centuries previously. Yes, the Jews remember. When they hear my name, Haman the Agagite, in the proclamation, they'll remember. They'll remember as they fall into hell, a whole nation put to the gallows. |
| HARBONA: | Can a five hundred year-old memory be so devilishly alive? |
| HAMAN: | The Jews are alive. Have you ever looked into their eyes? |
| HARBONA: | They're a conquered people; exiles weeping by the waters of Babylon. When a Persian official passes by they don't raise their heads. |
| HAMAN: | There's one of them here in Susa who sits each day in the palace porch. I look straight into his eyes and see that hairy dog Samuel, the foam and lice on his beard, butchering Agag in Gilgal. |
| HARBONA: | Haman, Haman, sir. I have nothing against hanging Jews, but you are the Chief Minister of the Empire; the King's ring on your finger, your dignity second only to that of Ahasuerus himself. No tramp of a Jew in the palace porch can possibly raise your hackles? |
| HAMAN: | All the King's servants in the porch rise and bow when I go by, but the Jew sits on his stool, without even lowering his gaze, and his face full of defiance. |
| HARBONA: | The King's command is that everybody should make obeisance to you. How does he dare not to? *(In the rear, Mordecai, the Jew, is seen ascending the stairs to the left, wearing sackcloth and ashes. He stops and turns to look at Haman.)* |

| | |
|---|---|
| HAMAN: | Talk of the devil! Do you see him?...That one!...That one! *(Mordecai goes out of sight.)* |
| HARBONA: | Mordecai! |
| HAMAN: | You know him? |
| HARBONA: | Everybody at court knows him. It was Mordecai saved the King's life. |
| HAMAN: | You believe that tale? |
| HARBONA: | Tale? |
| HAMAN: | Two half-witted room servants? |
| HARBONA: | They both confessed to be about to suffocate the King. It was Mordecai who revealed the treachery. |
| HAMAN: | Confessed under torture. |
| HARBONA: | And then they were summarily executed before they could be interrogated further... |
| HAMAN: | What else was to be done once they'd confessed? |
| HARBONA: | Before they'd named anyone else... |
| HAMAN: | There was no one else. |
| HARBONA: | Good...You were the judge in the case. |
| HAMAN: | Naturally; it was a clear-cut case. |
| HARBONA: | And you became Chief Minister. |
| HAMAN: | Yes, then, officially. But it had long been planned. |
| HARBONA: | Did you realise, sir, that some people at court expected that office to be Mordecai's reward? |
| HAMAN: | Mordecai as Chief Minister? That swine on the steps up there? |
| HARBONA: | But it was you who were chosen. |
| HAMAN: | I am of royal lineage. |
| HARBONA: | Mordecai was left at the palace porch. |
| HAMAN: | A Jew in the porch of the palace. It's disgusting. |
| HARBONA: | Still keeping the secret of the two servants. |
| HAMAN: | There was no secret. I have no fear of him. |
| HARBONA: | He's let it be and forgotten it by now. |
| HAMAN: | I won't forget it. We remember each other, Mordecai and I. He defies me mutely in the porch each day. |
| HARBONA: | Scorning the King's elect? That is an insult to the King. Why don't you punish him? |
| HAMAN: | That's what the proclamation you read just now is, my punishment for Mordecai. He'll hang with all Israel. He and his family, if he |

|            |                                                                                                                                                                              |
| ---------- | ---------------------------------------------------------------------------------------------------------------------------------------------------------------------------- |
|            | has a family, and the whole Jewish nation, they'll pay the price for being contemptuous of me.                                                                                |
| HARBONA:   | *(Laughing gently and unheedingly.)* Pretty good, sir. I understand that sort of revenge. But when you talked of revenging the wrong done to Agag five centuries ago, I didn't understand that. |
| HAMAN:     | Have you heard of the witch of Endor?                                                                                                                                          |
| HARBONA:   | No, I haven't. A hag, was she?                                                                                                                                                |
| HAMAN:     | She called Samuel back from hell to prophesy the death of Saul. And I shall summon Samuel, and Agag, to the threshold of the valley of the Son of Hinman—to Gehenna, to welcome the entire people of Moses. |
| HARBONA:   | That's what it means to be Chief Minister.                                                                                                                                    |
| HAMAN:     | The thrill of knowing that it's in my power to destroy a whole nation, a nation which claims to have been promised an eternal covenant!                                        |
| HARBONA:   | You're teaching me the meaning of politics.                                                                                                                                   |
| HAMAN:     | Have you ever envied Ahasuerus the King, Harbona?                                                                                                                             |
| HARBONA:   | Dangerous question, sir.                                                                                                                                                      |
| HAMAN:     | Now, now, lad, two servants of the palace are surely free to speak their minds in a relaxed way.                                                                              |
| HARBONA:   | Alright then, yes. I have envied him.                                                                                                                                         |
| HAMAN:     | Why?                                                                                                                                                                          |
| HARBONA:   | He's thirty years old, and Queen Esther is only twenty!                                                                                                                       |
| HAMAN:     | *(Laughing.)* Fair play to you, lad; fair play!                                                                                                                               |
| HARBONA:   | She's Empress of the whole kingdom, and yet no one knows where she comes from.                                                                                                |
| HAMAN:     | I hadn't thought of it. After Vashti had been exiled from the palace, all the fairest maids from each corner of the empire were gathered for the King to choose his beloved. And this was the young lady who won his favour. |
| HARBONA:   | Is he fond of her?                                                                                                                                                            |
| HAMAN:     | What do I know? He has other women. I don't think he's seen her for a month.                                                                                                  |
| HARBONA:   | She sits on her throne as if born to it. Do you know anything of her family?                                                                                                  |
| HAMAN:     | The King of the Medes and the Persians is too wise. He never has in-laws!                                                                                                     |

131

| | |
|---|---|
| HARBONA: | Nobody knows where Vashti went to. Nobody knows where Esther came from. |
| HAMAN: | Did you ever see Vashti? |
| HARBONA: | Esther is more beautiful. |
| HAMAN: | That's your opinion? I haven't taken much notice of her. |
| HARBONA: | Poor you, sir. There's nothing else worth looking at in Susa, to compare with her. |
| HAMAN: | You set your sights high? |
| HARBONA: | I wait upon her for at least part of each day, but she hasn't seen me yet. Who knows? A little hunger and tiredness? |
| HAMAN: | Is she supercilious like Vashti? |
| HARBONA: | She's gentle and leisurely, but even so I feel there is a sleeping tiger behind those eyelids of hers. |
| HAMAN: | For me, women are things for one's use. We can't have sons without them. And I suppose it's quite a useful arrangement. |
| HARBONA: | So you know nothing of pleasure? |
| HAMAN: | I have ten sons, seven of them officials at the palace or officers in the army. That is a matter of pleasure, deep pleasure. I came to Persia a foreigner; an unknown soldier. Today I'm Chief Minister of the whole empire. After me, my sons will be princes. The children of Agag. I have defied fate. All power is pleasurable. |
| HARBONA: | You're quite right, sir. You have no reason to envy anybody. |
| HAMAN: | I know better than you what envy is. |
| HARBONA: | You, too, are envious of the King? |
| HAMAN: | Envious of Ahasuerus? |
| HARBONA: | Of his pomp, perhaps? His greatness, his authority? |
| HAMAN: | Not at all; not one iota. I have little to say to pomp as such. And as to his authority, I hold it. I exercise it as I wish by now. |
| HARBONA: | That's alright as long as he doesn't suspect it. |
| HAMAN: | Not much likelihood of that. His mind is like yours, on Esther or some other one of his loves. |
| HARBONA: | Watch that you don't wake the sleeping tigress in Esther. |
| HAMAN: | Esther's role is to keep the King from seeing things. |

132

| | |
|---|---|
| HARBONA: | I'd give a lot to have her begin to see me. |
| HAMAN: | One must be young to be envious of the King. |
| HARBONA: | Or old enough to use Bigthana and Teresh. |
| HAMAN: | What are you suggesting? |
| HARBONA: | A joke, sir; just a joke. Palace gossip is harmless enough. |
| HAMAN: | Envy is the stuff of palace gossip. |
| HARBONA: | Who do you envy? |
| HAMAN: | You're too young to understand. |
| HARBONA: | Try me. |
| HAMAN: | The Gods, Harbona. The Gods who control death. |
| HARBONA: | Well, no. In that case, I don't understand. |
| HAMAN: | That's what politics is all about, Harbona: man yearning to be God. Death is the key to the secret. The ability to use death, command death, make death obedient, an instrument in one's hand, that's the politician's bliss. Today I'm God for the whole Jewish people, through the proclamation I'm announcing the death of the whole nation, and that will come to pass in an orderly fashion. That's what is intoxicating about politics. I can imagine one day a man, a Chief Minister or a general, being able to take a ball of flame in his hands and then, by throwing it, to destroy the whole of humanity; putting the world on fire. When that day comes, Harbona, that will be the end of the world. For no man could resist the temptation. No one who held the fate of living humanity in his hands and at his will, could refuse the experience, the experience of being God. That is the enchantment of politics. Today I am God for Mordecai, for the whole of Mordecai's people, for Moses and Samuel and their race. The order has gone out to the furthest reaches of the Empire. The hope of Abraham has been extinguished. The eternal covenant has been deleted. The Jews are going together into the concentration camp of the eternal night, the night I designated for them. Today the history of Israel closes, through the determination and command of one man; me, Haman the Agagite, the artist in politics. |
| HARBONA: | Yes, a real thrill. I can understand. And yet for |

all that, the sight of Mordecai on the palace steps, a sack about his waist, disturbs you.

HAMAN: I haven't lost my wits. I said that I envied God, not that I had become a God.

HARBONA: Mordecai's become a bit of a nightmare for you, sir.

HAMAN: I told you, I see Samuel in his eyes.

HARBONA: There's still some time till the day of the mass killings.

HAMAN: The thirteenth day of the twelfth month.

HARBONA: Will you accept advice from a young man?

HAMAN: I'll listen intently and weigh it.

HARBONA: The King is hardly likely to refuse you anything to do with the Jews.

HAMAN: As far as I can see, no.

HARBONA: Why be so dilatory when there is such urgency?

HAMAN: Before stringing up the Jews?

HARBONA: No, I can understand that. A matter of organisation. But the hanging of one leader amongst them? The hanging of your particular enemy, the spy of Bigthana and Teresh.

HAMAN: Hang Mordecai?

HARBONA: It would be possible, you know, to hang him today.

HAMAN: How can I persuade the King? He puts such stress on the Law, except in very special circumstances.

HARBONA: Show him what the danger is in waiting too long, giving people time to organise a rebellion.

HAMAN: Harbona, you have the mind of a politician.

HARBONA: Go home now and get the carpenters to set up the gallows beneath the windows of your house.

HAMAN: Then on to the King to persuade him of the danger to his throne.

HARBONA: You'll sleep peacefully tonight, with Mordecai twisting and turning at the end of a rope not far from the foot of your bed.

HAMAN: The crows and eagles picking the bones...Give me your hand, lad; I'll look after your career...I'm off to the carpenters at once.

HARBONA: Then to the King. I'll be there waiting upon him. *(Haman turns to go and comes face to face with Mordecai, spits towards him, and strides on.)*

MORDECAI: Harbona!

| | |
|---|---|
| HARBONA: | Well, well! Mordecai! How strange, we were just talking about you. |
| MORDECAI: | I'm not surprised. |
| HARBONA: | Have you heard? There's talk of the King having a special favour in store for you today; he and the Minister mean to elevate you. |
| MORDECAI: | I must ask a favour of you, Harbona. |
| HARBONA: | Another one! I've just read the proclamation. |
| MORDECAI: | You're suggesting I'm the cause of it? Yes, that could be true. |
| HARBONA: | What other favour can I do for you? |
| MORDECAI: | Go to Queen Esther, tell her I am here at the porch, asking for a word with her. |
| HARBONA: | The Queen? |
| MORDECAI: | Yes. |
| HARBONA: | Have you seen yourself, man? The dirt on your forehead. That sack about your waist. |
| MORDECAI: | Sackcloth and ashes, the symbols of submission and prayer for my people. I must have a word with the Queen. |
| HARBONA: | I can't ask the Queen to come to you like this. |
| MORDECAI: | You'll annoy her if you don't. |
| HARBONA: | Nobody has audience of the Queen without great cause. |
| MORDECAI: | The last time it was by talking to the Queen I saved the King's life. |
| HARBONA: | Is the King in danger again? |
| MORDECAI: | The Queen is in danger. |
| HARBONA: | The Queen in danger? Are you sure? |
| MORDECAI: | As sure as when Bigthana and Teresh were hanged for plotting to murder the King. |
| HARBONA: | The Queen in danger? *(Esther comes to the top of the steps, behind Harbona, in a long dress of black and purple.)* |
| ESTHER: | What's wrong, Harbona? *(He turns and kneels.)* |
| HARBONA: | It's Mordecai the Jew asking to see you, my Lady. |
| ESTHER: | Mordecai the Jew? |
| HARBONA: | *(Rising.)* Here he is, my Lady. *(Esther and Mordecai look at each other.)* |
| ESTHER: | What is the meaning of this? |
| MORDECAI: | Oh, that my head were not in deep waters, and my eyes a fountain of tears. |

| | |
|---|---|
| ESTHER: | Harbona, I wish to talk to this Jew without being interrupted by anyone. |
| HARBONA: | I'll arrange it, Lady, so that nobody at all will come near you. *(Exit.)* |
| MORDECAI: | Did you hear the proclamation? |
| ESTHER: | I've read it. |
| MORDECAI: | Your own nation, Esther. |
| ESTHER: | My nation. My family. I'm glad you acknowledge that. |
| MORDECAI: | Do you understand what the proclamation means? |
| ESTHER: | Death climbing up to our windows to destroy the little ones. Yes, I understand. |
| MORDECAI: | That happens all the time, in every part of the world. Wherever there are men, you'll find infants and babies being killed. This today is very different. |
| ESTHER: | Our people? Is that what you mean? |
| MORDECAI: | No. What does that matter? But God's people, Esther—the chosen nation. |
| ESTHER: | The God of Abraham, the God of Isaac, the God of Jacob. The God of the promise. |
| MORDECAI: | The only God. The living God. The God of Israel. We are his witnesses. The only witnesses he has throughout the world. That's our role, our task on earth, telling of his existence. This proclamation deletes that. |
| ESTHER: | It was you reared me, Mordecai; you who taught me. Behold, an everlasting covenant will I make with them. That was your lesson every Sabbath even though Jerusalem was so far away. Can the proclamation delete that? |
| MORDECAI: | Who can say? It's impossible to tell. |
| ESTHER: | He relies on *us*? |
| MORDECAI: | It's a covenant. It's through us he works. It's our task to avert the danger. We are responsible. |
| ESTHER: | You are responsible. |
| MORDECAI: | I'm responsible? |
| ESTHER: | The proclamation is your work. |
| MORDECAI: | Esther! |
| ESTHER: | That's what the palace maids all say. That's the gossip amongst the servants in the porch. |
| MORDECAI: | How could that be? |

| | |
|---|---|
| ESTHER: | Because you refuse to obey the King's command. |
| MORDECAI: | I see: Haman? |
| ESTHER: | The King's Chief Minister. It's the King's command that all his servants should bow to him. There used to be a lot of talk about why you refused to do it. The servants say the proclamation is Haman's revenge. |
| MORDECAI: | They're right. This is Haman's revenge; an old, old hate. An old, old score. The third and fourth generations of those that hate me. |
| ESTHER: | Do you still say it's through us he works? |
| MORDECAI: | What else can I say? |
| ESTHER: | If so, you can prevent this destruction. |
| MORDECAI: | That's why I'm here. |
| ESTHER: | All you need do is comply with the King's command. |
| MORDECAI: | How? |
| ESTHER: | Reconcile yourself to Haman. Show good will towards him; bow before him and ask him for mercy on the Jews. |
| MORDECAI: | *(Like thunder.)* Esther! are you mad? |
| ESTHER: | Mad? why? |
| MORDECAI: | Are you forgetting the old traditions? Everything I taught you. Bow before the Agagite? |
| ESTHER: | Is that too much to ask to save the people of Israel? |
| MORDECAI: | Do you think it was because of pride or envy or desire for glory for myself that I refused to honour Haman? |
| ESTHER: | It is not I who accuse you. |
| MORDECAI: | I call on God as my witness that I would be ready to kiss his footmarks for the salvation of Israel. |
| ESTHER: | Less than that could make your peace with him. |
| MORDECAI: | Between him and the God of Israel no peace is possible. Between me and him no peace is possible. The living God is his enemy. The purpose of the proclamation is to usurp God. To silence the witness to him. To avenge and remove God's punishment on Agag. That is why I can never bow to him. Bowing to him would be a betrayal. You know that. |

137

| | |
|---|---|
| ESTHER: | My soul is among lions, and I lie even among them that are set on fire. |
| MORDECAI: | You, too, are a Jew, my cousin. |
| ESTHER: | I never denied it. It was you put me in the bed of the uncircumcised. You who commanded me not to reveal to anyone to which nation I belong. If I have been torn away from my people, if I have been exiled from Zion, it was because I obeyed you; because it was you who reared me, and I was like a daughter to you; an obedient daughter, Mordecai. |
| MORDECAI: | And today you are a queen wearing the imperial crown. |
| ESTHER: | There's no crown on my head now. I never wear it except when I'm summoned to the King. |
| MORDECAI: | Has your elevation in the world made you too proud to care about the fate of your people? |
| ESTHER: | Did you find me proud? Did you find me uncaring? Must you be so cruel? If you only knew how lonely I am in this palace. I'm an exile amongst the exiles of Judah. |
| MORDECAI: | Are you willing to acknowledge your people now in the hour of their need? |
| ESTHER: | Your people are my people and your God my God. |
| MORDECAI: | Who knows but that you came into your kingdom for such an hour as this? |
| ESTHER: | What can I do? |
| MORDECAI: | I had a dream last night. |
| ESTHER: | A dream? With a message? Alright, tell me your dream. |
| MORDECAI: | There was the sound of thunder and a dark, misty day, pain and woe and great tribulation on earth. And two dragons appeared in combat, making enough noise to frighten the whole world. And at the noise all the nations prepared to attack the holy nation in order to destroy her. And she called on God, and at this a small fountain arose, and out of the fountain a mighty river flowed and light and the sun rose, and the lowly were raised up and the mighty and arrogant destroyed. That was my dream. |
| ESTHER: | Have you Joseph's talent? Can you explain the meaning of dreams? |

MORDECAI: The two dragons are myself and Haman. The nations are those in every corner of the empire preparing now to destroy God's own nation. Today is the dark, misty day and the proclamation this morning the sound of thunder.

ESTHER: And the small fountain which gave rise to the great river leading to the coming of the dawn.

MORDECAI: The small fountain is you, Esther.

ESTHER: Me? Me, who has been expelled from Israel? Who has been excommunicated and who lies in the bed of the uncircumcised? How can this be?

MORDECAI: By your going to the King and confessing that you are a Jewess, and pleading for the lives of your people. It is only you who can save us.

ESTHER: (Definite in tone.) No!...No!

MORDECAI: Esther!

ESTHER: No!

MORDECAI: Why not?

ESTHER: You know the law. You yourself are a servant at his porch.

MORDECAI: You are the Queen.

ESTHER: The law is quite clear: whoever goes in to the King's presence without being summoned, be he man or woman, queen or otherwise, shall be put to death.

MORDECAI: That is the letter of the law. But in the law itself there is an exception.

ESTHER: That the King extend his golden sceptre towards the person in forgiveness? An exception indeed. Nobody ever remembers it happening.

MORDECAI: But it can happen. The law provides for it.

ESTHER: It could not happen as well.

MORDECAI: And you're afraid of losing your crown.

ESTHER: The crown, of itself, is as despicable in my eyes as a sanitary rag.

MORDECAI: You think you can escape death within the King's household. The cadavers of your people will be falling to the ground as manure, and you lying in the emperor's bed.

ESTHER: It wasn't my choice to hide the fact that I'm a Jewess.

MORDECAI: You can't escape. If you keep quiet and conceal your lineage now, the salvation of the Jews will come from some other source, and you and your father's house will be lost forever.

| | |
|---|---|
| ESTHER: | Mordecai, I fear death just like everyone else. Not more than everyone else. |
| MORDECAI: | The proclamation is quite clear and definite. Not one Jew is to escape. |
| ESTHER: | I am a Jew. |
| MORDECAI: | So, you are to die even if you don't go to the King. You've nothing to lose. |
| ESTHER: | More, far more than you have imagined. |
| MORDECAI: | You have to die even without going to him. If you venture and go to him, there is a chance, a chance, that you could save your own life and that of your people. That means a chance to save everything. You can only lose that which is already lost. Don't you see that? You have nothing to lose, and you could win your own life and win the earth for the people of God. |
| ESTHER: | Mordecai, there are some things no one has a right to ask of a woman, even in the name of God. |
| MORDECAI: | What are they? |
| ESTHER: | Do you know a whole month has passed since the King last summoned me to him? Since I saw him last? Thirty nights. |
| MORDECAI: | You count them? |
| ESTHER: | Yes, I count them. Like any married woman. |
| MORDECAI: | But he is not just any married man. A King and Emperor. |
| ESTHER: | No man is an emperor between the sheets. |
| MORDECAI: | He has a houseful of lovers and concubines. |
| ESTHER: | You speak like one of the palace girls. They love to taunt me with that. |
| MORDECAI: | You might as well get used to it. |
| ESTHER: | But I'm his proper wife. |
| MORDECAI: | That's why he might well extend the sceptre towards you. |
| ESTHER: | A chance, a terrible chance, that he might not. |
| MORDECAI: | I acknowledge that. |
| ESTHER: | The law and tradition weigh against him doing it, especially after Vashti's disobedience. |
| MORDECAI: | I don't deny it. We are all, every living Jew, under a death sentence. |
| ESTHER: | That's not the point at all. I could suffer that. |
| MORDECAI: | What are you afraid of then? What can't you suffer? |

| | |
|---|---|
| ESTHER: | Must I tell you? If you were a woman, you'd have understood ages ago. |
| MORDECAI: | I'm not a woman. You have to tell me. |
| ESTHER: | Being alive for even one second after he's refused to extend the sceptre towards me. |
| MORDECAI: | I can't follow you. |
| ESTHER: | Mordecai, it wasn't my choice to marry the King. It was you who expelled me from Israel. There were months of preparation, do you remember? I was frightened by it and despised it. And then my turn came, and I went in to him. And the instant we looked at each other, well, everything was alright. I knew then, that moment, that it would not be a matter of one night only. The next day he gave me his hand formally, in front of the whole court, married me and placed the crown on my head, and the whole kingdom feasted in celebration for weeks. |
| MORDECAI: | And now? |
| ESTHER: | Thirty nights since I saw him. Not a word from him. No message. No sign. And between his palace and mine there are only fifty yards of path. |
| MORDECAI: | You're worried about it? |
| ESTHER: | At night in my bed I see my soul's adored. I walk the palace, walk the gardens, between the roses where I walked before with him. I keep my head high amid the women, and hold my tongue when I see them sniggering at me. I force myself to look like a queen, whilst feeling like crying my heart out like a lost baby. |
| MORDECAI: | My dear girl, what else did you expect? |
| ESTHER: | I'm lost, Mordecai, lost. Lost to Israel. Lost in the palace of Persia. Do you see? I love him. Not his majesty, nor anything that belongs to him, but he himself; the man who is my husband. |
| MORDECAI: | So why don't you go to him? Why must you fear death at his hand? |
| ESTHER: | It's not death I'm afraid of. I'm afraid of him not extending the sceptre. |
| MORDECAI: | That means death. |
| ESTHER: | The second death, coming before the first one. The death of the heart—death of the soul, the disappointment that's a living death, that he |

141

|  |  |
|---|---|
|  | could look down from his throne on me—and not extend his mercy to me. |
| MORDECAI: | Poor Esther, giving your heart to a king is an idiotic, nonsensical thing to do. |
| ESTHER: | Can I help it? |
| MORDECAI: | Women are things that come and go in his life, with a palace-full of lovers at his beck and call. |
| ESTHER: | Don't be so stupid, Mordecai. I know about the women's palace better than you do. I couldn't care a damn for them. What does it matter, what does it matter at all, as long as they come and go and I stay. It is me he loves. |
| MORDECAI: | Why don't you face facts? You're saying that in order to console yourself and to try to convince yourself. And you don't believe it. |
| ESTHER: | Yes, I do believe it. It's true. It must be true. My life depends on it being true. |
| MORDECAI: | The life of our people, the promise made to the world, the hope, the only hope of humanity, depends on it being true. I challenge you to prove it to be true. |
| ESTHER: | He loves me. You can't prove something like that. It's something between him and me. |
| MORDECAI: | You're lying to your own heart. There is proof. And you know there is proof. Love or death. |
| ESTHER: | Death is the law. |
| MORDECAI: | Love is not subject to the law. Love is free of the law. |
| ESTHER: | I have no right to gamble on his love. |
| MORDECAI: | Yes, you have a right, as you're waging your own life. But you haven't the faith. You don't believe in his love...You daren't. |
| ESTHER: | Shut up, you blackguard. Don't blaspheme. I'll go to see him. I'll throw my life before him. I'll tell him everything, about my family, my people, and you. And if it should mean my demise, let it be so. |

## END OF ACT 1

## ACT II

*The Council Chamber of King Ahasuerus. On the left of the room is the throne, on a high level. A wall with doors stands behind the throne. Rich drapes hang at the back and right of the chamber, which can be drawn back to reveal an ante-chamber. Apart from the throne, the only other furniture is a smooth couch, covered with a colourful cloth and cushions. The King is rising from the throne as the curtain rises. The couch is at the centre back, and the lighting from above.*

| | |
|---|---|
| AHASUERUS: | Who is waiting upon me? *(Harbona appears.)* |
| HARBONA: | I, my lord King, if it please you. |
| AHASUERUS: | Alright, Harbona. Is the sun fiery outside? |
| HARBONA: | Like a giant in golden armour, sir. Would you like a drink? |
| AHASUERUS: | Too early. I tried to sleep for half an hour, but in vain. |
| HARBONA: | You had a long and busy morning, sir. |
| AHASUERUS: | Only the routine things, and yet I got tired. |
| HARBONA: | You didn't sleep well last night, sir? |
| AHASUERUS: | No, not last night...the whole night. |
| HARBONA: | If I was King and Emperor, sir, that wouldn't happen to me. |
| AHASUERUS: | It doesn't happen to you now, is that what you're saying? |
| HARBONA: | You had no white arm for a pillow, sir? |
| AHASUERUS: | No; neither a white arm nor a white bosom. |
| HARBONA: | One must surely have been a King for a good while to be able to be so wasteful with your nights. |
| AHASUERUS: | How old are you, Harbona? |
| HARBONA: | Twenty three, sir. |
| AHASUERUS: | Six years younger than I. I have been King on this throne for twelve years. |
| HARBONA: | And already tired of the pleasures of the flesh? |
| AHASUERUS: | Did you see my first queen, Vashti? |
| HARBONA: | Yes, my lord King, many times, from afar, as a man in a prison dungeon glimpsing paradise. |
| AHASUERUS: | Her breasts were like paradise. The oscillations of her arms like the dance of a goddess. When she was mute, her conversation was like honey. And in one instant, night descended on her glory. |
| HARBONA: | Pride and its greed. |
| AHASUERUS: | She was like the sun beating down on one, sir. |
| HARBONA: | Every married man, be he Emperor or farmhand, likes to attend on his beloved and do according to her caprice in the bed chamber. |
| AHASUERUS: | But in public, the Queen too must obey? |
| HARBONA: | Disobedience is proof of contempt in the heart. |

| | |
|---|---|
| HARBONA: | Yes, sir, it is the contempt that is unforgiveable, not the disobedience in itself. |
| AHASUERUS: | A woman's spite is like a vile, venomous thing. |
| HARBONA: | Vashti was only twenty, sir. |
| AHASUERUS: | If a woman is not sensible by the time she's twenty... |
| HARBONA: | It is a King who speaks. For me, it is not that she be sensible that is important about a woman, but that she be twenty. |
| AHASUERUS: | Your choice is a safe one. It's easier to be twenty than to be sensible. |
| HARBONA: | Even for those who are twenty-three? |
| AHASUERUS: | You know nothing of loss of sleep? |
| HARBONA: | Only from choice, in order to win some pleasure. |
| AHASUERUS: | Win pleasure? You surprise me, Harbona. Another royal disadvantage. |
| HARBONA: | What's that, sir? |
| AHASUERUS: | I can't remember winning pleasure. Poor me, I only command pleasure. What would you most like to win of all things in the world, Harbona? |
| HARBONA: | Of real things or imaginary ones? |
| AHASUERUS: | Imaginary ones if you like. |
| HARBONA: | An empress's kiss, and her body. |
| AHASUERUS: | A lad's dream. |
| HARBONA: | Your turn to play now, sir. What would you most like to win of all things in the world? |
| AHASUERUS: | That which I can't command. |
| HARBONA: | And what is that, sir? |
| AHASUERUS: | The heart of an Empress. |
| HARBONA: | Was it thinking of Vashti kept you awake last night? |
| AHASUERUS: | Yes and no. I have another queen by now. |
| HARBONA: | A queen who would find it impossible to disobey. |
| AHASUERUS: | Who knows? Who knows?...Don't give your heart to a woman, Harbona. |
| HARBONA: | No danger of that, sir. I have no heart. |
| AHASUERUS: | You're not a king, and you have no heart. How lucky you are. You know nothing of jealousy? |
| HARBONA: | I have sometimes seen a sweet thing, and been jealous of its owner for a while. But before long, I'd get a taste of that sweet thing. No, life in Susa is wonderful; I know little of jealousy. I have patience. |

| | |
|---|---|
| AHASUERUS: | And I'm jealous of you. |
| HARBONA: | *(Laughing.)* Help me! Why jealous of me? |
| AHASUERUS: | Because you're a happy animal, living like a stallion in his prime. |
| HARBONA: | That's why I sleep at night, sir, though I haven't got a palace-full of ladies at my beck and call...But they do come. |
| AHASUERUS: | No lady has been near me for a month. |
| HARBONA: | A month! |
| AHASUERUS: | Thirty nights. |
| HARBONA: | Have you seen the doctor, sir? |
| AHASUERUS: | Abstinence not disease. |
| HARBONA: | A regal abstinence; much too regal. |
| AHASUERUS: | I choose every blow but those to the heart, and every wickedness but that of a woman. |
| HARBONA: | Can disappointment remain so painfully alive in a king's memory. |
| AHASUERUS: | It's disappointment that reminds a king that he's mortal. |
| HARBONA: | He needs to be a king to believe that. |
| AHASUERUS: | I learnt last night how easy it is to forget favours; how difficult to forget disappointments. |
| HARBONA: | Disappointment is a good counsellor. |
| AHASUERUS: | Its counsel is to shield the heart from a further blow; it's better to break things off suddenly, to stop before endangering the heart a second time. |
| HARBONA: | And that was Vashti's end? |
| AHASUERUS: | Not only Vashti. |
| HARBONA: | The price is loss of sleep. |
| AHASUERUS: | *(More lightly.)* Loss of sleep can turn out to be an advantage. Last night I got one of the scribes to read to me. |
| HARBONA: | Poetry? Love lyrics? |
| AHASUERUS: | Reading, not singing. |
| HARBONA: | I know! The Chronicle of the Times. |
| AHASUERUS: | Yes, the main events during my reign. |
| HARBONA: | Memoirs? |
| AHASUERUS: | And many a thing had slipped from memory, even recent events. |
| HARBONA: | What sort of things, sir? |
| AHASUERUS: | Two grooms of the chamber waiting upon me, as you do today, and plotting to murder me, and about to do so. |

| | |
|---|---|
| HARBONA: | Bigthana and Teresh? |
| AHASUERUS: | Yes, I remember. |
| HARBONA: | Everybody at the palace remembers it too well, and are terrified when they think about it. |
| AHASUERUS: | Do you know, it isn't hard to murder a king. *(Both laugh.)* |
| AHASUERUS: | Who are the servants waiting outside? *(Harbona goes to see.)* |
| HARBONA: | Haman, the Chief Minister, is here, sir. He has a special request for your majesty. |
| AHASUERUS: | And I one for him. *(He goes to sit on the throne, with his back to the other two as Haman enters.)* |
| HARBONA: | *(To Haman at the entrance.)* My lord Haman, the King summons you...Is the gallows ready? |
| HAMAN: | *(Quietly.)* Everything ready, the gallows, the rope, and the Jew...*(He comes forward and bows.)* My lord King. |
| AHASUERUS: | What news, Haman? |
| HAMAN: | The proclamation has been published, sir. |
| AHASUERUS: | Proclamation? |
| HAMAN: | The proclamation to each and every province of the realm putting an end to the Jewish nation. |
| AHASUERUS: | Of course, I'd forgotten. |
| HAMAN: | The messengers have gone out. It'll all happen together then, on the same day, the thirteenth. |
| AHASUERUS: | The thirteenth? That's clever, an unlucky day. |
| HAMAN: | After that day there will be no Jews, sir. They'll belong to the past, to history. Then the Persian Empire will enjoy peace and tranquility for a thousand years. One rule throughout the world, your word and your will. |
| AHASUERUS: | I don't know about that. It's your will which is being imposed on the Jews. |
| HAMAN: | For the welfare of your government, sir. |
| AHASUERUS: | I don't doubt it. The full report you gave me about them justifies the punishment. |
| HAMAN: | And removes a grave danger; a danger to your throne, even your life, sir. |
| AHASUERUS: | It's strange that I know nothing through business about the Jews. As far as I know, I never saw a Jew. Are there any of them amongst the palace servants, Harbona? |
| HARBONA: | I know of one, sir, a servant at the gate. |
| AHASUERUS: | A servant at the gate? Not a lowly servant. |

146

| | |
|---|---|
| HAMAN: | I was about to talk to you specially about him... |
| AHASUERUS: | Wait, Haman. I'm questioning Harbona now. What sort of women do they have? |
| HARBONA: | Jewish women? |
| AHASUERUS: | Yes. You're a well-known judge of the women of all nations. |
| HARBONA: | I saw Vashti in her glory, sir. I saw Queen Esther at her wedding feast. I saw her this morning. How could I look at a Jewess. |
| AHASUERUS: | Alright, fair enough. What sort of women do they have, Haman? |
| HAMAN: | Religious. |
| AHASUERUS: | I see: dangerous? |
| HAMAN: | Women and mothers who put their language and the beauty of Jerusalem before their daily bread. |
| HARBONA: | Such people could never be assimilated into the Empire. Putting bread first secures obedient slaves. |
| HAMAN: | They must be destroyed for the security of the throne. |
| AHASUERUS: | That's what I was talking about earlier. |
| HAMAN: | I'm glad to hear it, sir. It'll make it easier for me to put my request before you. |
| AHASUERUS: | I was saying how easy it would be to murder the king. |
| HAMAN: | Through the mercy of the gods, sir, it is not so easy. Every living man and woman knows the law, that to come even into the ante-room without being summoned by the King means death—without exception. |
| AHASUERUS: | Do you remember Bigthana and Teresh? |
| HAMAN: | I was the judge in the case, sir. I hanged them. |
| AHASUERUS: | They were about me constantly, servants like Harbona there. They were arrested just a quarter of an hour before they had planned to kill me. Do you see? |
| HAMAN: | That could never happen again, sir. That isn't the danger now. |
| AHASUERUS: | You're not planning to stab me suddenly with a dagger, Harbona? |
| HARBONA: | I have one consolation, sir. |
| AHASUERUS: | And what is that? |
| HARBONA: | If you did suspect me, you'd never ask the question. |

| | |
|---|---|
| AHASUERUS: | *(Laughing.)* You're shrewd. It was last night, in the early hours when I was listening to what happened with Bigthana and Teresh, that these things came into my mind first. We were in the middle of the wedding feast at the time. It was Esther, the Queen, who first told me of the plot, and saved my life. |
| HAMAN: | Once the treachery had been revealed, your officials acted immediately, sir. The two traitors were caught, they broke down under torture, and by nightfall they were strung up on a rope. |
| AHASUERUS: | Quite true. I realise that. It's important also that the King should honour those servants who saved his life. I have been neglectful. |
| HAMAN: | Saving the King's life was honour enough for us, sir. |
| AHASUERUS: | What do you think, Harbona? |
| HARBONA: | The King's honour demands the honouring of those who deserve it. |
| AHASUERUS: | Well, the King's life was saved. |
| HARBONA: | At the Queen's wedding feast, and she herself instrumental in it. |
| AHASUERUS: | Fifteen minutes before it was to take place. |
| HARBONA: | Proof that there's some good in marriage, sir! |
| AHASUERUS: | You're right, Harbona. If there is mercy, understanding and healing on her tongue, her husband shall not be like other men. Perhaps I lost my sleep in vain. |
| HAMAN: | My lord King, the King's life is more important to us, his servants, than anything else in the whole world. |
| AHASUERUS: | That's the sort of thing it's respectable to say, Haman. I'll do my best to believe you, though...Don't sulk. |
| HAMAN: | I'm not sulking, just worrying. |
| AHASUERUS: | Worrying about my life? |
| HAMAN: | Is that strange, sir? |
| AHASUERUS: | Where does the danger come from now? |
| HAMAN: | The Jews. |
| AHASUERUS: | But the proclamation this morning has settled their fate, surely? |
| HAMAN: | There is still some time before the great day. What have they got to lose now? |
| AHASUERUS: | A sudden rising, a rebellion? Is that your fear? |

148

| | |
|---|---|
| HARBONA: | The safest thing would be to break their hearts and spirits immediately. |
| HAMAN: | Yes, stun them, in case their poets begin to stir them into action by calling on their God. |
| AHASUERUS: | What did you say? Poets? |
| HAMAN: | They're a crazy nation, a tribe of uncivilised hotheads. When they lose a battle, when Jerusalem is destroyed, they never admit to defeat by an enemy. No, their poets lament because their God has been offended by their having turned their backs on him, and has let them be beaten as a punishment. Then they seek his forgiveness and call on their compatriots to rise in frenzied rebellion to defend their God. No terrorism is too dangerous for them then. They're like a gorse fire, sweeping destruction before it. |
| AHASUERUS: | That won't do. |
| HAMAN: | They must go to their deaths meekly, obediently, the whole nation. Don't you agree, sir. |
| AHASUERUS: | What is your counsel? |
| HAMAN: | Arrest their main leader in this city today, send soldiers to bring all the Jews to the law court, and hang him in their sight before nightfall. That'll break their hearts; they'll see that their God has no answer; then it'll be easy to round them up into concentration camps in order to exterminate them. |
| AHASUERUS: | A general's counsel...Alright, choose your Jew. Which Jew? |
| HAMAN: | The leader of the Jews in Susa. |
| AHASUERUS: | And who is he? |
| HARBONA: | *(Shouting suddenly.)* My lord King! The curtains! The ante-chamber. |
| AHASUERUS: | There's someone there! |
| HAMAN: | Jews! Jews breaking in! *(He draws his dagger, and runs to the door behind the throne, shouting.)* Soldiers! Immediately, to the defence!...Jews! *(Two or three soldiers rush in through the doors and form up in front of the throne.)* Shields and swords at the ready! Jews! |
| AHASUERUS: | *(Taking control.)* Open the curtains wide. Let us expose the whole ante-room! Come, Jews! *(The curtains are opened, to reveal Esther, magnificently arrayed and wearing her crown,* |

149

|  | *on her knees and extending her hands in silent supplication towards the throne.)* |
|---|---|
| ALL: | The Queen! |
| AHASUERUS: | Esther! *(She bows her head to the floor.)* Esther! *(Immediately, his sceptre in his hand, he leaps from his throne and down to her.)* Esther, what's the matter? Look at me, Esther, the sceptre is extended towards you! It is I who am here, your brother, your husband...You're alive! *(The two are on their knees, gazing at each other.)* |
| ESTHER: | Looking at you then was like looking at the Angel of God. |
| AHASUERUS: | Get up! Leave us, all of you! *(All the others leave.)* Come, sit with me on the couch...You gave me a fright, Esther. |
| ESTHER: | My lord, it was not disobedience brought me here. Nothing other than a terrible need. |
| AHASUERUS: | I believe you, Esther. |
| ESTHER: | My life is but a candle-flame between the thumb and forefinger of my lord. |
| AHASUERUS: | The wind of the law shan't extinguish it. |
| ESTHER: | I'm forgiven? |
| AHASUERUS: | Ask me up to half of my realm, and it shall be yours. |
| ESTHER: | My lord King, half of your realm isn't enough. |
| AHASUERUS: | There is nothing I could refuse you. |
| ESTHER: | You refuse me the only thing my soul craves for. |
| AHASUERUS: | What have I refused you? |
| ESTHER: | The thing I faced death just now, to seek it. |
| AHASUERUS: | Thirty nights I've closed my bed to you. |
| ESTHER: | You count the nights too? |
| AHASUERUS: | I'm a married man as well, Esther. |
| ESTHER: | It's a married women who's listening to you! *(They smile.)* |
| AHASUERUS: | Is that your complaint? |
| ESTHER: | No, that's not my complaint. I'd wait a year, lonely at night but happy as a cuckoo, without receiving any message, with no sign from you, if only I could have from you what I'm asking for. |
| AHASUERUS: | Ask what you will, Esther. |
| ESTHER: | Fear ties my tongue. |
| AHASUERUS: | What fear now? |

| | |
|---|---|
| ESTHER: | Fear of a 'Yes' on your lips and a 'No' in your breast. |
| AHASUERUS: | Ask and it's yours. |
| ESTHER: | *(Slipping to her knees beside him.)* I ask for my husband's heart and the love of my beloved. *(They gaze at each other.)* |
| AHASUERUS: | Was that what you risked your life for? |
| ESTHER: | My life is of little worth compared to the gift I ask for. |
| AHASUERUS: | I'm a king, Esther. |
| ESTHER: | And I the dust of the earth. |
| AHASUERUS: | You ask me to break with the customs of the Kings of Persia? |
| ESTHER: | Your will is my will. Why don't you simply enjoy your ladies. Love cannot say no. |
| AHASUERUS: | I put the crown on your head. Isn't that enough. |
| ESTHER: | My crown belongs to you. That's its only worth. |
| AHASUERUS: | I made you Queen of my household. |
| ESTHER: | My king's heart's the only realm for me. |
| AHASUERUS: | I have my empire. What are you? A wife, a girl, a female, an hour's pleasure, a night's rest, an escape? |
| ESTHER: | You have your ladies for all that. |
| AHASUERUS: | What can you give me then? |
| ESTHER: | Love. Love that tells the truth. |
| AHASUERUS: | Tells the truth?...A woman? |
| ESTHER: | A married woman, not a concubine for the night. |
| AHASUERUS: | Nobody tells the Emperor of the world the truth. |
| ESTHER: | That's why you need me. Love drives fear out. |
| AHASUERUS: | Where did you get your confidence? |
| ESTHER: | Love is strong like death. |
| AHASUERUS: | Not so the Queens of Persia. |
| ESTHER: | The blood of heroines flows in my veins. |
| AHASUERUS: | Oh, Esther...if it were only possible? |
| ESTHER: | I risked my life to prove it. |
| AHASUERUS: | ...Can I trust you? |
| ESTHER: | Look at me and judge. |
| AHASUERUS: | Vashti too was as beautiful as the dawn. |
| ESTHER: | Without the light of your eyes, I am nothing but night. |
| AHASUERUS: | You won't disappoint me, once again? |

| | |
|---|---|
| ESTHER: | Before you can doubt me, I'll be dead; quicker than a sword-stroke. |
| AHASUERUS: | You're not asking, Esther, you're stealing my heart! |
| ESTHER: | Ahasuerus, my beloved! |
| AHASUERUS: | Put me as a seal on your heart, as a seal on your arm. |
| ESTHER: | Now and at the hour of our death, amen. *(Ahasuerus rises and summons:)* |
| AHASUERUS: | Harbona!...Come here, and Haman also...Come to greet the Queen, both of you...There is no more need for the soldiers. *(The two enter and bow.)*...Haman is my right arm, Esther, the Chief Minister of the Empire. |
| ESTHER: | Good day, my lord Haman. |
| HAMAN: | And a good day to you, my lady. |
| HARBONA: | Our fright has turned to joy, sir. |
| AHASUERUS: | Did you see the soldiers with their shields around me, Esther? |
| ESTHER: | Soldiers? Were there soldiers here? |
| AHASUERUS: | Each with his shield and spear ready to pierce your heart. And you didn't even see them? |
| ESTHER: | Forgive me, my lord. I didn't notice. I saw you and your throne. That was enough. |
| HARBONA: | Didn't you hear the shouting, my lady? |
| ESTHER: | Yes, Harbona, before the curtains opened, indeed I did; their noise made my blood freeze. |
| AHASUERUS: | Haman was afraid there were Jews there, craving the King's blood. |
| HARBONA: | Fair play for the lord Haman, sir. A wife is sometimes more of a danger than an army! |
| AHASUERUS: | Depends on the army. |
| HAMAN: | This is the first time, in my experience, that anyone has trespassed in the ante-room and remained alive. My lady Queen is the bravest of all Persia's subjects. |
| ESTHER: | Not brave, but lucky, Haman. In my weakness I found forgiveness, with the sceptre extended towards me. You're a politican, Haman, have you room for forgiveness? |
| HAMAN: | This wasn't a political matter, my lady. |
| ESTHER: | No, I know that. But in political matters...? |
| HAMAN: | I'll tell you a story, a true one. Something that happened to a king in my family. He was beaten in battle and taken prisoner. Next day, |

|  |  |
|---|---|
|  | he stood before the enemy ruler, unarmed, and extended his hand in peace to greet him and beg forgiveness. He was struck dead then and there. |
| ESTHER: | Terrible! |
| HAMAN: | No, lady. In politics that was the right course. In politics it is only might that counts. Start forgiving rebellious nations, spare the life of just one of their leaders and your government is doomed. Showing mercy is the start of one's downfall. |
| ESTHER: | My lord King, I'll keep the Chief Minister's lesson in mind. When it comes to a question of politics, nation set against nation, I won't go on my knees like today, to plead for mercy. |
| HAMAN: | You know nothing of the experience, my lady. And it's obvious from your demeanour that you're not a member of a conquered nation. All those are cowards to the marrow of their bones. They'll go to their destruction like sheep. You could drown their country under water, and they'd simply cry and accept charity. |
| AHASUERUS: | Tonight, Esther, you must tell me about your background and history, your nation, your lineage, your family. I must get to know my Queen. |
| ESTHER: | I will, gladly, my lord King. I'll tell you all of it. I have found mercy today. |
| AHASUERUS: | Haman believed the King's life was about to end. |
| ESTHER: | And I was sure the Queen's life was about to end. |
| HAMAN: | And the King saved the Queen's life. |
| HARBONA: | Because the Queen had previously saved the King's life. |
| ESTHER: | When was that, Harbona? |
| HARBONA: | During your wedding feast. |
| ESTHER: | Me? |
| AHASUERUS: | In the case of Bigthana and Teresh. |
| ESTHER: | But I don't deserve the honour for that. I only delivered a message from someone else. |
| HAMAN: | And I then had the honour of removing the danger quickly and permanently. |
| ESTHER: | My lord King, if I have gained favour with you...? |
| AHASUERUS: | Anything I can do for you; anything in the world. |
| ESTHER: | I've promised to tell you my history tonight. |

153

| | |
|---|---|
| AHASUERUS: | That will be a feast for me, Esther. |
| ESTHER: | I've received my life today from my King's hand. |
| AHASUERUS: | That's a feast already. We ought to celebrate it. |
| ESTHER: | That is my wish. If I arrange a feast in my house, in the hall that opens out to the rose garden, tonight when the full moon is rising, will my King come to it? |
| AHASUERUS: | Harbona, I have that which I couldn't command. |
| HARBONA: | My lady, the King accepts your invitation. He has won something today, something impossible. Did I say it properly, sir? |
| AHASUERUS: | The heart of the truth. I'll come like a youth to your feast, Esther. |
| ESTHER: | You have the King's secret, Harbona. What did he win today? |
| HARBONA: | He won his sleep, and lost his abstinence. Isn't that it, sir.? |
| AHASUERUS: | Well answered, my stallion. |
| ESTHER: | And, Haman, my lord Haman, Haman the Agagite, the man the King honours before all others, it is right and fitting for the King's hand-maiden to honour him also. May I invite you to accompany his majesty tonight to my feast? No one except the King and Haman—and Harbona as groom? |
| HAMAN: | My lady Queen, your invitation is my command. But for that, I wouldn't dare accept such an in-comparable invitation. |
| ESTHER: | Thank you, Haman, I must honour the man the King honours. |
| AHASUERUS: | The man the King honours! Thank you, Esther, for those words. I was about to forget again. |
| ESTHER: | Forget what? |
| AHASUERUS: | The thing I summoned Haman here today to discuss. I must have your advice, Haman. |
| HAMAN: | If I can advise you, sir, I will. |
| AHASUERUS: | The Queen is giving a feast to honour the minister. Well, what if the King wished to bestow an honour on one of his servants, a special honour. What is to be done? |
| HAMAN: | To the man the King wishes to honour? |
| AHASUERUS: | Yes. What is the custom? |
| HAMAN: | A public honour or a private one, sir? |
| AHASUERUS: | A public one, in the city, in full view of the populace. A sign for everybody to see of the King's favour. |

| | |
|---|---|
| HAMAN: | You're not teasing, sir? |
| AHASUERUS: | I love to tease, but I'm not teasing now. The matter touches on my honour as well. |
| HAMAN: | If that's the case, I must answer according to the royal traditions of Persia—unless you prefer to consult with someone else, sir, someone more impartial? |
| AHASUERUS: | From whom should I seek advice but from the Chief Minister? |
| HAMAN: | I was afraid you might think me...well, bold. |
| AHASUERUS: | No danger of that. You are familiar with the ceremonials and customs. That's part of your office. So, let me have your advice. |
| HAMAN: | Alright then, sir, as long as you don't consider me impudent. |
| AHASUERUS: | I'm listening. |
| HAMAN: | I'll answer according to the tradition, quite impersonally. For the man whom the King wishes to honour, he must be given the royal robe, the one worn by the King himself in procession, and the steed the King rides, and the royal crown must be put on his head. |
| AHASUERUS: | Yes, I remember now. That's the custom. |
| HAMAN: | Then, the robe and the steed must be given to one of the King's greatest princes, and he then shall robe the man whom the King wishes to honour and lead him on the steed through the streets of the city, proclaiming before him: 'This is what is done for the man the King wishes to honour.' |
| AHASUERUS: | Exactly. That's the tradition. Those are the rituals. |
| HAMAN: | I don't press for them this time, sir. |
| AHASUERUS: | I press for them; the traditions of the Medes and Persians. |
| HAMAN: | So be it, sir, as it is your will. |
| AHASUERUS: | Harbona, where is the royal robe? |
| HARBONA: | In the cupboard in the ante-room out there, sir. |
| AHASUERUS: | Bring it here...Put it on the couch, beside the Queen...Take the crown too—there it is on the throne—and put it with the robe...Now, tell the soldiers to fetch my steed and bring it to the porch...Is that all correct, Haman? |
| HAMAN: | Quite correct and proper, sir. But I'm ashamed. |

| | |
|---|---|
| AHASUERUS: | Do you see, Esther, I couldn't sleep last night. So I called for candles and got two of the scribes to read the Chronicles of the realm to me. We came to our wedding, and then to the story of the two grooms, Bigthana and Teresh, and their plot to murder me by strangling me as soon as they came on duty. Do you remember? |
| ESTHER: | How could I not remember. |
| AHASUERUS: | Well, I forgot. Of course the two villains were hanged. According to the chronicles last night, you were the judge, Haman. |
| HAMAN: | It was I had the honour of securing your life, sir. |
| AHASUERUS: | But it wasn't you revealed the treachery. It wasn't you revealed it nor was it you who warned me. It wasn't you who saved my life. |
| HAMAN: | No, the Queen did that, my lord. |
| ESTHER: | No, I've told you already: I simply carried a message. |
| AHASUERUS: | A message from whom? |
| ESTHER: | One of the servants at the palace porch. |
| AHASUERUS: | That's what the chronicle says, 'one of the servants at the palace porch.' But his name was there too. What was his name, Haman? |
| HAMAN: | *(Almost choking.)* Mordecai!...The Jew. |
| AHASUERUS: | What? |
| HARBONA: | Mordecai, sir, the leader of the Jews in Susa. |
| AHASUERUS: | Jew?...Did you say Jew? |
| ESTHER: | The leader of the Jews. The tribe of Benjamin. A royal family. |
| AHASUERUS: | Haman!...Haman! |
| HAMAN: | Out of Hell! |
| AHASUERUS: | Haman! |
| HAMAN: | Yes, sir? |
| AHASUERUS: | You brought me a special request this afternoon? |
| HAMAN: | Nothing special, sir. Part of the routine administration. |
| AHASUERUS: | Asking me to hang the leader of the Jews in Susa? |
| HAMAN: | Yes, that's right, sir. |
| AHASUERUS: | This one, this Mordecai? |
| HAMAN: | No, sir. I didn't mention anyone in particular. It was a matter of teaching the Jews a lesson, removing the danger to your life, that was the only purpose. |

156

| | |
|---|---|
| AHASUERUS: | The leader of the Jews in Susa: those were your very words. |
| HAMAN: | That was the only way to smother a rebellion. The proclamation had created a state of crisis, sir. We had to prevent any tumult. |
| AHASUERUS: | You knew that this was the Mordecai who had saved my life? |
| HAMAN: | That didn't cross my mind at the time. |
| AHASUERUS: | And his deed didn't appear in your report either? |
| HAMAN: | I didn't think... |
| AHASUERUS: | I don't intend judging hastily. That is not my habit. You have been a zealous minister of the Crown...Perhaps there is some mistake. I must study your report on the Jews again. I must take time to consider matters...Harbona, where is this Jew? |
| HARBONA: | Mordecai, sir. |
| AHASUERUS: | Mordecai. |
| HARBONA: | In the palace porch, sir. |
| AHASUERUS: | Bring him here to me this minute. |
| HARBONA: | But, sir... |
| AHASUERUS: | Well? |
| HARBONA: | The fact is, sir, his head is dirty, he has a sack around his waist; he isn't fit to... |
| AHASUERUS: | Life in Susa is lovely, Harbona—whilst the King's servants remain obedient. |
| HARBONA: | Forgive me, my lord, he'll be here immediately. *(Exit Harbona. The King sits on the throne in a most regal manner.)* |
| AHASUERUS: | You know this Jew, Esther? |
| ESTHER: | It was he, as you know, who found out about the plot. It was he who rushed to me to ask me to warn you immediately. *(Harbona brings Mordecai in. They bow to the throne.)* |
| HARBONA: | My lord King, here is the man. |
| AHASUERUS: | Mordecai? |
| MORDECAI: | That is my name, sir. A Jew. |
| AHASUERUS: | What is that sack around you? |
| MORDECAI: | A shroud. My nation is preparing for its grave. |
| AHASUERUS: | And the dirt on your forehead? |
| MORDECAI: | Ashes to ashes, earth to earth, darkness on the Star of Judah. |

| | |
|---|---|
| AHASUERUS: | It was you who saved my life. |
| MORDECAI: | No, my lord King. Not I. It was the God of Israel who did it for the sake of his people. |
| AHASUERUS: | His people have been condemned to death. |
| MORDECAI: | We are prepared to die. Ready for the concentration camps up to the end of time. Israel is the altar of the world. |
| AHASUERUS: | My lord Haman, greatest of my princes, this is the man whom the King wishes to honour...Take the royal robe on your arm...Take the crown in your hand...Take now the right hand of my servant, Mordecai...Take him into the ante-room. Anoint his head with oil. Clothe him with the royal robe. Put the crown on his head. Then put him on the King's steed and lead him yourself through the streets of the city. Arrange a procession of soldiers to announce your coming, proclaiming: This is what is done for the man whom the King wishes to honour... *(Mordecai and Haman bow and turn to leave. They stand by the entrance of the ante-room and look at each other.)* |
| HAMAN: | Samuel! |

## END OF ACT II

## ACT III

*(A pavilion opening out onto a lawn and gardens. A table and couches on the left. It is moonlight. There is harp music. Women dance in silence. A contralto voice sings:)*

> Aromas of musk,
> Fragrance of roses,
> Harps playing,
> Moon-lit lawns sleeping,
> Goddesses dancing—
> Their ankles bangled—
> On a carpet of roses
> Lily-white bosoms glowing
> In the gardens of musk.
>
> Full moon,
> And moon-lit singing,

Roses kiss
The feet that tinkle on the gossamer lawns,
Arms like vipers—
Silver-adorned wrists—
Weave on the still
And sweet moraine
Of the tranquil night of Susa 'neath the full
    moon.

| | |
|---|---|
| AHASUERUS: | The singing has stopped. |
| ESTHER: | Stopped, yes. But a word from the King can call it all back. |
| AHASUERUS: | No, don't let's call it back; just throw it a kiss as it goes. |
| HAMAN: | I could throw those dancing women a kiss. |
| ESTHER: | Harp music and singing voices are lovely, but the silence afterwards is wonderful too. The reverberations of the music cling to us now like fragrances. |
| AHASUERUS: | The dancing has ceased as well. |
| ESTHER: | The moon is still with us. |
| HAMAN: | And the wine. |
| AHASUERUS: | Esther, if only tonight could last... |
| HAMAN: | The dinner, the wine, the singing and the dancing... |
| AHASUERUS: | And you, beautiful lady, by my side here in the garden. |
| HAMAN: | Then the King would indeed have become one of the gods. |
| AHASUERUS: | Those dancing girls were indeed goddesses. How does one explain the enchantment of dance? |
| HAMAN: | It's an intoxication, the joy of forgetfulness, an escape from bitterness and anxiety into a world of sensual dreaming. |
| AHASUERUS: | I haven't seen you dance, Haman. |
| HAMAN: | I'm a politician, a minister. |
| AHASUERUS: | I knew that from your answer. It wasn't that of a dancer. |
| HAMAN: | What is dancing for you, sir? |
| AHASUERUS: | A moving pattern, orchestrating the waves of the sea into an order and ceremony for the intelligence; complexity becoming harmony; a realm in its diversity and unity. |
| HAMAN: | An emperor's answer, sir. Each to his own. *(All laugh.)* |

| | |
|---|---|
| AHASUERUS: | And you, Esther, I know you dance. What does dancing mean for you? |
| ESTHER: | Worship. A King dancing naked before the Lord. A husband and wife worshipping each other through their bodies. That's what dancing is: a eucharist. |
| AHASUERUS: | And tonight, what sort of worship was that dance tonight? |
| ESTHER: | My worship of you, that's what they danced in the moonlight. Did they please you? |
| AHASUERUS: | I've already told you so. |
| ESTHER: | Tell me again; tell me once more. |
| AHASUERUS: | Tonight is a paradise, my dear wife; tonight is a paradise. I've said it twice now. |
| ESTHER: | Will you come to me tonight? |
| AHASUERUS: | I'll stay here with you tonight. |
| ESTHER: | Truly? |
| AHASUERUS: | Truly, truly! |
| ESTHER: | I'm in the Garden of Eden and can't believe it. |
| AHASUERUS: | We can lie and watch the dawn rising between the roses. |
| ESTHER: | The last time. The last night. I'll have my King in my arms. |
| AHASUERUS: | And not for the last time either! |
| ESTHER: | Afterwards, farewell. |
| AHASUERUS: | Farewell? |
| ESTHER: | Yes, my darling, farewell. |
| AHASUERUS: | What are you saying, Esther? |
| ESTHER: | I couldn't go without farewelling. I ventured everything to possess tonight. |
| AHASUERUS: | This night is the beginning of our life. It was tonight you came into your realm. |
| ESTHER: | I shall be queen of your heart tonight. |
| AHASUERUS: | You're there already; tonight and till the hour of my death. |
| ESTHER: | But after tonight, it's farewell. |
| AHASUERUS: | But why farewell? What do you mean? |
| ESTHER: | It's not of my choosing, my King; not my choice. |
| AHASUERUS: | Whose then? |
| ESTHER: | You know, you and Haman. |
| AHASUERUS: | Know what? |
| ESTHER: | Today I was condemned to be hanged. |
| AHASUERUS: | *(Laughing.)* Hanged! Esther! Impossible! By whom? |

| | |
|---|---|
| ESTHER: | In your name. By Haman, the minister... |
| AHASUERUS: | What? |
| HAMAN: | *(Shouting.)* Me? |
| ESTHER: | You and your proclamation. |
| HAMAN: | No! No! |
| ESTHER: | I am a Jewess. |
| HAMAN: | Jewess! |
| AHASUERUS: | Esther! |
| ESTHER: | The people of Israel. The tribe of Benjamin. A royal family. |
| HAMAN: | *(Twisting as if out of his mind.)* No, no! Fate can't play tricks like that...No! No! |
| AHASUERUS: | You've stunned me, Esther. |
| ESTHER: | What does it matter? I have tonight as mine. Tomorrow, farewell. |
| AHASUERUS: | You shan't say farewell; you are mine. Tonight and tomorrow and afterwards. |
| ESTHER: | Haman and the proclamation. |
| AHASUERUS: | They can't touch you. |
| ESTHER: | Yes they can, my lord, they can reach me. |
| AHASUERUS: | In the King's palace? |
| ESTHER: | In the King's arms. |
| AHASUERUS: | You are my Queen. You have no nation but myself. |
| ESTHER: | Today is the day of tribulation of my nation. Therefore I must be an Israelite. |
| AHASUERUS: | Why? |
| ESTHER: | Because I'm related to every Jew throughout the realm. I'm responsible for them. |
| AHASUERUS: | Who taught you that? |
| ESTHER: | Cain. |
| AHASUERUS: | Cain? |
| ESTHER: | My lord, listen to your handmaiden. If a Jew be hanged for thieving, for rioting, if he is hanged for shedding blood or breaking the law, for treachery, if he is hanged for treason against the King, I won't say a word in his defence, not a word to prevent his punishment. But this proclamation means Jews are to be hanged for one fault only, that of being a Jew. And I, your Queen, am a Jew. I shall die with my people. |
| HAMAN: | My lady, the King's proclamation can't touch the King's own family. The King and all his family and relations are above the law. |

ESTHER: Haman, Haman the Agagite, the day the sentence in the proclamation is carried out, if only on one Jew in Susa, that day my body, the body of the Queen, will be found hanging from the rafters of the King's palace. And you will be responsible.

AHASUERUS: Who are your family, Esther?

ESTHER: My father and mother were with the ten thousand slaves taken from Jerusalem to the camps in Babylon. They both died on the way. I was an orphan.

AHASUERUS: You ran away?

ESTHER: No. I was rescued by a cousin, a son of my father's eldest brother, and he brought me up as if I were his daughter. It was he who brought me to Susa after the destruction of Babylon. He taught me courtly and regal manners. It was he who taught me history and literature and fear of the Lord. It was he sent me to you to be your wife.

AHASUERUS: Who is your cousin? He reared a queen. He nurtured majesty. The King is in his debt.

ESTHER: Yes, my darling, the King is in his debt. It was he saved the King's life from the traitor's blade.

AHASUERUS: What? Saved my life?

ESTHER: It was he who was honoured today in the streets of the city.

HAMAN: Mordecai! Mordecai! A cousin of the King's!

ESTHER: Yes, Mordecai. It was he Haman chose to hang first of the Jews, the King's cousin; the man who saved his life.

AHASUERUS: What have you to say, Haman?

HAMAN: This is an earthquake, the earth is opening up under our feet.

AHASUERUS: My faith in you is quaking too.

HAMAN: Sir, I have been a long time in your service. You know of my loyalty. A minister's mind is guided by the policies and needs of the realm, not by anything personal. It's difficult for the Queen to understand this. Shouldn't we discuss these matters in Council without the Queen?

AHASUERUS: I must get to the bottom of this matter tonight, here and now.

HAMAN: The matter of the Jew?

AHASUERUS: The matter of Mordecai.

| | |
|---|---|
| HAMAN: | How can we do that with the Queen here? It isn't fair. I can't speak plainly. |
| AHASUERUS: | You may say anything. You've won my confidence in the army. I'd be very sorry to think that confidence was foolishly misplaced. |
| HAMAN: | The proclamation was the result of long consideration; the result of an official report on the Jews, sir. |
| AHASUERUS: | I remember the report. |
| HAMAN: | It showed that their religion made the Jews a people apart. They can never be assimilated into the unity of the Empire. Their whole desire is to win their freedom, re-possess Canaan, re-build Jerusalem. That means war and tearing asunder the united kingdom. It's a threat to the throne, a threat to the King's life. That was the reason for the proclamation, to ensure peace, to prevent rebellion and revolution. The Law of Union. |
| ESTHER: | And nothing personal came into it? |
| HAMAN: | I never dreamt the Queen was a Jewess. I didn't know Mordecai the Jew was related to her. Nor did you, sir. There was never a Jewess before in the royal palace of Persia. But there, government policy can't be dictated by a personal accident. |
| AHASUERUS: | Haman, you came here to complain about the whole Jewish nation, and to demonstrate their evil nature, and ask permission to get rid of the danger. I asked for a full report and charged you—do you remember?—to include the good and the bad; everything good that was known in favour of any of the Jews throughout the realm. And you knew better than anyone else that it was Mordecai the Jew who had revealed the treacherous plot of Bigthana and Teresh. There was no mention of that in your report. |
| HAMAN: | It wasn't concern for your throne prompted this action in revealing the treachery; that became clear. |
| ESTHER: | Isn't being related to the King reason enough for being concerned? |
| HAMAN: | If the Jew respected the King, he'd obey him. All the servants at the palace porch complain about his disobedience. |

163

| | |
|---|---|
| AHASUERUS: | What disobedience? |
| HAMAN: | It is the King's command that everyone should bow to the Chief Minister; a gesture of respect for the King's law and order. Mordecai the Jew spits on the King's command. |
| AHASUERUS: | By refusing to bow to you? |
| HAMAN: | It's easy to understand that now. He's a cousin of the King's, this Jewish slave. He's become drunk on the greatness of his fortune. He's grown to despise bending himself. |
| AHASUERUS: | And you came to me specially, today, to ask permission to hang him before nightfall. |
| HAMAN: | And I gave my reasons, to safeguard the King's life following the proclamation. |
| AHASUERUS: | By hanging the man who saved the King's life? |
| ESTHER: | By hanging the only one, apart from Haman, who knows the secret of Bigthana and Teresh. |
| AHASUERUS: | Bigthana and Teresh. |
| ESTHER: | The two traitors hanged without calling any witnesses, without interrogating them, without torturing them to find out their motives, without any official record of the trial. |
| HAMAN: | It was a time of festival and feasting. Time was short. There was no need for any witnesses. The two had confessed and were hanged. |
| ESTHER: | They very nearly succeeded. Another quarter of an hour, and there'd have been a new King of Persia, and Mordecai already hanged. |
| AHASUERUS: | Esther, you're suggesting new things, nasty things. |
| ESTHER: | Thirty nights; thirty days without you, my lord. |
| AHASUERUS: | Up to last night, I'd forgotten the trial during our long wedding feast. |
| ESTHER: | Think what would have happened had the plot succeeded... |
| AHASUERUS: | If it had succeeded? |
| ESTHER: | Think who would have become Chief Minister of Persia? |
| AHASUERUS: | *(Laughing.)* I haven't the faintest idea. |
| ESTHER: | The answer is simple, isn't it, Haman? |
| HAMAN: | *(Icily.)* I haven't the faintest idea, whatsoever. |
| ESTHER: | Really? Didn't you hear anything during that trial. It was all arranged. |
| HAMAN: | Nothing was said about the Chief Minister. |

| | |
|---|---|
| ESTHER: | Who would have been Chief Minister?After the murder of the King? Bigthana and Teresh, of course. That was to have been their reward...do you see?... The king has no son. |
| AHASUERUS: | *(Beginning to understand.)* And who, who perhaps would have been...instead of the son? |
| ESTHER: | His mind is guided by the policies and needs of the realm, not by anything personal. |
| HAMAN: | Evil lies! Lies! Queen or not, you're lying through your teeth. A serpent of a wife! |
| AHASUERUS: | We shall see. *(He calls.)* Harbona. *(He comes to them.)*...Send for Mordecai the Jew. Bring him here to me at once. Hurry! *(Exit Harbona.)* |
| HAMAN: | I'm warning you, sir, this is a trick by the Jews to destroy me. A trick to delete the proclamation. They've planned this, Mordecai and his family, to win the day for the Jews and bring down the Empire, to start a rebellion in the palace. There is malice and mortal danger behind this...For the Jews to win the authority. *(Harbona and Mordecai enter and bow; Mordecai being properly dressed by now.)* |
| HARBONA: | Mordecai the Jew, sir? |
| AHASUERUS: | Mordecai, the crown of the King of Persia was on your head today. |
| MORDECAI: | Yes, my lord King. |
| AHASUERUS: | You wore the royal robe. |
| MORDECAI: | Yes, in the streets of the imperial capital, and I a Jew. |
| AHASUERUS: | The man the King insists on honouring. |
| MORDECAI: | He has had his hour of elevation before the hour of his hanging. I thank you humbly. |
| AHASUERUS: | You know why this happened? |
| MORDECAI: | The King's gracious acknowledgment of the services of his citizens. |
| AHASUERUS: | You remember Bigthana and Teresh? |
| MORDECAI: | Yes, I do, well. |
| AHASUERUS: | You discovered all the details of the plot? |
| MORDECAI: | That was my duty. |
| AHASUERUS: | And yet you were not called as a witness at their trial? |
| MORDECAI: | It was a time of feasting and time was short. |
| AHASUERUS: | I heard that already, more than once. I want to know: who, besides Bigthana and Teresh, were involved in the plot to kill the King? |

| | |
|---|---|
| MORDECAI: | Sir, the life of the King of Persia, Emperor of the World, is sacred to the Jew. |
| AHASUERUS: | I heard differently, very differently. Why do you say this? |
| MORDECAI: | Because the word of the Lord, through his prophet promises Israel that it is through the patronage of the Persian monarchy that Jerusalem will be re-built. |
| AHASUERUS: | Alright, so the Jews are the defenders of the throne? |
| MORDECAI: | Not the Jews, but the God of the Jews—the Creator and Lord of kings. |
| AHASUERUS: | And so I can rely on you for help. Who was behind Bigthana and Teresh in the plot to kill the King? |
| MORDECAI: | Sir, Bigthana and Teresh were hanged. |
| AHASUERUS: | The rest will be hanged, everyone in the plot, on your word. |
| MORDECAI: | I and the whole people of Israel have been condemned to be hanged. |
| AHASUERUS: | That can be changed, and the Jews saved if I get from you the names of all the traitors. |
| MORDECAI: | Is this a promise, sir? |
| AHASUERUS: | The word of the King of the Medes and Persians. |
| MORDECAI: | Sir, even to save Israel I won't bargain with men's lives. |
| AHASUERUS: | Mordecai, the King has to defend his own life for the security of the realm. |
| MORDECAI: | The treachery was exposed. The King's life is not in danger now. Nobody alive today envies him, nobody alive is plotting to steal his throne. Bigthana and Teresh have been hanged. The danger to the King is ended. |
| AHASUERUS: | If there are men alive who once tried to murder him, then the danger is not ended. |
| MORDECAI: | I give the King my word: the plot ended with the deaths of Bigthana and Teresh. |
| AHASUERUS: | I honoured you today. |
| MORDECAI: | And I honour you now. |
| AHASUERUS: | There are ways of getting the information out of you. Torture can open men's lips. |
| MORDECAI: | I have heard that, sir. But I was called to save life, not to destroy it. |

| | |
|---|---|
| AHASUERUS: | For the last time, which of the King's servants was involved in the plot with Bigthana and Teresh? |
| MORDECAI: | My lord King, I never said there was anyone. |
| AHASUERUS: | You lie. You said it to the Queen. |
| MORDECAI: | No, not a word about anyone except Bigthana and Teresh. |
| AHASUERUS: | Harbona, arrest this Jew and take him into the ante-room. Send for the torturers and the instruments. Bind him hand and foot. Then wait for my instructions about him...*(Exeunt Harbona and Mordecai.)* Your cousin is stubborn, my lady. |
| ESTHER: | Stubborness can be a form of loyalty. |
| AHASUERUS: | Esther, you have accused the Chief Minister of the realm, the King's personal friend, of intending to murder the King and usurping the throne himself. The only witness is Mordecai the Jew. I must know the truth. |
| ESTHER: | Through torture? |
| AHASUERUS: | Torture is the usual method. |
| ESTHER: | There is another person living who could help you under torture. |
| AHASUERUS: | Another one? |
| ESTHER: | One who's sure to help you: he'd break down under torture. There he is! |
| HAMAN: | My lord, I've given my life to your service, in the army, on the field of battle, in the court and in Council. There has never before been a woman meddling in politics in the palace of Persia. Was it not to teach women manners that Vashti was thrown to the dogs? |
| AHASUERUS: | For disobeying the King, that's why Vashti was destroyed, for scorning the King. I must know today who is disobeying; who has scorn in his heart for the King today. |
| HAMAN: | Are you insinuating that it is me? You suspect me on the suggestion of a girl who's fighting like a cat for her little kittens, the Jews! |
| AHASUERUS: | Not a suggestion but an accusation. And a fair bit of evidence to back it. |
| HAMAN: | That is the opinion of my King! My career is in danger therefore? I, who guarded your throne like the apple of my eye, in battles, in camp and in court. Is that my reward? Are the hate and malice of the Jews to triumph tonight? |

167

| | |
|---|---|
| ESTHER: | The malice of the Jew! The Jew is in the ante-room bound hand and foot, waiting to be tortured, because he saved your life. |
| HAMAN: | You hate me. |
| ESTHER: | Yes, I hate you. I'll say more: it is because the Jew closed your path to the throne that this proclamation was made this morning to destroy us. |
| HAMAN: | Sir, I'm not going to stay here and suffer the bile of a crazy woman. There's the venom of an asp on her lips. If she were a man she'd have forfeited her life already. |
| AHASUERUS: | You will stay, Haman; you'll await my will. I haven't had an answer that satisfies any of the accusations against you. |
| HAMAN: | What answers can there be to baseless accusations? |
| AHASUERUS: | Baseless? Why were Bigthana and Teresh not interrogated before being hanged? Why wasn't Mordecai not called to give evidence? Why is there no record of the trial? All your answers are empty ones. You are not being accused of spilling innocent blood, Haman, but of treason; treason, Haman. |
| HAMAN: | Isn't fifteen years of ceaseless toil on behalf of the throne of Persia not enough of an answer? If not, I'm prepared to resign and return to my country. |
| AHASUERUS: | Resign! If falsity and treachery are proved against you, resigning won't save you. |
| HAMAN: | I've never heard my King snapping at me so unworthily. |
| AHASUERUS: | Haman, I'm a gentle person, eager to believe people, ready to trust them. An emperor is a lonely man. He has only servants around him. To befriend a servant is a dangerous venture. I elevated you to being a friend, put the imperial signet ring on your finger. And tonight, doubts shake the foundation of my trust. |
| HAMAN: | Unworthy doubts, sir. A woman meddling in politics, and a King forgetting his manhood to listen to her. |
| AHASUERUS: | Harbona, *(Calling out loud. Harbona enters.)* |
| HARBONA: | Sir? |

| | |
|---|---|
| AHASUERUS: | Keep a watchful eye on the ante-room and the gardens. Nobody is to leave the house without my permission. |
| HARBONA: | Yes, sir. *(Exit.)* |
| AHASUERUS: | Esther, I'll go to the gardens to stroll and ponder matters...*(He goes out slowly, standing a moment at the entrance before disappearing.)*...Esther! Come here. |
| ESTHER: | *(Going to him.)* My lord? |
| AHASUERUS: | You didn't utter a word of protest when I had Mordecai bound? |
| ESTHER: | I knew it was me who was on trial. *(Exit the King. Esther stands staring after him.)* |
| HAMAN: | *(Coming to her.)* The moon light, full of magic and enchantment, the garden where there was feasting and dancing, and we humans rowing and spitting like cats. That's not the way it should be on a night like this in Susa. |
| ESTHER: | It'll be a night like this on the thirteenth day of the month of Adar and the bodies of a hundred thousand Jews swinging on ropes, their children thrown into ditches and food for the wolves and dogs. |
| HAMAN: | A mistake! I confess it, my lady; a mistake. |
| ESTHER: | Not a mistake, but an evil soul. |
| HAMAN: | It's possible to rectify the mistake. With your help, my lady, I'm prepared to do that. |
| ESTHER: | It's possible to rectify it without your help. |
| HAMAN: | It's no easy matter to rescind a royal proclamation. After all, it was the King's proclamation, the law of the Medes and Persians. The honour of the King is at stake. My help may be valuable to you. |
| ESTHER: | Your repentance comes too late. |
| HAMAN: | You hate me. Fine! There is room for hate in politics, but it's a foolish thing to let hate colour your judgement. |
| ESTHER: | In politics it is only might that counts; showing mercy is the start of one's downfall. |
| HAMAN: | But we can come to some understanding? |
| ESTHER: | You are an enemy of mine. |
| HAMAN: | That's a mistake as well. |
| ESTHER: | Either you or I must hang. |
| HAMAN: | The choice is inconvenient. It isn't customary to hang the Queens of Persia. The King has a prejudice against it. |

| | |
|---|---|
| ESTHER: | You or I. He'll have to choose. |
| HAMAN: | Hang? Hanging is something that happens to other people. Nobody in his right mind can contemplate his own hanging. Imagination is fatal for a politician. |
| ESTHER: | You or I. It would be wise for you to get accustomed to the idea. You and your ten sons to the gallows or I and my whole nation. *(She sits on the couch.)* |
| HAMAN: | *(Beginning to be afraid.)* No, there's another choice; another way, a better way. I offer you peace, my lady, peace to the Jews, and co-operation between you and me. |
| ESTHER: | The Jews are appealing to the King; to the King only. |
| HAMAN: | Lady, you are young; but a young girl of a wife, and today you have got involved in politics; something never done previously by a Queen of Persia. Your situation is dangerous, like a rudderless ship at sea. You could lose the King's confidence at a stroke, lose his favour, lose sight of his face. And then you'd disappear like Vashti, and the Jews would be defenceless. |
| ESTHER: | It wasn't my choice to get involved in politics. It was you who forced me to. The difference between us two tonight is that I'm not afraid. *(Haman holds himself under tight rein.)* |
| HAMAN: | I'm offering you a bargain, offering co-operation. I have a lifetime's experience to put at your service. And you have talent, genius, bravery to a degree rare in women. Together you and I could guide the King's policies; I could help you re-build Jerusalem; and at the same time secure that the King's affections were for you alone. |
| ESTHER: | Do you think it's by trickery and intrigue that I'll keep the King's affections? |
| HAMAN: | How else? He's a King. |
| ESTHER: | *(Laughing long.)* The funniest of God's creations is a middle-aged politician! |
| HAMAN: | Lady, time is short. The King can return any moment. You have his ear tonight; he's listening to you; a word from you, and he does your will. I can save the Jews for you without bringing disgrace on the King or breaking with |

|  |  |
|---|---|
| | the traditions of Persia; you must say a word now to reconcile the King to me. There's no one else can help you in these dangerous next few months, nobody who can keep you from causing offence. Then you can provide the King with a son; and I'll keep the realm secure for him. I'll be the Chief Minister for you and your son. I'll put a Jew on the throne of Persia, as Emperor of the World. |
| ESTHER: | The King has another Chief Minister to call on. |
| HAMAN: | Don't believe that, lady, that's impossible. It is I who have the experience. I handle everything. You can depend on me. |
| ESTHER: | He's standing outside now. |
| HAMAN: | Chief Minister? Harbona? |
| ESTHER: | Mordecai, the King's cousin. I depend on him, on him as Chief Minister. |
| HAMAN: | *(Beginning to break down.)* Mordecai! No, no, lady, not Mordecai. Mordecai the Jew. Not Samuel! Mordecai as Chief Minister. You can't do that. You can't spit on me like that. |
| ESTHER: | The man who kept your secret, the man who saved the King's life when you had plotted to murder him... |
| HAMAN: | A moment of weakness. Bigthana and Teresh persuaded me. |
| ESTHER: | Haman the Agagite, you are an evil one. But your career is at an end tonight. You dared raise your fist against the Almighty, against the God of Israel. You planned to exterminate the chosen nation, the nation which is part of Creation. Every time that happens, God prepares a saviour. And that is my privilege tonight. I will stand with Miriam and Judith amongst the women of the Hebrews. From the small fountain a mighty river has flowed and you will be drowned, you and your sons, in the flood. Woe to you, Haman, woe to your birth. |
| HAMAN: | Lady, Esther, Queen, you're beautiful, Esther, lovely and young and awesome. I could worship you. I could serve you. I could love you, Esther...Be merciful, be gentle, be kind. Look, you're a young woman, and my life is in your hands... |
| ESTHER: | Keep your hands off me you rascal! |

171

| | |
|---|---|
| HAMAN: | You're beautiful, Esther, beautiful like an army at arms. You are my queen. My life is under your feet. Spare me, save me from the King's wrath. Save me from hanging, Esther. Do you see, I can't be hanged, I can't...*(Esther laughs aloud.)* Don't laugh, Esther, don't. You're not a woman but a tigress! |
| ESTHER: | Jewess! |
| HAMAN: | Mercy, Esther, mercy! Don't hang me, don't...*(Ahasuerus has come in and seen this.)* |
| AHASUERUS: | Haman!...Are you trying to rape the Queen? *(Harbona and two soldiers rush in and take hold of Haman.)* Bind him!...Give me the ring off his finger...Cover his face...*(That is done.)* |
| HARBONA: | What shall we do with this scum, sir? |
| AHASUERUS: | What should be done with a knave who defiled the Queen with his hands? |
| HARBONA: | In his malice, this very morning he erected a gallows in front of his window in order to hang Mordecai the Jew. |
| AHASUERUS: | Take him, and hang him on it. Send Mordecai the Jew to me. *(Exeunt Haman, Harbona and the soldiers.)*...Esther, how did you find out that Haman was behind Bigthana and Teresh? |
| ESTHER: | Nothing was easier. Mordecai refused this morning to give that as an excuse for not bowing to Haman. Then I knew. *(Mordecai comes in.)* |
| MORDECAI: | My lord King. |
| AHASUERUS: | My cousin, will you accept the office of Chief Minister of the Persian Empire? |
| MORDECAI: | If it please you, sir, I shall—on two conditions. |
| AHASUERUS: | State them. |
| MORDECAI: | That a royal letter be sent tomorrow to all the provinces of the empire rescinding Haman's proclamation and declaring peace to the Jews. |
| AHASUERUS: | We'll compose it together. |
| MORDECAI: | If I forget thee, Jerusalem...May I have a part in re-building Jerusalem? |
| AHASUERUS: | Always Jerusalem? |
| MORDECAI: | Jerusalem is the centre-point for mankind. |
| AHASUERUS: | Give me your hand...There's the imperial ring on your finger. You may re-build the walls of Jerusalem as a thank-offering for Esther. |

THE END

# Have A Cigarette?—Excerpt From The Third Act (1956)

*Have a Cigarette?* is a play set in a mid-European country in the 1950s, and was based on actual incidents in the Cold War. It deals with a young couple, Mark and Iris, who met as partisans during the war against Hitler, and subsequently married. Mark is a member of the Communist party; Iris a clandestine Catholic. She realises she is pregnant, and is dying to tell him the news. But when he returns home she has, first, to listen to his news about his promotion to the rank of commisar in order to go to Vienna to carry out a mission. The mission is to execute the traitor, Phugas, the leader of the emigre community in Vienna, who is sending Christian literature and young priests back to his homeland by plane and parachute. There is an impending crisis as all priests are due to take an oath of allegiance to the state.

Phugas turns out to be not only a close friend to Iris's father, one who had even visited him in his condemned cell, but also Iris's God-father. This means to Iris (though not to Mark) that the two are related. She vows to Mark that if he kills Phugas he will never see her or their unborn child again. But she urges him to go to Vienna, see Phugas, and then seek political asylum. She can then, she says rather unrealistically, seek asylum in the United States Embassy and be smuggled out of the country.

He goes to Vienna in turmoil, hardly able to accept the seriousness of her threat. He is armed with an electronic, cigarette-case pistol. He gains access to Phugas by means of a letter from Iris, which describes him as 'an unbaptised thing but I own him.' But when he tries to shoot Phugas, Iris's rosary falls out of the cigarette case, and foils his intention.

Mark is persuaded by Phugas's sister Callista, to seek political asylum from Captain Christopher, the US officer in charge of Phugas, who contacts the US Embassy in the homeland to seek help for Iris. While they are waiting for a phone call from the embassy, Phugas tells them how the men who had been waiting to take Mark back to the Russian sector

173

had, instead, kidnapped Phugas's young pilot, a man who lived with his girlfriend and their imbecile child, who was the result of her rape by a soldier as Vienna was liberated. The pilot's girlfriend is distraught at the loss of her lover, and Phugas can do nothing for her:

MARK: There's nothing you can do for her?

PHUGAS: Nothing; just leave her alone with her suffering and her half-wit child.

MARK: Phugas, how on earth can you believe in God?

PHUGAS: I know, I know. Nobody has an explanation which even begins to make sense of the pain in the world.

MARK: I've heard some of your priests boast that the Church has an answer to everything.

PHUGAS: God forgive them their blasphemy.

MARK: For the communist, pain is part of the historical process. It'll disappear with the class war.

PHUGAS: Could you say that to a girl whose lover has just been kidnapped and strung up by a band of murderers?

CALLISTA: Mark isn't arguing the toss; he's just asking for help.

PHUGAS: I've no hope to offer him. Nothing to offer anyone. I've made a mess of the lives of everybody who depends on me. I send fine young men, who happen to be priests, to slave in the salt mines of Siberia. I am the best *agent provocateur* the government has got in Vienna. Think of the poor lad: he's been a pilot with me for months, in many a dangerous situation. One time we had to land within miles of the capital two hours before daybreak. You'd have thought from the way he behaved we were within the American Sector of Austria! Without even a mention of the dangers involved, he told me the whole story of his beloved while repairing the carburetor at the same time. She refused to marry him because she had this mongol baby, and she didn't want to burden him. Today, he was snatched away from her, in broad daylight, and I can do nothing at all on his behalf or on hers...Part of the historical process!

| | |
|---|---|
| CALLISTA: | What'll you do tonight? |
| MARK: | I'll have to pilot myself. |
| CALLISTA: | You haven't done so for a year. |
| PHUGAS: | I've held a pilot's licence for twenty-five years. |
| CALLISTA: | You've a right not to value your own life. You have no right to endanger the life of a young priest on his first mission. You know you could die in the pilot's seat. |
| PHUGAS: | I know that it is necessary to go over there tonight. |
| CALLISTA: | You could postpone it. |
| PHUGAS: | The regime won't postpone the oath of allegiance. Therefore I can't postpone. It's the regime that arranges my timetable. Enemies are as faithful as lovers. |
| | *(Enter Capt. Christopher.)* |
| MARK: | *(Abruptly)* Do you believe there is a God? |
| CHRISTOPHER: | An improper, un-American question! |
| MARK: | Un-American? What does that mean? In my country to call something un-American is a term of praise. |
| CHRISTOPHER: | Forgive me. Your question came so unexpectedly that I forgot with whom I was talking. For us—if I may say so—the meaning of un-American is something contrary to the standards of behaviour considered appropriate for an officer in the service of the United States. |
| MARK: | What's improper in my question? |
| CHRISTOPHER: | It's difficult to explain to a foreigner. I admit that you do get Americans who ask such questions, even more personal—ruder—ones. But in the American society I'm used to, belief in God is a private matter, not something to throw at someone in a salon. |
| MARK: | That is, asking about God is rather like asking about the toilet? |
| CHRISTOPHER: | *(Seriously)* For us each is as private as the other. |
| MARK: | Is one as important as the other? |
| CHRISTOPHER: | Private matters are the most important ones for us Americans. |
| MARK: | As I understand it, your specialty is the problems of the countries of south-eastern Europe. |
| CHRISTOPHER: | Correct. |

| | |
|---|---|
| MARK: | There are only some six hours since I was expelled from my country and from the party. Believe me, in my country and in all these countries the question of whether there is a God is not a private one. It is an intensely private one, of course. But it is also the most important political and public question in all Europe. The future of the Proletarian Revolution depends on the answer. You haven't begun to learn the A-B-C of Europe if you're not aware of that fact. Every communist in Europe and in Russia is agreed on that. |
| CHRISTOPHER: | I'm glad to hear your testimony on that point. It confirms much of what Phugas has told me from time to time. But why do you ask this question of me now? |
| MARK: | Because I don't have an answer. Because I'm neither a communist nor a Christian. Because my uncertainty, my doubts have destroyed my life today. I came here an atheist, to carry out the instructions of my government, and a rosary and a crucifix fell across my pistol. Because of that the life of my wife—and the child in her womb—are in danger. And I am here waiting for the phone to ring—like a man expecting a revelation...If only I could hear her voice... |
| CHRISTOPHER: | That's what I came to tell you about. |
| MARK: | You've got news? |
| CHRISTOPHER: | We've investigated and followed up all the answers you gave us during those two hours of interrogation. They've all been found to be correct and useful. We'll be glad to have the opportunity of further questioning. But my message now is to tell you that the authorities will shortly grant you political asylum, and that you are as of now a free man within the American Sector. |
| MARK: | Thank you. Callista has offered me a bed for the night. |
| CHRISTOPHER: | That's a good idea. It would be unwise for you to venture forth too soon. |
| MARK: | Have you any further news? |
| CHRISTOPHER: | We've been talking to officials in our embassy. They've promised to move quickly, and report |

|           |                                                                 |
|-----------|-----------------------------------------------------------------|
|           | back immediately. The message will come through to you here, Phugas, over the phone. It should come any minute... |
| PHUGAS:   | Are you a gambler, Mark?                                         |
| MARK:     | In the casino, at the tables?                                   |
| PHUGAS:   | Or on the horses, or aeroplane races?                          |
| MARK:     | In the airforce at the beginning of the war we all bet heavily. In the casino, when we could get there. Then, on each *sortie* we'd bet on the number of us who'd get back. It was an arrogant thing to do, betting on our own lives. After that, in the partisans, nobody had any money to bet with. |
| PHUGAS:   | In the partisans, life itself was a gamble.                     |
| MARK:     | That's true. To see the end of any day, or any night, was a matter of chance. |
| PHUGAS:   | Why then do you ask for certainty from life now?                |
| MARK:     | Certainty?                                                       |
| PHUGAS:   | Certainty that there is a God; that he exists.                  |
| MARK:     | My present situation is the result of Iris's choice; not mine. And if God does not exist, then that choice was a cruel one, a crazy one. Communists call it bourgeois morality. By now, I'm not simply an exile but a piece of flotsam, without country or party or family or a relative of any kind in this world. I've nothing to give meaning to my life except Iris, who threw me on to this shore, and the off-chance that she may be safe. I have a rational right to know whether or not the choice she made was a crazy one, her faith a form of madness; was it madness led to me being thrown here into Vienna. I have to know... |
| PHUGAS:   | It's impossible to know. Nobody knows that there is a God.     |
| MARK:     | So you have no answer to madness?                               |
| PHUGAS:   | Some of us believe there is a God.                              |
| MARK:     | I know: Paul Claudel, the unbeliever, goes into Notre Dame in Paris. He stands by the third column and stares at a statue. And at that instant he comes to believe; believes as if he knew, and doubt is impossible for him for the rest of his life...That's no help to me. It isn't a |

normal experience. You can find scores of people in asylums who believe like that; who believe like those who know they're walking on their heads, and that the nurse is an owl.

PHUGAS: You're right. Belief is a gift. Not everyone receives it.

MARK: And what if I didn't receive that particular gift? If I can't believe? What if belief is a word which has no meaning for me?

PHUGAS: There's nothing left but to gamble.

MARK: How do you gamble on God?

PHUGAS: You've been thrown here, into life's casino, in Vienna. Escape is impossible; the doors have been closed; and you're not allowed to stay without gambling—that's the rule of the house. So, why not wager that there is a God! Stake your life on his existence; that's the minimum wager at these tables. It's a perfectly reasonable wager, and you have to bet, as it's impossible to know that there's a God and you can't make yourself believe in him. And it's no good refusing to bet because that's equivalent to betting that there is no God. That's why there is no escape from having to play at these tables. Mark, you can't wager that there is no God. That wouldn't be a reasonable one. It's too late. You lost any benefit you might have gained from that wager this morning when you failed to shoot me. Your career is finished. You've already lost everything except your life. Throw your life on the table and bet with it that God exists. Think of it: before you've seen whether you've won or lost, you'll already have given some meaning to your life in Vienna, for once you have placed your bet there will be no madness, just waiting for events. You could win the wager—if that happened, your reward will be great. If you lose—well, what have you got to lose that you haven't lost already? You said yourself you'd lost everything...

MARK: *(Like thunder)* Lies! Lies! I haven't lost everything, yet. Christopher here is my witness, I haven't lost Iris, yet. I have Iris to hold...and to hold at the tables...I'll use her in my wager.

| | |
|---|---|
| CALLISTA: | What will you do with Iris's life? |
| MARK: | Hold it as ransom for proof of God's existence. Iris is a believer. She trusts in God. Let God save her now and I'll believe too. If I hear her voice on the phone, in safety, I'll give my life to God! |
| CALLISTA: | You can't bargain with Iris's life. You can't wager her life. You have no right to do it. |
| MARK: | Why can't I? Why haven't I the right? She is my life. |
| CALLISTA: | How do you know she hasn't struck her own bargain? |
| MARK: | What bargain could she have made? |
| CALLISTA: | For your sake. Hard bargains can be made. |
| MARK: | If I hear her voice...*(The phone rings shrilly.)* *[He hears her voice, from the headquarters of the Secret Police chief, Krechlen, where she is being tortured. Her message is an official one: for him to use his spare gun to kill Phugas, and his wife's life will be spared. But she abandons this message to tell him to kiss her rosary, before her voice is cut off.]* |
| MARK: | She's gone...in the middle of a sentence...Did you hear? |
| CALLISTA: | Just the last words..."to kiss..." |
| MARK: | You didn't hear her message? *(All shake their heads sadly.)* There'll be no more messages...nothing more...never. *(He puts the phone down.)* |
| CHRISTOPHER: | It's clear that Krechlen has a spy working in our embassy. I've worried about that all morning, but we had to take the risk. That's how he found out we'd promised to try to let you talk to her on the phone. That devilish humour is typical of him...*(He goes to Mark.)* I'm sorry, friend; terribly sorry. We did our best, but we were too late. |
| MARK: | Half an hour too late. The half-hour I wasted this morning. |
| CHRISTOPHER: | Don't say that. We don't know the details yet. I'll go straight away to enquire. *(Exit.)* |
| CALLISTA: | Can you tell us what she said? |
| MARK: | An official message from *them*. Nothing personal except that last word and last sentence. |
| PHUGAS: | What was the official message? |

| | |
|---|---|
| MARK: | That I have a second electronic gun, and a promise to save Iris's life if I completed my mission here in Vienna. *(He has taken the cigarette case gun out of his pocket.)* |
| PHUGAS: | What about it then? |
| MARK: | It's too late. |
| PHUGAS: | Callista wouldn't move for half an hour. You have the freedom of the American sector. You could walk out of the house and into the Russian sector without any trouble. Then you could phone straight away. |
| MARK: | Iris said one word at the end: "excuses, Mark." That is, pretence, lies. She wouldn't have said that if she was in their clutches. She stopped in mid sentence... |
| PHUGAS: | Iris is safe. *(Callista picks up Iris's rosary from the desk.)* |
| MARK: | I heard her voice in safety!...What trick is it that life has which makes man challenge and prophesy his own damnation...Life is bedlam; all Europe is a madhouse. |
| CALLISTA: | Mark, give me that gun. *(She gets hold of his arm.)* |
| MARK: | Don't worry. I won't offer your brother a cigarette. |
| CALLISTA: | The purpose of the message wasn't to make you shoot my brother. |
| MARK: | What then? |
| CALLISTA: | The thing you're about to do now. |
| MARK: | How do you know? |
| CALLISTA: | That's why they carted Iris to the phone—so that her dying voice might send you to your doom, to shoot yourself. Today your death is much more important to them than even that of Phugas. And you intend carrying out their wishes? |
| MARK: | I don't care what they want. My life is finished. |
| CALLISTA: | Your life is, indeed, finished. But isn't it your vocation, your calling, now to carry on living when your life is finished? |
| MARK: | Vocation? What calling is there for me? |
| CALLISTA: | Iris is calling you, Mark. It was she who sent you here to us...She who gave up her life for you, to deliver you from evil. She didn't escape from her pain. She chose her pain and you |

know that; she drank her cup to the full—for your sake, in order to secure that you would be with her for ever. And you, now, must, though your life is finished, must live, not your life but that of Iris. She left you a gift: the rosary of her prayers. Take her rosary, and give me the pistol. *(They exchange objects.)*

MARK: What'll I do with it?

CALLISTA: Do as Iris did, kiss it.

MARK: *(Falls to his knees, and raises the rosary to his lips.)* Iris, Iris, pray for me. *(A moment of silence. Callista buries her head in her hands.)*

PHUGAS: Mark, I have a journey to make tonight, by air. It's an important mission. It would be safer if I had a pilot...Will you come with me?

MARK: *(Rising)* Will you have me?

PHUGAS: It's a dangerous mission. This morning's tragedy shows how close they are on our tracks.

MARK: I have nothing to lose but that losing it would be a great gain.

PHUGAS: In my service you have to guard your life, bitter as it is, as a miser guards his gold.

MARK: I'm beginning to learn.

PHUGAS: I need not only a pilot, but also a colleague and a successor. The work must go on after me. I'll take you on, if you're willing.

MARK: *(Giving him his hand.)* I've kissed the crucifix.

CALLISTA: *(To Mark.)* This is your home from now on.

PHUGAS: We must get ready to go. We must collect the priest and the special edition of the paper. Just in case of accident, it would be better for us to carry arms...*(He goes to the desk and puts a pistol in his pocket.)* Callista, give Mark the electronic gun. That'll do for him tonight. *(Callista gives Mark a parcel and the gun.)*

CALLISTA: Take this as well.

PHUGAS: What is that?

CALLISTA: A pound of coffee for the priest.

## THE END

# The Arts, Artists and Thinkers—Testimony of the Poet

*In 1957 a symposium on the arts was held at Downside Abbey, England. Lewis took part.*

Inviting me to take part in this symposium, Mr. Todd wrote: 'I am inviting you to contribute as a poet. Your contribution could include some indication of how in your view art mediates truth, both to the artist himself and to those who listen to his work. How would you describe the experience of artistic creation?'

May I take that as my agenda? The fact that none of you knows anything at all of my work is an obvious advantage; it gives me a sort of anonymity. I can say 'he' as though it were 'me.'

I suppose it is normal to begin writing verses in adolescence, perhaps in the last two years of school life. It is a consequence of being taught poetry. A poet is a schoolboy who likes poetry even after being taught it. Lines and verses stick in his mind, are exciting, and he tries to do something similar. Then he discovers that the most absorbing of all verse is that of his slightly elder contemporaries. Poets are largely formed by their seniors, whether in their image or in revolt against it.

May I pass-by the question, how does a poem start? There are so many answers by so many poets in as many languages. I venture a generalisation: however the poem starts, what sets the poet working at it is the realisation that what is vaguely in his mind has the promise, the shapeability, of a poem. A poet is a man who has formed the habit of making poems. By practice he acquires proficiency in recognising and collecting the sort of material that is capable of being shaped into a poem. He lives on the watch for it. In medieval Wales and Ireland the material of poetry was part of the curriculum of the poets' schools. Today it depends on the caprice of fashion and the caprice of the individual.

But whatever it be, the matter of poetry is not an unwritten poem in the poet's mind. It is not a completed experience for which the poet has to find adequate symbol. A poem is not the expression of anything already existing, nor of anything that has already occurred unexpressed.

When you are making a poem you are aware of two activities, both essential and continuous. The first is complex. Your poem has started, perhaps a line, perhaps more, perhaps—in spite of Mellarmé—an embryo idea. So you begin churning up, inventing, discovering, phrases, half-lines, lines, sentences that grope into the right rhythmic shape, or else that won't, and your poem builds up. You depend, of course, on what the doctors call your foreconscious for memories and associations of all kinds and periods of your life, and you find you are fed with images and suggestions of matter appropriate for that or this particular point of your poem. You don't know what may not turn up. It is not that you've got an idea but cannot find the right word for it. It simply is that you haven't yet the idea, you are suspended, waiting, willing, experimenting, evoking, perhaps by chanting a phrase repeatedly to yourself, fishing for the thing, despairing; and then when your headache is so bad that you give up and think to go to bed, suddenly it comes—or no, it doesn't come, but there it is, proton-like and Proteus-like, having crossed no intermediate space, impossibly virginal, nothing like anything you expected, but so absurdly inevitable that with glaring untruthfulness you dub it *le mot juste*.

So the poem is not the completion of anything foreseen or preconceived. It is not the carrying out of a previous intention. Certainly it is necessary to have some initial intention, but you launch your intention, you entrust it to the co-operation of all that seems chance or at least is unknown and incalculable in the foreconscious and the unconscious. So that the poem does not recollect or recreate an experience. The poem is the experience: it creates the experience for the poet just as much as for his first audience. The Dante of the *Inferno* was not a man who *had been* through Hell, but a man who went into Hell a-making.

Yet I must not suggest that it is all a game of tennis between the conscious mind and the foreconscious. There is a third player; let us call him *technique*. Poetry is normally made in verse, all kinds of verse, from such strict forms as sonnet or *englyn* to *vers libre*. Verse, all and every verse, implies rules, relations, semantic and phonetic relations, formal constructions, both rhythmic and metric. These are never ornaments of verse, in the sense of being superfluities, but essential and major concerns. No craftsman of verse can give his constant attention to these factors without observing that they profoundly and incalculably contribute to the texture, to the themes, to the development, to the ultimate shape of the product which is the poem. Paul Valèry once wrote that Racine would change the character of one of his *dramatis personae* if a rhyme demanded it. That is not a *boutade*: it holds truth, though it might be more carefully said. It is not that a rhyme for Racine modifies a character already decided, already entire, but rather that the rhyme discovers the character, contributes to the character, adds its own unforeseen quality to the character. When Monime tells Mithridate:

> ...*cet aveu honteux, ou vous m'avez forcée,*
> *Demeurera toujours présent à ma pensée.*
> *Toujours je vous croirais incertain de ma foi;*
> *Et le tombeau, Seigneur, est moins triste pour moi*
> *Que le lit d'un époux qui m'a fait cet outrage.*

both Racine and Monime are surprisedly discovering that she has become this kind of person, that there are in her these unplumbed depths, and hence to the end of the play he has to treat her accordingly.

Characters don't have the same sort of life in the dramatist's mind before he starts writing and after starting. Characters take flesh from the words fastened to them, from the rhymes they find, out of the unfolding situation. They grow into and through the technique.

Some modern critics have written blame of Aristotle because in his discussion of tragedy he said that the thing of first importance was the plot. They are shocked that he did not give priority to characterisation. That is a sadly academic criticism. Aristotle was examining how plays were made. He was analysing tragedy from the point of view of the practical maker, and I think he was right and most percipient to put plot first. Plot also is technique, and for the working playwright it is the exploration of the plot that contributes most to the shaping of the tragic hero. I remember reading the advice of an English literary critic to young aspiring playwriters. Put half a dozen living characters together on the stage, he advised, get them talking, and then see what happens to them. For my part I cannot imagine even a Pirandello play being written that way. You don't put living characters into a play. You start your plot with mere ciphers or ghosts. You fasten words to them while you fasten them into a plot. Then, if your words have life, they may emerge from the plot living characters. I think that is as true of *Uncle Vanya* as of *Odeipus Rex.*

Technique, in this view, is the poet's major ally; the technical controls of verse, far from being restrictions or impediments, are an ever-present fount of happiness. Rhymes create character and alliteration may tangle a hawk in a sprung rhythm. The poet is a craftsman who has learnt to trust technique. This, I suspect, is a point at which I ought to bow to the ballet dancer.

The second constant activity in the making of a poem is that of critic. 'Would he had blotted a thousand,' said Ben Jonson rightly of his better. You cannot control what the foreconscious offers. Half-lines leap up, phrases, new combinations of words; images and memories take word-shapes, sometimes nimbly, sometimes sluggishly. But there you are, the appraising critical you, alert, watching, rejecting, selecting, moving the pieces about, building the chosen into a satisfactory unit, testing them on your ear, speaking them in different tones, scrutinizing them on the paper. Have you got the necessary patience? Can you reject steadfastly enough or do you surrender to what you know is second-rate? Can you lie in wait long enough, like a fisherman over a dark pool? Is the critic in you—the essential poet in you—resolute enough, inflexible, fine and subtle enough? Everything depends on that.

Making poems, like making a picture, is applied criticism. A single line may destroy a lyric or a painting. Even to recognise when your poem is finished is a vital critical decision. For I have said that I do not understand a poem as the reproduction of anything previously complete in the mind. Therefore to find the poem finished is to be critically satisifed with the whole shape of it, since there is no criterion outside the poem itself. That is why fixed forms such as sonnet or *ballade* are so tempting, and why success in them is now all but impossible. Technique can also betray. One needs immense critical sureness to succeed with the fixed forms.

Mr. Todd's second question was: how does art mediate truth? I am no philosopher and I must try to avoid the snares of the metaphysicians and the analysts. The account I have offered of poetic composition posits that the poet does not 'tell the truth.' He is not a witness in any legal sense. He is not relating or recollecting or symbolizing a previous experience. The fact that memory provides very much of the unshaped material of a poem does not, I trust, invalidate this account. One may remember the Abbé Bremond's theory of the relation of poetry to prayer. It seemed to me a most depressing theory in its implication for poets. I am anxious to avoid giving my two nouns, poetry and truth, capital letters, and I am more interested in poems and in plays than in poetry. And yet, truth in poetry—the phrase has its honest meaning, just as it is sound sense to talk of sincerity in a poem. Any poem, even the slightest lyric, is a complex thing. Let me go to neutral territory and consider for a moment 'The Banks o' Doon' by Robert Burns:

> Ye flowery banks o' bonnie Doon
> How can ye blume sae fair!

It is a hackneyed theme. In six simple verses the poet uses images that had been used a thousand times before him. Nothing is new; the rhymes are most obvious, the rhythms those of commonplace song. Yet is is one of the lovely and immaculate things. Truth and sincerity are words you need to describe its quality. An adjective too literary, a smear of sentimentality, might have toppled the thing into a falsehood. Burns goes serenely by his dangers and achieves a song that is as pure as a crocus.

So I would offer for your consideration that the truth of a poem is the recognition of the poet's critical control. It is the criterion of the poem's spiritual unity. The truth, the integrity—and I thank goodness for this—are not all in the poet or in his mode of life or even in his immediate mood, but they are in the poem, in the thing made, which, once completed, stands independent of the poet. Integrity is not a virtue of the poet transferred to the poem as though the style were indeed the man, but is a quality achieved objectively in the poem through the poet's craftsmanship and critical control. Even so, I do not offer that as a dogmatic statment about all poetry. I offer it as a means of protecting my own integrity. Poets are not as good as their poetry and are not served by being identified with their poems. There is wisdom in *Hamlet* that there never was in William Shakespeare. The truth of the poem depends on no reference outside itself. Its validity is its oneness, and its truth is its being. It has the truth of a thing, a *res*.

I do not deny, of course, that there is a large body of poetic work in many languages that is autobiographical, that poets have had experience which they have recorded in poems. What I am trying to maintain is that the making of the poem changes, transforms the experience, frames it in a new context so that its truth now is the truth of the poem. It cannot be veracious, it cannot be witness, just because art demands an absolute unity, and every poet knows that in composing he surrenders his experience to the poem. I venture to maintain that this is true even of the Song of the Ascent of Mount Carmel.

A good poem is an impersonal thing; whereas bad verse is personal. I wonder will the dancer tell us that at the supreme moment of a well-achieved dance she is like Wordsworth's Lucy:

She neither hears nor sees;
Roll'd round in earth's diurnal course,
With rocks, and stones, and trees.

I believe it must be a common experience for a poet, having some time written something good, to read it again after an interval and say to himself 'How did I ever happen to write that? I cannot imagine myself today thinking or saying anything at all like that.' When you come out of the dance you are just ordinary and normal. It is when you surrender your being to the technique that you achieve things beyond your knowledge of yourself.

I stop here. I know that there are implications unexplored in more than one of my paragraphs, but I have tried not to trespass on the philosopher's ground. Nor have I discussed 'poetic vision' as a means of approaching Truth. Frankly, I do not know what poetic vision means. It is the adjective that I don't understand.

## A Television Interview With Aneirin Talfan Davies in 1960

(Mr. Davies was a friend of Lewis and of David Jones.)

*Well, Mr. Saunders Lewis, since you were born in England, some people, and critics among them, claim that somehow or other you are a man without roots. What would your answer be to that?*

My answer to that, first of all, is that it brings back to me all at once a rather unhappy memory. I remember when I was at the University in Liverpool, arguing about something or other with my father. He turned to me suddenly and said "Look, Saunders, nothing at all will come of you until you come back to your roots." And that is one of the *personal* things my father said to me that I still remember vividly today. The idea that because I was born in Liverpool I was born an exile from

Wales, is completely false. I don't know what the statistics are, but I'm pretty sure that there were round about a hundred thousand Welsh-speaking people in Liverpool during the period of my boyhood. And I should say that at least half of those were monoglot Welsh speakers who could hardly manage a word of English. For instance, girls would come as maids to our house and to my aunt's house in Liverpool, from Anglesey and Caernarfonshire, absolutely monoglot Welsh girls. They would come with us to chapel for a few years, then they would get married and go back to Wales with just as little English as when they came to England. In Liverpool in my time there was a society as monoglot Welsh as in any village in Anglesey. I remember learning English at school, and other boys making fun of me because the little English I had was full of Welsh words. So I was not born in English-speaking England at all, but into a society which was completely Welsh and Welsh-speaking.

*What about your parents—where did they come from?*

My father came from Carmarthenshire, and many of the family are still there to this day, around Llan-non. My father grew up in the Church—the Church of England as it was at that time. He was confirmed in the church at Llan-non. The family graves are in Gors Las to this day. My mother's family: she was born in London. My aunt was born in Liverpool. But the family, Owen Thomas's family, was from Bangor and Anglesey, and my family is still there in Anglesey today. And since Anglesey was closest to Liverpool, it was there we went every summer to the family. If you asked me what part of Wales I came from, I should say from Anglesey.

*So North Wales Welsh is your natural tongue?*

I think it's my mother's and aunt's Welsh, Anglesey Welsh, more or less.

*What about your father's influence on you?*

That's a difficult question to answer. I've never really thought about it properly—his influence on me. My father was a man of letters and a scholar. He was a man who was frightened of the public. He wasn't fond of company. He was a man who liked solitude and the study. He was a natural man of letters, a natural scholar. He studied at Glasgow University. He collected old Welsh books. When I was working on Williams Pantycelyn, I didn't have to get hold, myself, of any first edition of any book of Pantycelyn's, from a library. My father had them all. The result was that I inherited, I'm sure, from him, my idea of what a scholar's library should be. I think that was my father's chief influence on me. He was, like every good scholar, a very lazy man. He much prefered study and reading to publishing. He wrote many occasional pieces for Welsh periodicals. For the *Cymro* [i.e. when the *Cymro* was the weekly paper of the Calvinistic Methodists] in particular, but study was what my father loved doing above all else.

*If I might throw in a recollection of my own at this point: where I met you first, I think, was in your father's study in Swansea. I remember your saying at a dinner in Swansea on the publication of* Monica, *that one of the weaknesses of that novel was that you had failed to avoid the temptation to preach. Were you ever tempted to become a preacher?*

You say "Were you ever,"—it's natural for preachers' children, preachers' sons, to play at being preachers. I'm sure *you* did.

*Many a time!*

And so it was natural when we were children, that preaching was the way we spent our leisure hours on Sunday, for example. So preaching was a constant part of our pantomime, our play-acting. So I can say that as a child preaching was very important to me. After that, no. After that, the only time I have been a preacher was in politics! I am afraid of preaching, because of my father, grandfather, great-grandfather, indeed on my father's side preaching goes back even further than that. By this time, I think I have no desire at all to preach, or any desire to persuade anyone of anything.

*What kind of thing did you read when you were a child and a young man?*

I think I can say that the only Welsh books I read during the period I was a boy at school, were the Bible, the Hymn Book, and commentaries for Sunday School. I don't think I read much Welsh apart from that. I think all my reading, all the time I was at school, was in English. I read widely, as everyone reads at school, throughout the whole range of English literature. The school was a private one, middle-class, where the whole community read very widely. And so I had the kind of knowledge of English literature common at that time.

*And you were completely unconscious of the Welsh literary tradition, as it were?*

Absolutely, absolutely. I think my father was rather shy of urging me to read Welsh and Welsh literature—he had a very rich collection in his library but he left us to read the things we were learning at school, and to read around them. Then, I remember quite well, we were living on the Cheshire side of Liverpool, in Wallasey, and my father was the minister of Liscard Road Church. In Wallasey there was a library, a really excellent public library. Earlston Library it was called. It was there I began to look for contemporary works in English. And I remember very well, the last years, the last two years I was at school, I discovered Yeats in particular, Yeats above all. Contemporary English literature began to take its hold of me. From that time to this, I have considered Yeats to be one of the greatest poets of the century in English.

*I'm sure you're right. Would you say that reading Yeats, for instance, created a desire in you to search in the literature of your own nation for what was to be found in Yeats about his country's literature?*

You have put your finger on it. It was through reading the works of Yeats, Synge, Patrick Colum, the Irish or Irishry—it was through those that I came for the first time to understand what patriotism and the spirit of a nation meant. And I soon began to think that things like those, which had seized hold of them in Ireland, were the kind of things I should seize hold of in Wales.

*How old were you when all this was going on?*

Say the last two years at school, that is, I can't remember the exact years; I'm not sure, but when I was seventeen and eighteen years old.

*But it was natural, I suppose, since your education was entirely English, for you to study English at Liverpool University?*

I had already begun to write in English, before leaving school. If you want to look for my first published work, there was a weekly paper called *The Wallasey Chronicle,* I think it's still in existence. When I was in my last year at school, I began to write reviews in the *Wallasey Chronicle,* and so to obtain books. Then, soon after that, in my first year at University in Liverpool, I started to go once a week to the theatre in New Brighton, and to write a theatre review for the *Wallasey Chronicle.* And so I got the theatre for nothing—the *Wallasey Chronicle* didn't pay me, but I got my theatre for nothing, as I got the books for nothing. And so the idea of writing for the theatre came to me during my first year at college in Liverpool.

*Would it be true to say that at that time you wanted to be a writer in English?*

I am afraid that this is the whole truth and nothing but the truth. Unfortunately, the notion of writing in Welsh had not occurred to me at that time, and I think that was the time my father told me that I should have to return to my roots before any good would come of me.

*Well, when would you say you made the first conscious decision to master the Welsh language as a literary medium?*

Strangely enough, it was in France. I was in my third year at college in Liverpoool when the war broke out. The 1914 war. That August, I was in the army. Then I went out to France. I had learned French pretty well at school and had followed courses in French at the University in Liverpool. I could read French easily, and in France I came to be able to speak it fairly easily. Now, over there, I came across a French novelist called Maurice Barrès. And I read a series of books by Barrès entitled *The Development of My Own Mind,* or my personality. *Le Culte du Moi.* And through reading those, I learned from Barrès that the only way to cultivate your personality as an artist and to develop your own resources, is to go back to your roots, just as my father said. That you had to go back to your own past and use your own inheritance in order to construct your own self. And I think it was Barrès after Yeats and the Irish, it was Barrès that made me a Welsh nationalist of conviction. Then I determined that I had to master the Welsh language and read Welsh literature. After that, on leave, I came home to Wales—my father had moved to Swansea while I was out in France, and there, in Morgan and Higgs's shop in Swansea, about 1916 I think it was, I got hold of T. Gwynn Jones's biography of Emrys ap Iwan, and that confirmed everything for which Barrès had prepared the way.

*It's obvious to me that Wales is in a state of crisis at the present moment. Now, would you say that a Welsh-speaking Welshman has a duty to stick to Welsh? Because it is a temptation to many a young writer to turn to English. What would you say to a young writer today?*

I don't know what to say to him. I think one must say this: it isn't a matter of choice. For instance, I didn't choose to write in Welsh either. I had intended first of all, it's true, to write in English—but when you begin to look around, suddenly the thing gets hold of you, and you can't write in any other language. Well now, if a young writer is able to choose what language he is going to write in, Welsh or English, all I can say is that I am dreadfully sorry for him, dreadfully sorry. Because I'm fairly certain that it is very exceptional for anyone to have mastered writing well in two languages. There are a few exceptions where people have written well in two languages. There are a few exceptions where people have written masterpieces in two languages. I think there are a few exceptions. But they are so infrequent, they don't provide a model for anyone.

*Well now, time is going on; may I quickly ask you another question? It's clear that it was drama that attracted you almost from the start—your interest, as you have mentioned already, was the theatre. I wonder whether the fact that there was no professional theatre in Wales made you have doubts about the worth-whileness of writing plays in Welsh?*

Yes, it makes me have doubts, even today. It's painful for me to write plays that I know no-one can act. It's extremely painful, I recognise that. But you see, it's at that point that I come face-to-face with this problem: the only kind of writing that appeals to me at all strongly, within creative writing, is drama. For one thing because, like every creative writer, I have an exceptional gift for telling lies. Every creative writer has it, so that surely the only way to tell the truth is to write a play. Your characters express every aspect of any event or any person. You can tell the truth in a play.

*I wonder whether the fact that you are such a good playwright explains why you have failed as a practical politician?*

Yes, well, I have said that myself. I had a desire, no small desire either, a very great desire to change the history of

194

Wales—to change the whole course of her history, to make of Welsh-speaking Wales something lively strong and powerful, a part of the modern world. And I failed completely.

*Why do you think you failed?*

I was rejected by everyone. I was rejected in every election in which I offered myself as a candidate; every one of my ideas—I started with sociology, and the sociology of nationalism—every single one has been cast aside. That being so, I had nothing to turn to, to express my vision, except writing the history of Welsh literature and writing plays.

*Yes, but isn't the politician's function in the long run inimical to the artist's way of life, and the best thing that happened in Wales was for you to have abandoned politics and entered the literary world?*

Well, that may be so, because I was warned once as a young man in Liverpool not to do anything except write, for I should be sure to fail at everything else. I was given that warning once by a phrenologist. So it is possible that I should have been a failure anyway, if I had continued in politics. But the result is that you put into your writing what you have failed at in your life.

*Yes, I notice that in your plays you deal with politics—in nearly every one of your plays. Is this an attempt to do what you have just mentioned, that is to achieve what you have failed to do in actual fact?*

Yes, I think so. Any psychologist would say that what I am doing in my plays is taking revenge, making amends to myself for my failure. I think he would read into them a pitiful failure.

*But, Mr. Lewis, was not one of the reasons for your failure, perhaps, that through your conversion to the Church of Rome, in one way or another you made it impossible for yourself to be able to understand or to sympathise with Welsh life as it is at present?*

I don't think I stopped understanding Welsh life by turning to the Church of Rome. But I think I alienated Welsh people from me and made them suspicious and afraid of me because I became a Catholic. I think that the attitude of Wales, particularly at the time I became a Catholic, towards Catholicism, makes it impossible for her to accept a Catholic as a political leader. I acknowledge that at once. But I don't think it estranges me from Wales, nor from the Welsh Nonconformist tradition.

*But it has inflicted some kind of exile upon you, hasn't it? Would you say that that exile has helped you to look at Wales from outside, so to speak, and to be more honest than most of our politicians, or most of our writers for that matter?*

You know, I don't think it makes me look at Wales from outside, but rather to look at Wales with more *perspective*; that is, I see that it is absolutely necessary for us to stop thinking of Wales as beginning with the radical movement and the political nonconformist movement of the nineteenth century. We must bring all the past ages into our vision of Wales today, and I believe that Catholicism helps one to do that. But may I say one word on the subject of politics, and that is this: I became a Catholic not because anything in the social philosophy of Catholicism appealed to me in the least, not at all. I became a Catholic for one terribly simple reason, that I believe that in the Catholic Mass, God is worshipped as he should be worshipped by men and women. And that is the only reason I became a Catholic.

*When did you begin your journey to Rome? What first impelled you to turn towards Rome?*

Well, I told you that I began by reading Irish literature—not Irish but Anglo-Irish, Yeats, Synge; they directed me towards people like Lionel Johnson, Alice Meynell, and from them I went into French literature, and gradually Catholic Europe brought me to try to understand what Catholicism is.

*But Yeats would not have led you to Catholicism? Yeats rejected Irish Catholicism.*

Entirely. But he used the images of Catholicism, and that made me want to understand that imagery. That's how it was at first.

*May I ask you a question: our time is coming to an end, I'm afraid, and I want to ask you one last question without more ado, because we are all concerned about the fate of the Welsh nation, and in particular about the fate of our writers and our literature. Now, in an article in* Y Faner, *at about the end of the war, you made quite a violent attack on young Welsh writers and poets, comparing them pretty unfavourably with the* Anglo-Welsh. *Has anything happened since that twilight time—it was in 1945, if I remember rightly—has anything happened since to make you change your mind?*

Yes a great deal. But what make you change your mind are people. John Gwilym Jones makes me change my mind; Bobi Jones makes me change my mind; Islwyn Ffowc Elis makes me change my mind. I have a great admiration for the energy involved in the good, dogged work of an author who puts all his strength into his work, as he does. And not only that, the increasing maturity of Bobi Jones brings me great hope for the future of Welsh literature. And again, just recently, I was listening to a radio play by Miss Lewis, a student at Bangor, [Eigra Lewis Roberts, the prose writer] and I was tremendously cheered. She was so obviously thinking and creating in Welsh. Things like that make me believe the future is much more hopeful than I had thought.

*May I say one thing personally at this point. I am glad to hear you say that, and to hear you naming these people. I have a feeling, a nagging conviction that the older generation in Wales has been very ungenerous in its praise of the new generation. Many of them, I believe—I talk a great deal with young writers, and have been in close contact with them—tend to despair because they have only heard themselves criticised, almost from the day they first put pen to paper. Don't you feel it is essential for an artist to be praised from time to time?*

I'm quite sure you are right. Not only that, but it is natural for an artist—he is sure to do more work and harder work if he feels that someone understands and appreciates him.

*But you see what I'm getting at: a generation has grown up in Wales—I would call it the post-war generation, and it is represented in the little periodical I edited,* Heddiw. *They have grown up mostly in industrial villages and valleys, and their Welsh is not quite as faultless as that of someone brought up in a monoglot Welsh background. Isn't it perhaps our duty to give such people some help, and not to condemn so bitterly anyone whose Welsh is not quite as pure as that of some monoglot Welshman who was brought up in the country?*

Yes, I'm sure, I agree entirely. May I say one thing only: if you write, it is possible, wherever you were brought up, it is possible with dedication at least to achieve complete accuracy in the Welsh tongue. And I think there is no excuse at all for anyone not to manage that. Poor Welsh is not, in any circumstances at all, a virtue in a writer.

*No, it is not a virtue, but bearing in mind our educational system, that many children have to choose between Welsh and other subjects in our intermediate schools, there is a danger that the language is becoming poorer from year to year.*

At the same time, I believe it is right for us to set the highest standard possible for writers. You cannot write poetry without great accuracy in the matter of language.

*And so, a last question to finish with. What would be your advice to a young writer today, at the start of his career?*

Steep yourself in the literature of your language. Dedicate yourself to it and appreciate it to your utmost. Everything else comes second. Being in the fashion, following the fashions of London or Paris, is of wholly secondary importance compared with knowing your own Welsh tradition.

## Forever Oscar
BOOK REVIEW (1962)

**THE LETTERS OF OSCAR WILDE, edited and published by Rupert Hart-Davis; 84s.**

Oscar Wilde began his literary life in Ireland, publishing poems and essays in Irish journals. He was modestly yet plainly an Irish nationalist:

> My mother and father had bequeathed me a name they had made noble and honoured not merely in Literature, Art, Archaeology and Science, but in the public history of my own country in its evolution as a nation.

He visits the House of Commons in 1891:

> I was dining in the House of Commons on Thursday and proposed to some Scotch and Welsh members that...all of us who are Celts, Welsh, Scotch and Irish, should inaugurate a Celtic dinner, and assert ourselves, and show these tedious Angles or Teutons what a race we are and how proud we are to belong to that race...

George Bernard Shaw published his first play in 1893. Oscar Wilde wrote:

> My dear Shaw, I must thank you very sincerely for Op. 2 of the great Celtic school.

Op. 1 was his own *Lady Windermere's Fan* and Mr. Hesketh Person comments:

> Wilde paid Shaw the compliment of ranking their works together though he had just scored his sec-

ond huge success with *A Woman of No Impor-tance,* while Shaw's *Widowers' Houses* had prac-tically been hooted from the stage.

## Classic

It is Wilde's dramatic work that lives. He himself comments in a letter on *The Importance of Being Earnest*:

I like the play's irresponsiblity and its *obiter dicta,* but it is essentially an acting play: it should have been a classic for the English Theatre, but alas! the author was struck by madness from the moon...

It stands today a classic of the English Theatre even when dramatic prose in English is the prose of Harold Pinter. It re-mains diamond-perfect, the brilliant materpiece of English ar-tificial comedy. Wilde's judgment on his plays remains perti-nent also:

My plays are difficult to produce well; they require artistic setting on the stage, a good company that knows something of the style essential to high comedy, beautiful dresses, a sense of the luxury of modern life...

and in a letter to Alfred Douglas after his release from prison, when his stage career was all past, he sums up his own achieve-ment:

I would say that my unique position was that I had taken the Drama, the most objective form known to art, and made it as personal a mode of expression as the Lyric or the Sonnet.

How truly personal this art was is revealed in a letter written by his heroic friend Robert Ross after Wilde's death.

These were the *obiter dicta* of *The Importance of Being Earnest.*

Of the rest of Wilde's prose works it seems to me that this complete edition of his *Letters*, superbly edited and published, alone will live. Not his essays and tales. Most of them are ter-ribly eighteen-ninetyish. Robert Graves's *Goodbye to All That* put an end to that Pateresque English prose as surely as *The Waste Land* put an end to Sturge Moore poetry. But these Letters are alive, eloquent, gorgeous, pathetic, roguish, witty and wicked, and they tell the tragedy of his life.

They give us the man as Robert Ross describes him better than all his formal prose compositions. The collection includes the first complete version of the *De Profundis* letter from prison to Alfred Douglas, a tremendous thing. But to show what prose he could write let me quote a fragment from a letter he sent to his publisher from Italy after he had rejoined Douglas:

> I lived in silence and solitude for two years in prison. I did not think that after my release my wife, my trustees, the guardians of my children, my few friends, such as they are, and my myriad enemies would combine to force me by starvation to live in silence and solitude again. After all in prison we had food of some kind. The scheme now is that I am to live in silence and solitude and have no food at all. It is proposed to leave me to die of starvation, or to blow my brains out in a Naples urinal. I never came across anyone in whom the moral sense was dominant who was not heartless, cruel, vindictive, log-stupid, and entirely lacking in the smallest sense of humanity. Moral people, as they are termed, are simple beasts. I would sooner have fifty unnatural vices than one unnatural virtue. This, of couse, is the usual way in which poets write to publishers.

### A 'pervert'

There are perhaps people who think of Oscar Wilde as a "pervert," whatever that may mean today, and who seek a prurient interest in his letters. Perhaps one may venture two comments here:

(1) Wilde committed nothing that English law today would consider criminal.

(2) The years of his intercourse with Alfred Douglas and with London "renters" were the years in which he wrote his brilliant comedies and made his immense impression on the high society of London and Paris. They were the years of his greatness. He was intellectually in complete health and sanity and genius. Moveover his wit and vast sense of fun never deserted his judgment of himself even in his hours of despair. For example, it was suggested to him after his wife's death that he should marry again. He answered:

> As regards my marrying again, I am quite sure
> that you will want me to marry this time some sen-
> sible, practical, plain, middle-aged boy, and I
> don't like the idea at all. Besides I am practically
> engaged to a fisherman of extraordinary beauty,
> age eighteen. So you can see there are difficulties.

Anyone who can't delight in the sheer mischief of that ought to leave literature alone and go and play bingo.


## Dafydd ap Gwilym
(A review of the collected poems, for **Blackfriars**, 1963)

Until recent years Dafydd ap Gwilym was the only Welsh poet with a high reputation outside Wales. This was not so strange. He fitted into the conventional picture of medieval poetry. He shared themes and modes with Guido Cavalcanti and with Thibaut de Champagne. He stretched a hand to Rutebeuf and another to the early Chaucer. Sir Idris Bell tackled English translations; Stern treated him as a Welsh *Minnesänger;* a Dutch scholar, Theodor Chotzen, killed later in a Nazi prison, had in 1927 published his *Recherches sur la poésie de Dafydd ap Gwilym*, a large volume which remains still a most valuable survey of much of the poetry of Northern Europe in the four-teenth century. Now Professor Parry, of the University College of North Wales, Bangor, gives us the long-awaited edition which is based on a study of all the manuscript sources. One must not speak of a final edition, for the simple reason that oral tradition admits of very little finality; but here are the text and critical apparatus that will be the starting point of study for the rest of this century. What I propose to attempt now is to give English readers a glimpse of Dafydd ap Gwilym from the point of view of the Welsh literary tradition.

This is no longer too difficult. The first volume of the *The Growth of Literature* by H.M. and N.K. Chadwick—a great and noble work despite necessary lacunae and some errors—has revealed to English students the tradition of heroic panegyric that is the main stream of Welsh poetry from the sixth century onwards. The Welsh poets themselves used to call it the tradition of Taliesin, from the sixth-century poet of that name. The Norman conquest of England and the consequent threat to the Welsh that began in the closing years of the eleventh century gave fresh impetus to the heroic praise of the defending princes in the three princedoms of Wales. The struggle and its verse lasted till 1282 and later; but with the extinction of the principality and of the North Wales dynasty, the poetic activity that had made panegyric of the princes its main theme and heroic lyric its mode came to a difficult period.

For some two generations, say 1290 to 1330, there was multifarious and robust confusion. It is a still uncharted patch of Welsh literary history. The poets were professionals, organised in a *confrérie* that had points of likeness to the French cooperations, or *puys*, and the Chief of Song exercised offices not dissimilar from those of the *Roi des ministraux* of the French and Anglo-French thirteenth century. But the high rank and the panegyric function of the *prydydd* or the court poet seemed (or seems) at this period to be merging with those of the bohemian *ioculatorum turba*. Then out of the confusion came, before the middle years of the fourteenth century, two strong movements of renaissance.

The first was a reorganisation of the poets' corporation and a re-statement and enlargement of the tradition of panegyric. I must deal with it summarily, since it is a big matter. It is represented by a new chapter in the official grammar books of the poets, a chapter that describes the function of each class of poet and the appropriate modes of high panegyric. This reorganisation with its emphatic separation of the noble panegyrist from the miming and railing clown, is akin to the only little earlier movement of poetic reform in France, that is specially reflected in the work of Watriquet de Couvin and Jean de Condé. There are moral exhortations in Watriquet:

> *Menestrieus qui veut son droit faire*
> *Ne doit le jongleur contrefaire,*
> *Mais en sa bouche avoir tous diz*
> *Douces paroles et biaus diz*

and again in Jean de Condé:

> *Sois de cuer et nés et jolis*
> *Courtois, envoisiés et polis*
> *Pour les boines gens solacier*

which have their exact equivalent in the sentences in the Welsh grammar books that describe the moral qualities required of the poet of panegyric. Moreover, panegyric itself, the tradition of heroic praise as the highest poetic function, was now attached both to the *Lauds* of the daily Office and to the dialectic taught in the Cistercian schools, and so given new significance and *raison d'être*. Thus reorientated it became the basis of the great *cywydd* and *awdl* poetry of the next two centuries. That corpus of poetry is the major glory of Welsh literature.

The second movement, contemporary with this, is the work specially linked with the name of Dafydd ap Gwilym. Baldly, this response to the predicament was a turning aside from the tradition of heroic panegyric in order to embrace what Dafydd himself called the 'art of Ovid.' This meant all the varieties of invented love lyric and 'feigning' that stemmed from the *Roman de la Rose* or found in it (particularly lines 2265—2580 in Langlois' edition) their widest-known exemplars. It was a turning from what the Chadwicks have called the tradition of the Northern Islands to the continental and classical modes of *jongleur* and *trouvère*. Dafydd ap Gwilym himself, very aware of the challenge he was involved in, proudly maintained the equal dignity and honour of the Ovidian tradition he had elected for his own:

> The dignity of feigned love-song, however
>     resisted,
> Is no less than that of panegyric.

> (Nid llai urddas, heb ras rydd,
> Na gwawd geuwawd o gywydd)[2]

How came he to make his choice? Let us say that it was all around him. We shall not get a proper idea of the cultural climate of the late Middle Ages in Britain unless we recognise that Anglo-French and Middle English and Welsh were all cheek by jowl in the Welsh Marches and Crown Lordships. In the thirteenth century Brother Simon of Carmarthen writes French didactic verse that seems to betray the influence of the monorhyme of the Welsh *awdl*. Dr. Carleton Brown has shown that the most remarkable English lyric poet of the late thirteenth century was a Welsh-speaking Welshman 'between Wye and Wirral' who makes the North Wind his love-messenger:

> Blow, Northern wind,
> Sent thou me my suetyng,

and whose curiously contrived *Annot and Johon* is notably influenced both in imagery and technique by the Welsh love *awdl*.[3] Dafydd ap Gwilym was nurtured in a household that belonged to the king's service, did the king's business, and met with political trouble. Pembroke and Carmarthen and Cardigan were within easy reach, a busy, turbulent, polyglot region. One might hazard the suggestion that it is in the verse

---

2. I have to disagree with Professor Parry's reading and interpretation of this most important poem (p. 392).
3. No. 76 in Brown's *Lyrics of the Thirteenth Century*. See the notes, but Dr. Brown fails to observe the *concatenatio* between the last half-line of the monorhyme and the first half-line of the final couplet throughout the poem.

of Dafydd ap Gwilym that French-Flemish-English-South Pembrokeshire makes its most signal contribution to Welsh literature. Certainly he was early acquainted with castle and abbey, town and tavern. He learned the cosmopolitan fashion of minstrel and *jongleur* and wandering poor clerk. He sings the courtly high-born love-song, esoteric and learned with literary allusion. He sings as often the broad song of tavern druery and all the irreverent parody and farce and adventure of the goliard tradition. There is nothing that can precisely be called *fabliau* in his work, but his spirit is frequently that of the *fabliaux* writers. He is the gay, insouciant hero of his own misadventures, and so brilliantly master of the mood and manner that he turns *l'esprit gaulois* into *esprit gallois* and gives it for two centuries the freedom of Welsh verse.

Yet the tale of misadventure is rarely the purpose of a poem by Dafydd ap Gwilym. Unlike the *fabliaux* writers he is a true poet, and what is most typical of him, what imposes itself as the chief device of all his verse, is as ancient as the Heroic Age. The Chadwicks have a chapter on the riddle poetry of Old Norse and English and Welsh. It was a species of descriptive poetry, and they give this riddle of a fog as a Norse example:

> What is that huge one that passes over the earth,
> swallowing lakes and pools? He fears the wind,
> but he fears not man, and carries on hostilities
> against the sun.

There is a kindred but longer and more elaborate riddling of the wind in old Welsh, the only early Welsh example surviving. The Welsh poets of the fourteenth century, and Dafydd ap Gwilym especially, developed this riddling description into clusters of metaphor and fantastic simile bound together metrically by strong *concatenatio,* a poetic junction of intense rhetoric and contemplation. He walks over the moor to meet his mistress and a bramble catches his foot; the bramble becomes the theme of his riddle. He rides at night in a strange country, perhaps Cheshire, and he and his horse stumble in a peat-pit, and the bog is wondrously riddled. Mist blocks his love journey or the stars light it, thunder frightens his lady; or an echo, icicles and a gander disturb his serenade; a ruined house on his road where once he made love, his own heart and his deep sigh, they all—and a score more—become themes of his riddling. And, of course, his love-messengers, stag or wind or wave or bird:

> Flashing gull on the full tide,
> Hue of snow or white moon,
> Speckless in loveliness,
> Ball like a sun, fist of foam,
> Gaily-winged fish-swallower,
> There at anchor I'd have you float
> Linked hand with mine, sea lily,
> Like a paper glistening,
> A nun cresting the flowing tide.

It is as compulsive as Dylan Thomas for the English. All Dafydd's themes seem to rise like Goethe's songs out of moments of experience, realised with swift intensity, accidents, and occasions for incandescence. At the very same time Petrarch was teaching all Europe a slow and measured pace for poetry, but Dafydd ap Gwilym's verse is as nimble as his imagery; his mind is all turned out to see, to hear, to be with the fox and hare and blackbird, to climb the sky with the skylark, in a rapture of entranced living. They tell us his life was short. It could not but be so.

# Letter to David Jones Which Goes On to Discuss Death

158, Westbourne Road, Penarth, Glamorgan

8 - 1 - 1963

Dafydd Annwyliawn,

It was very comforting to have a letter from you, but I felt very guilty. For I know what a strain letter writing must be for you this weather. Your awfully inadequate gas fire makes me shiver for you. It is dangerous. Please do get an oil Aladdin stove and a 4 gallon tin for storing oil as soon as the weather improves, and get the oil delivery man to come *to your room* every week or fortnight to fill up. There's nothing else possible; that *and* your gas fire will do the trick and bring you warmth.

*Entre nous*, the English translation of my elegy on J.E. Lloyd in the Cymmrodorion transactions is pretty bad. But it gives me joy that you find more than one echo of Dante.

Wednesday, 9th Jan.

I had written thus far yesterday when I got a telephone message that my former colleague, Prof. G.J. Williams, best known outside scholarly circles as the Iolo morgannwg expert, has had a seizure, thrombosis and pneumonia, is unconscious and not likely to live beyond tonight. It was in his home that he and I and Ambrose Bebb started the Welsh Nationalist Party. He is actually the most complete Welsh scholar of this century, and of the encyclopedic knowledge in Celtic affairs of Edward Llwyd. We have been close friends since 1922. And now any minute will bring news of his death.

I've been thinking much of Michael Angelo at 80 working away at night at that Pietà in the Florence Cathedral, intending it for his own sepulchre and not letting even his close friends see it. I've been intending a story of it, but he was mentally such a giant I'm afraid of tackling it. He too had seen all his contemporaries die; he only had disciples. It's horrible and heroic, Titanic.

People who talk about "ripeness is all," "nothing is here for tears," etc. are just averting their gaze. Death even at Michael Angelo's 85 is a cutting off, a mutilation, and every friend's death is a kick in the stomach and unbearable, a foul dirty trick.

You see what sort of Catholic I am.

Keep alive, David. Keep warm. Buy a bloody oil stove and fug over it.

Saunders

Don't answer this till you're warm and well. But if ever you get unwell send for me by phone or telegram and I'll see you in a decent nursing home, and get you better.


# A Member Of An Older Breed

(Book Review—1964)

If you publish poetry today in any of the major languages of Europe or in any of the European-derived languages of America, you are implicitly laying claim to genius. You may be the most modest of men, but you have published a book of verse: it is an act of immense self-assertion. You must out-Rilke Rilke to justify your daring, to prove yourself Poet. You have to whip yourself to an existential vitality, build your personality, become your mask.

Or—for there is an alternative—you can turn Chinese or Welsh. In China poetry has normally been written by sedate, rather pot-bellied and polite civil servants. It is traditionally a form of courtesy. Its theme is the friendship of men.

The nearest thing I know to that in Europe is the tradition of Welsh poetry. This also, from its beginning in the sixth century, has been mainly a male affair, a form of polite after-dinner entertainment and social compliment.

The quite recent romantic revolution of Europe came of course also to Wales. We have had, we still have, poets of the romantic tradition, who will seek the mescalin experience in order to write the poetry of unique vision. Such poets, most of them under 40, are busy today in Welsh.

But there still exists in Wales another breed, an older breed. These are the heirs of Taliesin, of the court poets of Llywelyn the Great, of the country house poets of the 15th century gentry. We have a name for these poets of aristocracy today; we call them *beirdd gwlad*. Simple as the two words are, they are untranslatable. "Country poets" makes no sense in English; it would be taken to mean Wordsworth or Clare or Mr. Blunden. I think the best rendering would be "local poets," using "local" in the sense in which posh brewery advertisements call a suburban pub the "local."

In the Welsh areas of Wales poetry has still a social function. People actually like it. It is used to celebrate local festivals, such as deaths and marriages, hunt meetings and preaching meetings and eisteddfodau. The local poet is completely a member of his community, perhaps a farmer, a quarryman, or barber, or grocer; most probably a chapel deacon.

The heirs of Caradog Evans may throw a fit on hearing the chapel deacon, that arch-philistine, that arch-villain of the Anglo-Welsh romantic agony, called Poet. But you see, Wales is so like China. A chapel deacon is quintessentially a member of his community, planted in it like an elm. He belongs, as Taliesin his ancestor belonged to the court of Urien.

He writes and reads or recites his verses as part of the social life and entertainment of his group. He sanely ignores the existentialist dilemma. He needs no marijuana. For him Poet is no other than the normal average neighbourly countryman endowed with a happy skill of verse to please his fellows, to give them on occasion laughter or to commemorate their griefs. He cultivates, not his personality, not even his hair, but his craft: not an ecstasy, nor yet a guitar, but an *englyn*.

Local poets of course vary. We have good ones and we have the commonplace. Among the very good ones, among the masters, is one whose friends have recently collected his occasional work and made a book of it and published it: *Cerddi Alun Cilie*. Cilie—I write for English readers; to explain Cilie to a Welsh audience would be like telling Mr. Alun Owen about Lime Street—Cilie, then, is a farmstead in South Cardiganshire.

Alun Cilie is (for you) Mr. Alun J. Jones, a competent and up-to-date farmer who was born the last of seven sons about the beginning of this century. All seven sons were wits and poets and their names have travelled Wales. So have their much quoted epigrams. Not all have been printed. Many are of Bellocian flavour and quality. Mr. Alun Jones farms the old homestead and is the acknowledged prince-poet of his sea-fringed neighbourhood.

The Rev. D.J. Roberts, of Cardigan, has written a preface to this book of his poems and epigrams and says:

> Nothing gives more pleasure to his neighbours
> than to hear Alun Jones read his poems in their
> meetings.

Just like that. Just as if it were Homer. Just as if it were the normal, natural, lovely thing, this practice that has been transmitted from two-and-a-half millennia back, this residue of the oldest and greatest literary tradition of Europe. I confess that the reading of that simple sentence moved me even as the plain Latin of the low mass would move me before this confounded Vatican Council laid vandal hands on the liturgy.

Alun Jones is a master craftsman. First in language. A poem is destroyed by a single fault in grammar, by a wrong preposition—for prepositions are in Welsh the Achilles heel of unhappily bilingual writers. You can trust yourself to Alun Jones. He is simply, simply right and sure. He knows his language and he knows his fields. He was brought up in it and them. His Welsh is not a glove he puts on. It is the skin of his mind.

So also his verse-craft. He writes no *vers libre*, but the old alliterative Welsh metres and sonnets and lyric patterns of the 19th century. His elegy on a poodle would have won acclaim from the master parodists of the 15th century. His book is a chronicle of the change in farming techniques from the human skills and horse skills of the years before World War I to the mechanised farming of today.

This *bardd gwlad* is disarmingly unassuming. No tragic attitude: no apocalypse. Only the human note and a Greek acceptance. Some of the things in this book should find their way to any future edition of the *Oxford Book of Welsh Verse*.

## Incurably Involved in Religion

(Newspaper article—1964)

This year there have been two important debates or groups of discussions in the Welsh vernacular Press. The first has been about the future of the University of Wales; it is a debate that continues.

While it was at its height an advertisement appeared in some of the glossy coloured English weekly magazines appealing to honours graduates of British universities to join one of the great industrial companies of Great Britain.

The coloured advertisement showed (if I rightly remember) four master gowns of Oxford, Cambridge, Edinburgh and Wales, with an emphatic suggestion that these four represented the academic cream of Great Britain. I was surprised that none of the participants in the University of Wales debate remarked on the advertisement or drew the obvious and most relevant moral. Not even the alert Mr. Alwyn Rees.

Western Mall readers had their share of that debate. The second, not less poignant in interest, has not, as far as I know, spilled over into English. And that for a valid reason: it is concerned with religion and the condition of religious thought in Wales.

We Welsh-speaking people, however degenerate, however little moral, remain incurably involved in religion. Even our philosophers, even our actors. Our addiction takes curious and comic forms. A cranky minority of us became papist converts.

The result is delightful. A letter or article may by chance appear in one of the Welsh weeklies criticising some recent

212

display of the usual Catholic dark age mentality. Immediately the entire pack of fresh Welsh papal hounds flings itself on the quarry. The next number of the weekly paper or monthly journal can hardly contain all our letters.

It matters little whether the theme be the Virgin Birth or the contraceptive pill. Indeed, it is an obvious sign of divine providence that we have no Welsh-speaking or Welsh-reading bishop.

The present debate is most Protestant. The protagonist is Dr. J.R. Jones, professor of philosophy at University College, Swansea. He gave a television lecture that caused a shindy. He analysed the reaction of the Welsh pulpit to the materialism and indifference to spiritual shibboleths so general in Wales today. He found that the Welsh pulpit still, as a century ago, called people to repentance and salvation.

Today, he said, it is a call that has no meaning. At this moment of time we are not interested in personal salvation. We face a more ghastly abyss. We are caught, entangled in the meaninglessness of all human existence. Because for us life has been emptied of meaning, which is as much as to say that for us God is dead, we cannot take personal responsiblity seriously, and we don't.

We make life tolerable by distraction—while we wait for the inevitable hydrogen bombs to end this tale told by an idiot, full of sound and fury, signifying nothing.

Dr. Jones called on the Christian pulpit to restate Christianity, not in the cliches of an outworn evangelicalism, but in terms significant for men and women without belief, yet desperately anxious to find a *raison d'être* for living.

There were many answers from traditionalists, some sour and sardonic. There was a cool, lucid, logical traditionalist answer in a radio talk by another philosopher, Professor Hywel Lewis of London University. Then the BBC brought the two philosophers to confront each other in a television discussion.

I was privileged to listen to a tape-recording of this debate. I have listened on many occasions to discussing philosophers in three or four languages. I have not heard a fairer, more serious or nobler half-hour of argument.

Now Dr. J.R. Jones has amplified his postion in a pregnant pamphlet: *Yr Argyfwng Gwacter Ystyr*—The Crisis of Meaninglessness. He states at once that he is the Welsh interpreter of the theses of Dr. Paul Tillich.

Much of his pamphlet is a restatement of the fifth and sixth chapters of Tillich's impressive work, *The Courage To Be*.

But Dr. Jones makes the matter his own by thinking it out in Welsh and by joining it all to the Welsh theological tradition, which is centred on the doctrine of Justification, or on the linked doctrines of Justification and Atonement.

Dr. Tillich is Lutheran while the tradition of Welsh Protestantism is Calvinist. Dr. Jones follows Tillich's extension of Lutheranism in recognising a "justifying faith" in the truth-embracing agnostic who embraces the unavoidable unbelief of today in anxious groping arms, desiring desperately that life should have meaning, though unable to guess at it.

In such tragic scepticism, Dr. Jones insists with Tillich, there is already true faith, and his pamphlet ends comfortingly with a quotation from the German-American:

> "We cannot transform our lives unless we allow them
> to be transformed by grace. When this happens it is as
> though a voice were saying: 'You are accepted, ac-
> cepted by that which is greater than you, and the name
> of which you do not know.
> " 'Do not ask for that name now; perhaps you will
> find it later. Do not try to do anything now; perhaps
> later you will do much. Do not seek for anything.
> Simply accept the fact that you are accepted.' If that
> happens to us, we experience grace..."

I have tried to show the interest of Dr. Jones's writing without criticising it or meddling in the controversy. But perhaps I may venture to say that I find the above quotation very Billy Grahamish, so that I wonder whether new presbyter be not old priest writ large.

Dr. Tillich in his book has much to say of the Existentialists who share his starting-point. But there is no word of

Jean-Paul Sartre in Dr. Jones's essay and only an indirect reference to the Marxist answer to his problem.

A Catholic contribution to the discussion may easily be overlooked; there is a piece of splendidly muscled Welsh philosophic prose in the Reverend John FitzGerald's long essay in the 1964 number of *Ysgrifau Catholig*.

# Welsh Literature and Nationalism

(Newspaper article 1965)

Welsh literary critics are shy of emphasising what distinguishes Welsh literature from other literatures in Europe and especially separates it from its neighbouring English. This is perhaps because the discordant elements are not in the modern world fashionable. I take two modern examples in this essay.

The religious revival of the 18th century made Wales, for a century and a half, a Nonconformist and Calvinist community. There are historians and critics who are rather sorry about this. Today, Nonconformity is in sad and sullen retreat and Calvinism is almost a dirty word.

For English people of the upper-middle class—that is, the literary English—both Nonconformist and Calvinist have been rather smelly lower class attributes since the 18th century. That is the gulf that divides 19th century Welsh literature from English.

The Methodist revival gave Welsh prose and verse a separate character, a new idiom. One may complain that the 19th century Welsh literature lacks the broad secular liberal interest of French or German or English. True enough. True also of the 19th century Spanish literature; even of modern Italian letters. Welsh literature since the 16th century has been a minor literature. Nevertheless it is unique. It tells of an experience no other nation knows in the same fashion; and no other literature relates.

For Methodism was the form that the Romantic revolution took in Wales. Williams Panty-celyn and Ann Griffiths are for us what Blake and Wordsworth are for the English, what Man-zoni is for the Italians. There are no religious hymns of the 18th century in the Oxford Book of English Verse. That may be a correct judgment.

On the other hand, the greatest Welsh lyrics of the 18th and 19th centuries are certainly hymns. Their grandeur and intellectual power make them major poetry. These are national characteristics that a literary historian, be he Christian or unbeliever, must in loyalty to objective truth maintain.

I take my second example from a more recent past. It is now 40 years since the Welsh Nationalist Party began its career at Pwllheli. By the 1930's, it had become an established phenomenon in Welsh life. How much it has influenced Welsh political development and Welsh political thinking is a matter of petty dispute. Historians who rely on statistics are not impressed. Welsh socialist members of Parliament deny it an atom of importance. Welsh nationalists of an ardent optimism claim that only they have put the Right Honourable James Griffiths where he is now.

I make what I believe to be a statement of fact: the majority of Welsh poets and writers, novelists, dramatists, critics, have since 1930 onwards been avowed members of the Welsh Nationalist Party.

This is not a political argument. This is not a political article. I don't proclaim this as a challenge or in the least as a proof of the rightness of the nationalist cause. I am ready to grant that these men and women may be as daft as Sligo crofters thought W.B. Yeats. What interests me here and now is that this political allegiance has been a gulf between Welsh writers and their English and other contemporaries.

In the thirties, English poets and writers, from the public schools and from Oxford and Cambridge, were frenziedly trying to proletarianise themselves, engage themselves, joining the Communist party and the Left Book Club, enlisting for war against Franco in Spain. The influence of that period in English drama and poetry remains today, even if today it is an influence of disillusion.

In the same period, Welsh creative writing was profoundly moved by the development of the nationalist party. It was the period of Williams-Parry's great sonnets. Then came the poetry of Gwenallt and Waldo Williams and of Euros Bowen and the generation of Bobi Jones. It is the crisis of Wales that has given that period of poetry its *angst*.

It shows equally in the prose of D.J. Williams, the plays of John Gwilym Jones, stories and novels from Kate Roberts to Islwyn Ffowc Ellis.

Propaganda is not what groups these writers together. Only one or two write at all on politics. Dr. Kate Roberts, whose unfailing activity is a joy, does much political journalism, but she rigidly shuts the door on the least breath of propaganda in her stories and novels.

What these writers and poets have in common is an awareness that the Welsh nation may be dying of indifference and sloth and that a literature of a thousand years may end with a whimper.

In that they have, as it were, an epitome of what now overhangs all Europe, of what threatens humanity, a destruction of civilisation through apathy.

There is no longer any faith that makes the deferment of the nuclear war very urgent. So that a particular Welsh experience of this century, the crisis that the Welsh Nationalist Party evokes and was organised to avert, takes on universal reference and significance. Civilisation must be more than an abstraction. It must have a local habitation and a name. Here, its name is Wales.

Alas, there is one sad difference between the Welsh Nationalist Party of the 1960's and the Welsh Methodists of the 1760's. The Methodists in their day roused hate, violence, persecution, prison. That is why they triumphed.

# The Tradition of Taliesin

(A review of *The Penguin Book of Welsh Verse* — 1967)

A young poet, Mr. Anthony Conran, has translated into English a selection of Welsh poetry from the sixth century to today, and his translations are to be published this year in a popular series. It seems a moment to discuss a main tradition of Welsh medieval verse-making, the panegyric tradition that has its source in the sixth-century poetry of Taliesin.

Taliesin is the first known poet of the Welsh language. Tradition associates him with the court of Maglocunus or Maelgwn Gwynedd, king of North Wales. But the poems safely attributed to him belong specially to a more northern kingdom, the kingdom of Rheged which is the modern north-west of England from the Solway Firth southwards and perhaps across the Pennines to the Swale river.

The first certain reference to Welsh poets is in the well-known work of Gildas, a Latin treatise on the Ruin of Britain, *De Excidio Britanniae*. It is a moral tract, containing some history and much severe condemnation of five local Welsh kings, and most especially of Maglocunus, the king of North Wales. Until recently it was thought that this mightiest and most interesting of Gildas's tyrants had died in the year 547. But Count Nicolai Tolstoi, in a newly published study has given valid reason for putting his death at 575. This allows us to place Gildas's *De Excidio Britanniae* in the third quarter of the sixth century, and not a few previous difficulties are removed.

There is one recognised anomaly in Gildas. After describing the Ruin of Britain he turns to attack the morals of his contemporary Welsh regional kings. There are five of them, from the king of Devon in the South to the great ruler of North Wales. But the Welsh lands of Britannia in the second half of the sixth century extended much further north than North Wales. Our earliest poetry is associated with the North-West of England and the Scottish lowlands. On the kings of these regions, on the king of Rheged in particular, which perhaps bordered on North Wales, Gildas is utterly silent. While he was writing his indictment of the other rulers, his contemporary, Taliesin, who could have been among the poets he lashes for their false flattery in the North Wales court, was actually singing, in the very manner he condemns, the praises of Urien, king of Rheged. It is unlikely that Gildas penned his fierce attack on the Welsh rulers in any territory where they had jurisdiction. Welsh sixth-century kings were not as liberal as all that. 'Many have they bound in prison and ill-used with heavy chains,' says Gildas, thanking his lucky stars. He needed security and protection, *dinas pellennig (sanctuary for the traveller)*, to write his accusations. His silence about Rheged becomes understandable. It suggests that he wrote his arraignment of the other kings in the safe refuge of Urien's kingdom—he may indeed have been a native of it—and that while he penned his scorn of the poets of North Wales, Taliesin himself was teaching just that sort of panegyric to the courtiers of Rheged, and that their coincidence was not fortuitous.

Panegyric, poetic praise of the ruler in his court, be he emperor or king, was an ancient Latin tradition. It survived in such Latin poets as Sidonius in the fifth century and Fortunatus in the sixth. Frankish kings in Gaul took over this court custom from their defeated predecessors. In the Welsh language, as one would expect, it is our earliest, our sixth-century poetry. I have translated from Welsh to English a poem in praise of Urien by Taliesin as an example of this court panegyric:

Urien of Yrechwydd,      most generous of Christian men,
much do you give      to the people of your land;
as you gather      so also you scatter,
the poets of Christendom      rejoice while you stand.
More is the gaiety      and more is the glory
that Urien and his heirs      are for riches renowned,
and he is the chieftain,      the paramount ruler,
the far-flung refuge,      first of fighters found.
The Lloegrians know it      when they count their numbers,
death have they suffered      and many a shame,

Their homesteads a-burning,        stripped their bedding,
and many a loss        and many a blame,
and never a respite        from Urien of Rheged.
Rheged's defender,        famed lord, your land's anchor,
all that is told of you        has my acclaim.
Intense is your spear-play        when you hear ploy of battle,
when to battle you come        'tis a killing you can,
fire in their houses ere day        in the Lord of Yrechwydd's way.
Yrechwydd the beautiful        and its generous people,
The Angles are succourless.        Around the fierce king
are his fierce offspring.        Of those dead, of those living,
of those yet to come,        you head the column.
To gaze upon him        is a widespread fear,
gaiety clothes him        the ribald ruler,
gaiety clothes him        and riches abounding,
gold kings of the Northland        and of kings king.

Now, direct from that paean I want to move to the quite elaborate character study of Maglocunus, king of North Wales, that we find in Gildas. It is unlike his attacks on the other four kings. Those are brief and black. Of Maglocunus he reports exceptional qualities, royal virtues, but yet, and constantly, worse faults and infamies. Listen to Hugh Williams's translation of the opening paragraph:

> And thou, the island dragon, who has driven many of
> the tyrants previously mentioned, as well from life as
> from kingdom, thou last in my writing, first in
> wickedness, exceeding many in power, and at the same
> time in malice, more liberal in giving, more excessive in
> sin, strong in arms, but stronger in what destroys thy
> soul, thou Maglocunus...

You notice, of course, the antitheses, 'exceeding many in power, at the same time in malice, more liberal in giving, more excessive in sin.' I want to drop these rhetorical antitheses, though they have a touch of Tacitus about them, and examine only the theses. I make a list of them:

Island dragon *(insularis draco)*
overthrower of rulers *(tyrannorum depulsor)*
exceeding many in power *(major multis potentia)*
more liberal in giving *(largior in dando)*
strong in arms *(robuste armis)*
superior to almost all the kings of Britain, both in
    dominion and in physical stature *(tam regno quam*
    *status liniamento editiorem)*
accompanied by soldiers of the bravest whose
    countenance in battle appeared not unlike that of
    young lions...

I don't think that anyone acquainted with the poems of
Taliesin can doubt, after this catalogue, that here in Gildas's
Latin we have all the themes and imagery of the poet's
panegyric taken up, put into Latin, and made the basis of
Gildas's character study of the king of North Wales. In the
poem that was quoted above you will find phrase after phrase
corresponding with the Latin phrases of eulogy in Gildas. It
was, I conclude, the Taliesinic poems of panegyric that Gildas
took as the basis of his moral condemnation of Maglocunus;
he would be hearing them in the very court of Rheged; and it is
to Taliesin and his school that he points when he speaks of
'False tongues of flatterers singing at the top of their voice.' I
would even submit that these coincidences cannot be utterly ignored when the period of the Taliesin poetry is in question.

Gildas writes of Maglocunus with an intimate knowledge
both of his court and his career. It is accepted as probable that
they had been pupils together in the monastic school of Saint
Illtud in South Wales. That will explain a personal note in
which he reproaches the king for not listening to him in spite
of the difference of status between them. The king, Gildas tells
us, had once abdicated and returned home to become a monk.
His vows, however, had failed to hold him; he had abandoned
the monastic choir and the praise of the liturgy, and had
resumed his throne. But he had had a Latin education under
the most distinguished teacher of his age. Scholars have always
looked askance at Gildas's prolix and unclassical Latin prose.

Yet Gildas knew large parts of his Vergil by heart and if the Ruin of Britain is also somewhat a ruin of Latin, there are very frequent phrases and echoes from the *Aeneid* thoughout the first thirty-six chapters of the book. The king of North Wales had had a training that allowed him to appreciate the Vergilian echoes. He had shared in the same teaching. And it is impossible not to ask, what of Taliesin?

We know nothing of Taliesin except through such poems as are with confidence attributed to him. But when one reads the poems and Gildas's Ruin of Britain together, one notices more than one simile and many a phrase where the Latin and the Welsh are strikingly akin, and where the Latin is certainly a reminiscence of Vergil or of later Latin historians borrowing from classical Latin. A simile in Taliesin is apt to fill a line, as when he sings of invaders coming—

Like waves with mighty roar over the grounds.

It is a Vergilian simile, and Gildas has this description of Roman soldiery in attack: 'Just like a mountain torrent, swollen by numerous streams after storms, sweeps over its bed in its noisy course.' This is a direct borrowing from lines 496-99 of the second book of the *Aeneid*. This book, with its tale of the fall of Troy, is constantly in Gildas's mind throughout his account of the Ruin of Britain, as, for instance, when he speaks of 'swords gleaming on every side and flames crackling.' And has not something of it rubbed off onto many phrases of Taliesin, who tells of 'fire in their houses ere day in the Lord of Yrechwydd's way.' Gildas tells of the Saxons admitted to Britain 'like wolves into the fold,' while after the Roman withdrawal the Irish had leapt 'like rapacious wolves into the fold' and had cut down their victims, 'reaping them like ripe corn.' These figures all have their models in the *Aeneid*, and we find them again in Taliesin, for whom Owain ap Urien is 'reaper of his foes' and punishes them 'like wolves ravening sheep.' The Romans are said by Gildas to have exhorted the Britons 'to fight bravely so as to save their land, property, wives, children, liberty and life.' Taliesin describes

Urien addressing his troops in Roman General style before battle—'If there is to be a fight for our kinsfolk.' But let us quote the entire poem in Anthony Conran's English version; it is both scholarly and poetry, and the poem has a Roman ring.

## THE BATTLE OF ARGOED LLWYFAIN

There was a great battle Saturday morning
From when the sun rose until it grew dark
The fourfold hosts of Fflamddwyn invaded.
Goddau and Rheged gathered in arms,
Summoned from Argoed as far as Arfynydd—
They might not delay by so much as a day.

With a great blustering din, Fflamddwyn shouted,
'Have those hostages come? Are they ready?'
To him then Owain, scourge of the eastlands,
'They've not come, no! They're not, nor shall they be
     ready!
And a whelp of Coel would indeed be afflicted
Did he have to give any man as a hostage?

And Urien, lord of Erechwydd, shouted,
'If they would meet us now for our kinsfolk,
High on the hilltop let's raise our ramparts,
Carry our faces over the shield rims,
Raise up our spears, men, over our heads,
And set upon Fflamddwyn in the midst of his hosts
And slaughter him, ay, and all that go with him!'

There was many a corpse beside Argoed Llwyfain;
     From warriors ravens grew red
And with their leader a host attacked.
For a whole year I shall sing to their triumph.


I would not be thought to claim that Taliesin borrows his Vergilian lines from Gildas nor at all directly from the *Aeneid*.

But the evidence is there that Gildas and Taliesin were in touch. Hitherto Gildas has been left entirely to the historians. Welsh literary criticism has taken scant notice of him. I submit that Taliesin cannot be read apart from Gildas; the *De Excidio Britanniae* provides not only a key to the understanding of the Taliesinic panegyric, but reveals the mental climate, the cultural background and body of traditional imagery, in which the earliest Welsh poetry that we know had its formation. It belongs to the main stream of European literature rather more than we appreciate.

Finally I turn to Taliesin's picture of this Northern Welsh king, Urien of Rheged. Panegyric, in spite of Gildas, is not merely or mainly fulsome flattery. It is also idealization; it establishes an ideal, a standard of behaviour. So it is essentially creative. Taliesin's picture of Urien is the poet's greatest achievement, his major creation. Urien became, through Taliesin's portrayal, the accepted model of the Welsh Christian king, of the Welsh leader of his people. He is no adventurer. He does not win a kingdom. He is the acknowledged heir, the inevitable defender of his inheritance, his country's anchor, its shelter. He has the example and the qualities of his father and grandfather, and around his throne and his table are his sons, especially Owain, who learn from him, go to battle with him, take over from him, continuing the line and the tradition. He is renowned for his riches, for his exuberant generosity, for his physical strength, for his immensity in battle, for his victories, for his delight in poetry and song, for his rewards to warrior and bard. His nobles are like young lions around him.

This picture of the ideal Welsh king became the foundation of the entire Welsh poetic tradition for a thousand years, right up to the sixteenth century. It was the basis of the poetic schools. But I do not believe that we can study this portrait of Urien, considering its background, considering the impressive evidence of Gildas, without remembering another idealization, another heir and re-founder and father of kings, great in war as in generosity, the hero of Vergil's *Aeneid*. Taliesin's picture of Urien is far, far slighter, far less subtle, but it is in that

224

mould, in that tradition; it has that inheritance. Let me end, then, with Mr. Conran's translation of the most classical of Taliesin's poems, his short elegy on the prince or king, Owain ap Urien. It is one of the big things of Welsh poetry, and it has a Horatian quality:

## DEATH SONG FOR OWAIN AB URIEN

God, consider the soul's need
    Of Owain son of Urien!
Rheged's prince, secret in loam:
    To honour him was honour!

A strait grave, a man much praised,
    His whetted spear the wings of dawn:
That lord of bright Llwyfenydd,
    Where is his peer?

Reaper of enemies; strong of grip;
    One kind with his fathers;
Owain, to slay Fflamddwyn,
    Thought it no more than sleep.

Sleepeth the wide host of England
    With light in their eyes,
And those that had not fled
    Were braver than were wise.

Owain dealt them doom
    As the wolves break sheep;
That warrior, bright of harness,
    Gave stallions for the bard.

Treasure as from miser's greed
    For his soul's sake he gave.
God, consider the soul's need
    Of Owain son of Urien!

# Et Homo Factus Est, Crucifixus...

And he was made man. He was crucified.
What other course, what other fate
Could await the Son of Heaven?
Killing is the primal instinct of mankind,
The drive in the amoeba;
Poems of pain and songs of danger
Have been the most deeply felt poetry of the myriad victims
Since stone axes were chiseled
At the entrances to caves;
Millions of generations of woe
On the insignificant planet
Lost in the unending emptiness of existence.

And here in the pit of darkness
In the winter of the earth,
In the deepest hell in the history of our broken race,
We light a candle because a son is born to us
And we lift him from his cradle—
He's heavy, the weak babe,
Carrying on him the weight of all the aeons of sin,—
But we lift him up and kill him,
I Caiphas,
You Tiresias,
And place him up above
A hewn altar
Of the world's anguish
For one who is, except in Him, an unknown God.

1972

# Terminal Prayer

It's an experience for everyone that nobody else can know of.
Each one on his own and in his own way
Owns his own death
Throughout the millenia of existence.
One can look at it, sometimes even identify its exact moment;
It is impossible to empathise with anyone at that moment
When the breathing ceases and the person becomes but a
　　memory.
Afterwards? There is nothing which extends into that
　　afterwards except a groping prayer.
How pitiful is man, how infantile his imagination:
"In my father's house there are many mansions,"
As poor as us, as earthly limited
Was his genius in the days of his self-emptying.
And we therefore cannot portray hope:
"He is seated at the right hand of God the Father Almighty."
A general paraded in triumph through the streets of Rome
After the wars in a Persian universe
And crowned Augustus. Co-Augustus with his father,—
How comic are the supreme declarations of our faith.
And around us there remains muteness, and the pit of
　　annihilation
That our whole universe will fall into some night.
Our words cannot reach the edges of muteness
Nor say God with any meaning.
There remains one prayer for everyone, to go mute to the
　　mute.

1973